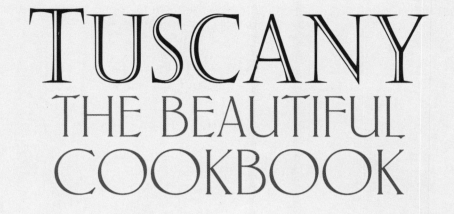

TUSCANY
THE BEAUTIFUL
COOKBOOK

AUTHENTIC RECIPES FROM THE PROVINCES OF TUSCANY

Fried Noodle Nests (top, recipe page 82) and Wide Noodles with Hare Sauce (bottom, recipe page 73)

AUTHENTIC RECIPES FROM THE PROVINCES OF TUSCANY

TUSCANY
THE BEAUTIFUL
COOKBOOK

TEXT AND RECIPES BY
LORENZA DE' MEDICI

FOOD PHOTOGRAPHY BY
PETER JOHNSON

STYLED BY JANICE BAKER

SCENIC PHOTOGRAPHY BY
MICHAEL FREEMAN

HarperCollinsPublishers

First published in the USA by Collins San Francisco.

Produced by Weldon Owen Inc.
814 Montgomery Street
San Francisco, CA 49133 USA
Phone (415) 291-0100 Fax 415 291-8841

Weldon Owen Inc.:
Chairman: Kevin Weldon
President: John Owen
General Manager: Stuart Laurence
Co-Editions Director: Derek Barton
Manging Editor: Jane Fraser
Project Coordinator: Laurie Wertz
Translator: Jennifer Grillo, with Monica Smith
Editor: Sharon Silva
Proofreader: Jonathan Schwartz
Production: Stephanie Sherman, Mick Bagnate
Design: Tom Morgan, Blue Design
Design Concept: John Bull,
    The Book Design Company
Map: Mike Gorman
Illustrations: Neil Shigley

Library of Congress Cataloging-in-Publication Data:

De'Medici, Strucchi, Lorenza.
    Tuscany, the beautiful cookbook : authentic
recipes from the provinces of Tuscany / recipes
and text by Lorenza de' Medici ; food photography by Peter Johnson ; scenic photography by
Michael Freeman.
Includes Index.
ISBN 0-00-255032-6
1. Cookery, Italian—Tuscan style. 2. Tuscany
(Italy)—Description and travel—1981. I. Title.
TX713.2.T86D4 1992
641.5945'5—dc20   91—42832

ISBN 0-06-757600-1 (pbk.)

99 00 01 02 03 TOP 6 5 4 3 2 1

Printed by Toppan in China

Pages 2–3: A solitary rower glides past the Ponte Vecchio.

Right: The crew from Ardenza trains for the Palio Marinaro race in Livorno.

Pages 8–9: Dipped Celery (recipe page 37) and Deep-Froed Baby Artichokes (recipe page 37).

Pages 12–13: Farmhouse and newly planted olive trees near Bibona.

Endpapers: Detail from Lorenzo Ghiberti's bronze doors, Baptistry, Florence.

Fried Red Mullet in Tomato Sauce (recipe page 165). Photographed in Livorno.

CONTENTS

Flag throwers dazzle the crowd during the Palio parade in Siena.

INTRODUCTION

It is no exaggeration to say that traditional Tuscan cuisine goes back three thousand years. Ample evidence of the Etruscan diet has been found at many archaeological sites, from the famous Tarquinia tombs near southern Tuscany to recently discovered house remains near Lucca in the north. These findings confirm that Tuscan eating habits have maintained a continuity through the centuries.

It is the Tuscans' attitude toward food that appears to have changed the least. The approach is based on a love of wine, freshly pressed olive oil and bread. In fact, the secret of Tuscan cookery is, and always has been, its simplicity. Sole or lamb described as *all'etrusco* on a Tuscan menu is not mere whimsy. These dishes actually forge a solid link with the past and incorporate the three basic elements of wine, oil and bread, which to the Tuscans are almost sacred.

Bread and olives were the food of slaves in Etruscan times, and today bread and olives are still found together on the shelves of most bakeries. Garlic, onions and leeks were often eaten with bread, not only for their taste but because they were considered good for the health, stimulating, and even, it was said, aphrodisiac. Bread continues to play an important role in Tuscan cuisine. The classic unsalted loaf is the perfect foil for the assertive flavors of country ham, sheep's milk cheese and salami. To a Tuscan, nothing is more satisfying than a slice of coarse country bread toasted over the fire, rubbed with garlic and sprinkled with oil.

Bread is never thrown away in Tuscany. It is the basic ingredient of several of the most popular dishes. *Ribollita* (or *frantoiana*—the name changes from place to place) is a thick, comforting soup made from bread, green vegetables, beans, black cabbage and extra virgin olive oil. Its summer equivalent is *panzanella,* a salad composed of bread, tomatoes, onion and oil.

Good olive oil is also vital to Tuscan cooking. Olives for the production of extra virgin olive oil must be picked very carefully, in the same way that they have been harvested for two thousand years. Olives for pressing should never touch the ground, so large tarpaulins are placed under the trees to catch any that fall while the others are carefully gathered by hand. It is essential that the olives be dry when they are harvested and that they be pressed immediately, so that none of their fragrance is lost. The grindstones used today for cold pressing are more or less identical to those used by the Etruscans.

There are, of course, large plants where olive oil is produced in quantity, but those operations use chemical solvents to release the oil, which changes the flavor and, even more importantly, increases the acid content. The production of olive oil is strictly controlled, and only cold-pressed oil may be described as "extra virgin olive oil." In the market there are same-sized bottles of oil that differ widely in price. Remember, an inexpensive bottle of oil cannot contain extra virgin oil, because the costs of producing it are far too high.

Many scholars agree that the first people known to have used olive oil for seasoning their food were the Etruscans. And now, after almost three millennia, dietitians all over the world, led by American scientists who have thoroughly investigated the original Mediterranean diet, have discovered that the oleic acid present in olive oil is the only fat that does not increase the cholesterol content of the blood.

The use of olive oil is common not only to Tuscany but to all of central and southern Italy. Interestingly enough, the famous Gothic Line that divided the part of Italy liberated by the Allied forces from the rest still held by the Germans in the last war, more or less coincides with the dividing line between the Italians who use oil and those in the north who cook with butter and lard.

One of the first physicians known to have emphasized the importance of limiting the use of lard and animal fat was Michele Savonarola, who informs readers in his sixteenth-century work *Libreto de tute le cose che se manzano communamente* ("All the things we generally eat") that it is much healthier to eat meat cooked on a spit, which, incidentally, is another Tuscan custom. He also insisted that olive oil should be used whenever possible. In Savonarola's day, however, it was not easy to find olive oil outside the areas where it was produced. In fact, in the poorer homes of northern Italy, olive oil was only used on special occasions until quite recently.

The third great element of the Tuscan kitchen is wine. Strong and light, red and white wines were drunk by the Etruscans and are still essential to the Tuscan table. The Etruscans were inclined to infuse their wines with honey and herbs, to enhance their taste and their own good spirits. Tuscany remains very much a civilization in which wine is not just a drink but a flavoring and an ingredient, a solace and a boon.

Catching up on the latest news is a favorite pastime in the Piazza del Duomo, San Gimignano.

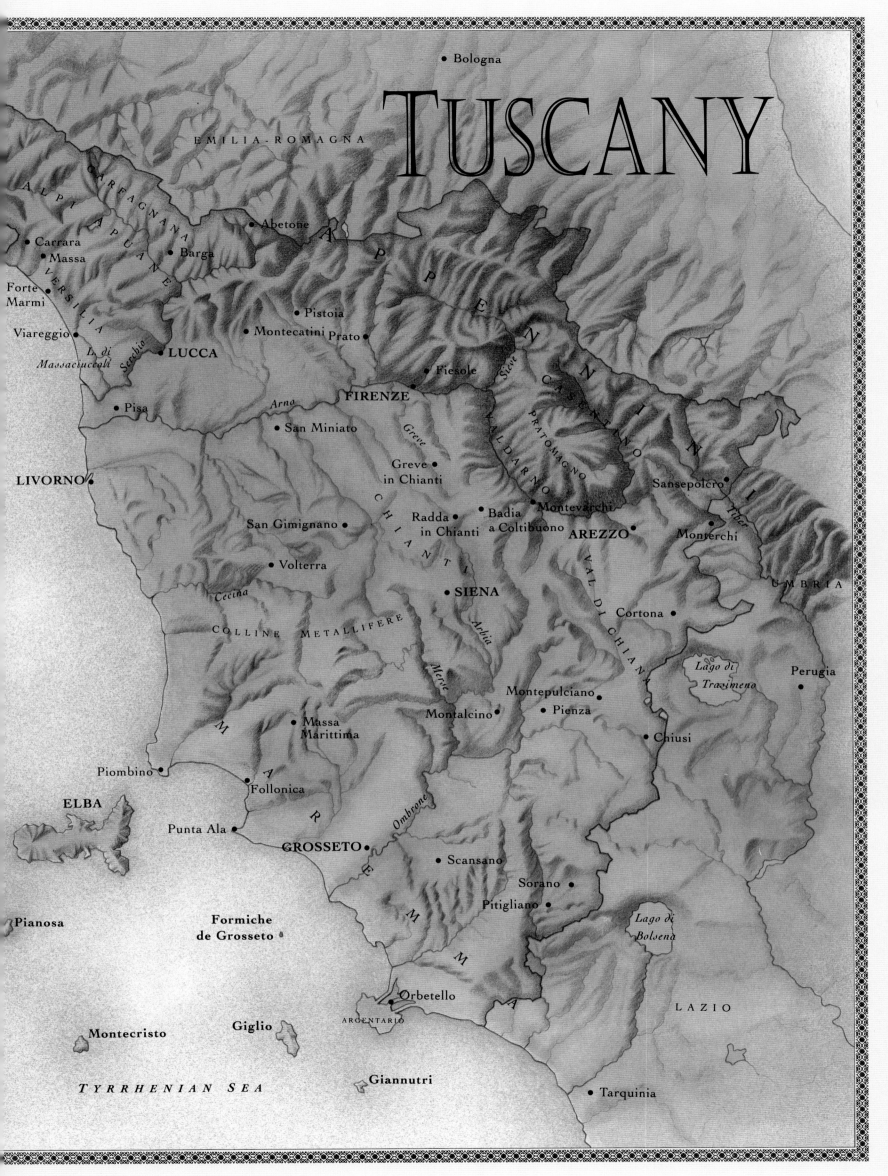

TUSCANY

Bologna

EMILIA-ROMAGNA

ALPI APUANE

GARFAGNANA

Abetone

Carrara

Massa

Barga

VERSILIA

Forte
Marmi

Pistoia

Viareggio

Montecatini   Prato

L. di
Massaciuccoli

Serchio

LUCCA

Fiesole

APPENNINI

Pisa

Arno

FIRENZE

Sieve

CASENTINO

San Miniato

Greve

PRATOMAGNO

VALDARNO

Greve
in Chianti

LIVORNO

Sansepolcro

Montevarchi

Radda
in Chianti

Badia
a Coltibuono

San Gimignano

CHIANTI

AREZZO

Monterchi

Volterra

Cecina

VAL DI CHIANA

UMBRIA

SIENA

Cortona

COLLINE   METALLIFERE

Arbia

Lago di
Trasimeno

Merse

Perugia

Montepulciano

Massa
Marittima

Montalcino

Pienza

MAREMMA

Piombino

Chiusi

Follonica

ELBA

Punta Ala

GROSSETO

Ombrone

Pianosa

Scansano

Sorano

Formiche
de Grosseto

MAREMMA

Pitigliano

Lago di
Bolsena

Montecristo

Giglio

Orbetello

ARGENTARIO

LAZIO

Giannutri

TYRRHENIAN   SEA

Tarquinia

17

Cypress trees nestle up to a chapel near San Quirico d'Orcia. Planted to mark boundaries and flank entrances to churches, cypresses are the unofficial sentinels of the Tuscan landscape.

Gastronomically speaking, Tuscany covers a large region made up of seacoast and hills, plains and mountains, cities, suburbs and villages, all populated by individualists. As Ugo Tognazzi, the very popular Italian film star and cook, said, "In Florence, if there are eighteen apartments in a building, there will be eighteen different recipes for *ribollita* soup." For simplicity's sake, Tuscany may be divided roughly into the coastal region and the interior. The former does not have a venerable history, because for so long it was a malaria-ridden marsh and therefore sparsely populated. It is true that Etruscans probably cooked *cee* (baby eels) and Livorno's famed *cacciucco* (a fish soup now prepared all along the Versilia coast), but it is not biased to say that the great Tuscan culinary traditions of roasts, stews, soups and *pappardelle* (wide noodles) originated in the inland areas.

Until a few years ago, Tuscans did not even know how to cook spaghetti. But the tradition of fresh pasta is centuries-old: *pappardelle* are said to have been unearthed in an Etruscan kitchen, together with a serrated wheel for cutting pasta dough. *Pappardelle* are still enjoyed today, along with *pici,* a type of thick, fresh spaghetti from Montalcino; *ravioli* filled with spinach and ricotta; and, in Lucchesia, meat-filled pasta called *tordelli.*

Another feature of Tuscan cookery, both ancient and modern, is the presence of certain herbs, including sage, rosemary, parsley, thyme, marjoram and bay leaves. The Etruscans made particular use of bay leaves and parsley. Herbs are now central to the Tuscan pantry. They are used to enhance the flavors of foods, which results in less fat being needed and thus a lighter final result. In fact, long before the first recipe book appeared in Tuscany, information on cooking was gleaned from herbals and medical books, indicating that there is a long tradition of attention to the medicinal and dietetic properties of the herbs used in cooking.

Not many cakes and desserts are native to Tuscany, although the excellent *panforte* a rich, flat fruitcake, comes from Siena, and there are a few fine sweet breads. *Brigidini,* large flat wafers from Lamporecchio, are sold at village fairs, and *castagnaccio* a chestnut flour cake, originally came from Lucca.

Chestnut trees have always thrived in the Garfagnana, the mountainous region in the province of Lucca, and until the last war chestnut flour was used to prepare a variety of dishes. The chestnuts were gathered and taken to a *metato,* a chestnut oasthouse, where they were spread on lattice frames and dried by the heat from a slow-burning fire on the floor below. The dried chestnuts were then ground into flour. Although there are only a few such mills left in Lucchesia, the flour is still available in grocery stores. During the chestnut season, friends gather around their fireplaces to roast chestnuts or to cook *necci,* chestnut flour pancakes baked over the embers in round iron molds. They are eaten either plain or filled with ricotta.

There is another Tuscan cuisine well worth remembering, and it is the one that was almost lost. Until a few years ago, those who knew and loved the old dishes based on variety meats and the tougher cuts complained bitterly that they had practically disappeared. Now, thanks to a few intelligent restaurant owners and keen private cooks, dishes like *cibreo* from Florence, *frittata di fegatini* (chicken liver frittata) from Prato, and *scottiglia* from Arezzo (made with various meat and chicken cuts) have been revived.

Caterina de' Medici was very fond of *cibreo.* Made of cockscombs and chicken liver and served on a bed of artichokes, she took it, and Tuscan cooking in general, with her to France. *Scottiglia* was originally a very humble dish made from the meat that stuck to the calf skins when they were taken to Arezzo to be tanned. It is believed that the Tuscans' fondness for these more unusual cuts goes back to ancient times when men and children gathered in the kitchen to keep the women company while they watched over the slowly simmering meat.

The popularity of vegetables in Tuscany has an equally long history. During the Renaissance, Florentine monks prepared great dishes of leeks and meat for the feast of San Lorenzo. Tuscans often cook fish and vegetables together; cuttlefish with Swiss chard and salt cod with chick-peas or leeks are, for example, typically Tuscan preparations. Bean dishes and molds made from spinach, fennel, carrots or all manner of other vegetables are delicious and frequent fare in Tuscan restaurants and private homes as well.

Almost everywhere in Tuscany, meat is grilled over open fires. What could appear more simple, yet at the same time be more difficult, than to match perfectly the quality and texture of meat with the temperature of burning embers? Everywhere in Italy, except in Florence, people ask for a grilled *fiorentina,* meaning a

Florence's Palazzo degli Uffizi was designed by Vasari as administrative offices for the Medici. The dramatic U-shaped building now houses one of the world's most important art collections.

T-bone steak. Although to the uninitiated a *fiorentina* is symbolic of Tuscan food, it is actually a fairly recent acquisition, born out of the custom of English noblemen ordering steaks when they stopped on the Grand Tour to winter between Fiesole and the Ponte Vecchio.

Tuscans have a preference for earthenware pots and pans; they believe cooking in them brings out the true flavor of sauces, stews and soups. Indeed, the presence of a special ceramic bean pot, in which beans can be simmered slowly and very gently, is de rigueur for the classic Tuscan kitchen.

Traditional Tuscan cheese is also much the same as it was in Etruscan times. Most of it is made from sheep's milk or goat's milk, although cow's milk is now frequently substituted for the latter. As Panunto, an early Florentine writer, explained, "Sheep's milk cheese is much healthier than cheese made from cow's milk because it smells nicer, the flavor is better balanced because it is made with milk that has a better complexion, and, furthermore, cow's milk cheese makes your blood thicker because it is more fatty than sheep's milk." *Pecorino,* a sheep's milk cheese produced around Arezzo, the Maremma, Volterra, Chianti and Pienza, is never missing from a Tuscan table. There is an old Tuscan proverb that says, "If you want good cheese and a good time, send your sheep to graze on thyme." Another old Tuscan saying declares that a dinner is not a dinner if you do not finish with cheese.

Not surprisingly, Italy's first known book on gastronomy appeared in Tuscany, where food has always played an important role. *Il libro della cocina* ("The kitchen book"), by an anonymous Tuscan author, appeared toward the end of the fourteenth century and probably refers to even earlier sources. It contains suggestions for special occasions and includes the following recipe entitled The Garden: "On important feast days, such as Easter, make a large tree, vine or trellis out of pasta. Then make pastry apples, pears, birds, bunches of grapes or whatever else you fancy and brush them with egg. Fill them with the mixture mentioned above [the recipe is provided] and color them yellow, green, white or black. Then hang them on the branches of the trees. Decorate the top of the tree with a cage filled with real birds. You may also hang seasonal fruit from the branches of your tree. When you carry the tree or vine or trellis out into the courtyard or garden, build a fire of a variety of sweet-smelling twigs nearby."

This effort certainly cannot be compared with the sumptuous banquets of the Tuscan nobility served during the Renaissance, a time when Italian cuisine led Europe, thanks mostly to Caterina de' Medici. Much of the literature on medieval banquets was written by Tuscans such as Folgore from San Gimignano, the Sienese Pietro di Viviano Corsellino, and Pucci from Florence. The first person to introduce science to the Italian kitchen was a Tuscan by adoption. In 1891, Pellegrino Artusi published *La scienza in cucina e l'arte di mangiare bene— manuale pratico per le famiglie* ("Science in the kitchen and the art of eating well—a practical family manual") in Florence, and it is still one of the most frequently consulted cookbooks in Italian households.

Many of the restaurant owners in northern Italy were originally from Tuscany. One wave of migration began in the nineteenth century, when the first grand hotels were opened on the shores of Lake Maggiore and Lake Como. Whole families moved there to work in the

Tourists flock to Pisa to see the Leaning Tower, the famous belltower that has been inching its way toward horizontal since its completion in 1372.

Fishermen cast their nets at the mouth of the Arno River in Marina di Pisa. In wintertime the catch will be tiny baby eels called cee, *a local specialty.*

hotel kitchens and they were followed by others, who stayed on in the large northern cities. Some Tuscans started as vendors of bread made out of chick-pea flour or chestnut flour; others sold tripe. Later they opened trattorias and, more recently, the better chefs started their own restaurants. This Tuscan tradition of preparing and serving food, however, began much earlier. There was, of course, the army of chefs who went to France with Caterina de' Medici's court in the sixteenth century, but even before then, in the Middle Ages, the Knights of Altopascio were known to ring a bell at night to call passing travelers to share a bowl of soup. It is no surprise that today all over the world there are literally thousands of restaurateurs who originally came from Altopascio or the neighboring towns of Montecatini and Lucca.

From the earliest times, Tuscany has been a leader of the arts. So it is not surprising that Tuscan cuisine is a leader of the culinary arts. All the basic ingredients are finer in Tuscany than in any other region of Italy. The mountains are rich in mushrooms and chestnuts. All kinds of berries, from raspberries to blackberries, grow wild, and the hills around Abetone are carpeted with blueberries. Trout are caught in the streams, and fish are taken straight from the sea to the markets.

Vegetables are cultivated in abundance in the reclaimed Maremma soil. Game birds, wild boar and hare are bagged throughout the area. In the Val di Chiana the famous Chianina cattle are raised for their meat, generally considered the best in Italy. Sheep and goats graze on the hills around Siena, and pigs are raised everywhere, hence the excellent Tuscan ham, sausages and salamis.

A famous Florentine restaurateur loves to tell about the time he was invited to present a Tuscan dinner at a grand hotel in another region of Italy. He was not very keen on the idea, but he was assured that he would have no problems. All he had to do was bring his cooks with him. Wisely he sent his chef ahead to check the situation. But the chef called in despair. The oil came from Liguria, and although it was very good, it was much lighter than Tuscan oil, which is greener, thicker and sharper. The peas were canned. The asparagus were by no means Tuscan. And instead of the hearty Tuscan bread there were dainty little rolls, probably perfect for a grand international hotel, but quite unsuitable for Tuscan cooking. Thus the restaurateur—and it should be said that Tuscans are not famous for their tact—loaded a truck with local ingredients and set off, taking all the necessary supplies with him.

FIRENZE

FIRENZE

T here are many splendid cities in Tuscany, all with their marvelous art and atmosphere and food. But it must be granted that Florence, the Tuscan capital, is supreme in art and cuisine. This accolade is not so much due to present-day Florentine cooking as it is to the very significant contribution made by Florence to the history of Italian gastronomy—and to the European table as well.

During the Renaissance, women played a fundamental role in this story. Curiously enough, most of the poulterers and greengrocers were women, and toward the end of the fifteenth century Florence had eight woman-run shops selling game woodcock and hare, venison and foxes, wild boar and peacocks. At the market, women presided over fruit, vegetable and flower stalls and also sold medicinal herbs, the most common of which were nettles, calamint and mallow.

It is, however, thanks to the ladies of the Medici court that Florentine cooking was developed and refined. Noblewomen from all over Italy and even from abroad joined the court. They were women who knew how to combine their native dishes with local recipes so that a real cuisine, as well as the art of entertaining, evolved and reached a peak during the Renaissance. Clarice Orsini, Lorenzo the Magnificent's wife, introduced elements of Roman cooking, while Eleonora of Toledo, wife of Cosimo I, brought the specialties of her Spanish homeland. Yet other new ideas arrived with Giovanna of Austria, the first wife of Francesco I, and Bianca Cappello

Left: Just south of the bustling streets of Florence, across the Arno, lies a serene world of grand villas and country retreats. Previous pages: The city's oldest bridge, the Ponte Vecchio, was originally home to blacksmiths and butcher shops until a Medici ruler replaced them with jewelers in 1593.

25

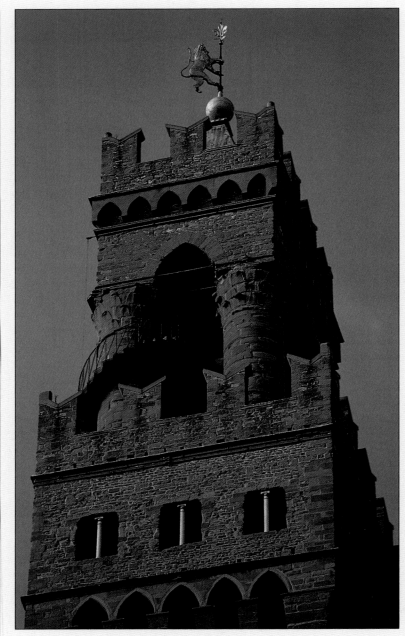

The Palazzo Vecchio has served as Florence s political center since medieval times. Today it is the town hall. Perched on the mast are a lion and a lily, the city's symbols.

from Venice, his second wife. All of these women influenced the food and style of entertaining in Florence, until the dishes and decorations at the Medici court were considered works of art. Dinners became veritable banquets, with an infinite number of ever subtler courses.

Sorbets made with oranges and lemons plucked from the citrus trees in the formal gardens were regularly served at the Florentine court, and even nowadays they are considered a refinement. Not far from the church of Santa Maria Novella, carefully collected winter ice was stored in specially dug deep trenches to prevent it from melting during the hot summer months. Sorbets generally came at the end of the meal, but if the banquet was particularly rich they were served between the main courses to stimulate the diners' digestion.

Although usually thought of as French, béchamel sauce actually came from Tuscany. One of the royal chefs apparently aroused the envy of other courtiers who would have preferred he name it for them rather than for Louis de Béchameil, Marquis de Nointel, who was majordomo to Louis XIV. No doubt the chef was right to do so, because when Caterina de' Medici introduced the sauce to France it had the rather unfortunate moniker of *colla,* which means "glue." As the fourteen-year-old bride of Henry II of France, Caterina took with her a great gift

for politics, a battalion of cooks, and the dishes of her native land.

At court, good wine was always present on the table. Trebbiano and Greco, imported from the islands of Giglio and Elba where the Greeks had planted Ansonica vines, were particularly prized. From a letter written by Lorenzo the Magnificent we learn that "vermiglio" from the vineyards at Badia a Coltibuono was also enjoyed. However, it appears that white wine was preferred to red at the time.

By the Renaissance, the Tuscans' love of good wine was already well established. When Leonardo da Vinci, who was born in wine country, moved to the court of Ludovico il Moro in Milan, he asked for vines to be planted in the garden. And during those same years, many of the Florentine noble families were selling wine from their country estates.

Church prelates did not lag far behind the Medici court when it came to food. They seem to have had a weakness for *biancomangiare*—pounded chicken or veal and ground almonds cooked together to make a white meat jelly. A sweet version made with honey, almonds and sheep's milk eventually became *blancmange.* We also have to thank the ecclesiastic cooks for being the first to introduce to Italian regional cooking the novelties brought from the East by the crusaders.

The first expert to recognize the importance of Arab confectionery was Bartolomeo Scappi, whose *Opera dell'arte di cucinare* ("Work on the art of cooking") is the most important book on this subject published during the Renaissance. Scappi, for example, gave detailed and accurate instructions on how to prepare the wafers that are still made in Montecatini. Wafers have been popular in Florence for centuries, and wafermakers were considered important enough to be members of the Bakers' Guild. Many of these culinary craftsmen came from Sicily, where there had been a strong Arab influence. *Brigidini* are famous Tuscan wafers that take their name from the Convent of Santa Brigida in Pistoia.

Another very famous Renaissance cook, Bartolomeo Sacchi, was strongly influenced by Tuscany. Although he was born near Cremona in 1421, he spent many years

An explosion of poppies and daisies graces a hillside near Buggiano. The Tuscan landscape has inspired centuries of artists and writers who have come here to surround themselves with natural beauty and human genius.

Late-afternoon traffic crowds the Ponte Santa Trinita in Florence. Despite the constant roar of motorcycles and buses the city remains a walker's paradise, a treasure trove of Renaissance art, architecture and spirit.

in Florence, where he evolved a unique philosophy of food. Sacchi is just as well-known for the advice he gave about eating as he is for his recipes. Some of his suggestions are still valid today: "First eat all those things that activate the stomach and give light and measured nourishment, such as an apple or some pears . . . also lettuce or anything that can be eaten either raw or cooked, dressed with oil and vinegar. Then eggs, and confectionery sweetened with spices, honey and sugar."

There was also a middle-class kitchen, which was slightly richer than the Florentine cooking of today. This is a list from a sixteenth-century recipe book that is not far removed from a modern shopping list: "Mullet from the sea, eel from the Ombrone or from Orbetello; pike, carp and tench from Lake Bolsena; partridge, hare, larks, peacocks, pullets; lambs and half a kid; herbs and leaf vegetables; cabbages, beans, chick-peas; horseradish, lupine seeds, leeks, garlic; pasta, barley, spelt; wafers and sheep's milk cheese; anise, sage, cloves and cinnamon for biscuits."

Among the middle classes, capon was the most popular meat and was prepared in several different ways. It was stuffed and sometimes seasoned with bunches of herbs. Bay leaves, thyme, rosemary, marjoram and sage were as popular in Florence as they were in the rest of Tuscany. Capon was also roasted in the same way as duck and goose, with the cooking juices used as a pasta sauce. *Arrosto morto,* meat slowly cooked in wine and chopped vegetables, was another classic roast of the era.

The same tradition brings us mixed cuts of meat roasted on a spit, slowly turned over embers sprinkled with cloves, pine needles and juniper berries to enhance the flavor. Braised meat, which before the discovery of America and the advent of the tomato was cooked in *agresto* (the juice of unripe grapes and thyme), is still very popular. Florence is celebrated for its stews simmered in shallow earthenware casseroles and seasoned with wild fennel, garlic, lemon peel and mixed spices.

Yet another feature of Florentine cooking is the sauce called *dolceforte,* or "sweet and pungent." It is often used with wild boar and tongue and is made very simply by dissolving sugar in vinegar to which raisins, pine nuts and a little chocolate may be added.

The diet of the poorer Florentines consisted of bread, millet, fava (broad) beans and chestnuts, and many of these ingredients remain important. A variety of wild plants were and still are used to flavor bread and eggs. A soup called *panata* stems from those times and is made with stale bread, which is ground and mixed with egg, grated cheese and nutmeg. Many lower-class families had some connection with the well-to-do houses and were given leftovers, which they ate with *agliata* and *porrata,* sauces made with garlic and leeks respectively. Even today busy women who work and cook for their families prepare double portions and serve the leftovers with these same sauces.

Undoubtedly one of the most vivid descriptions of sixteenth-century Florentine food that is still relevant today was written by the Italian satirist Pietro Aretino. He describes the peaches as "lusty and greedy," the melons as "pandering to one's palate" and the oysters as "delighting the appetite." He was also an expert on salad: "It is certainly not unimportant to know just how to mitigate the sharp and bitter flavor of some leaves with the sweeter and gentler flavors of others, creating such a smooth mixture that you would keep on eating it . . . scentless lettuce and chicory, a handful of wild radicchio, sprinkled with a little calamint, lemon balm and rue. I think that the creator of such a thing could only have been a Florentine. It could not have been anyone else, because setting the table, decorating it with roses and shining glasses, putting plums in syrup, dressing up livers, creating dishes with millet, and serving fruit after a meal all came from Florence."

GLI ANTIPASTI

A selection of cured meats on display along the Via di Citta in Siena.

GLI ANTIPASTI

During the Renaissance, antipasti were already being served in Tuscany. Although the word literally means "before the meal," in early times this course was called *primi servizi di credenza,* or "first services from the sideboard."

White meat and almond aspics, hams, salamis and small game birds were included in this opening course. Nowadays we still meet them in the antipasti, with different names but very similar flavors. For example,

The everpresent sign of good taste, olive oil is a staple in every Tuscan pantry. For the best flavor and health benefits, it must be extra virgin, which means the olives have been hand picked and cold pressed.

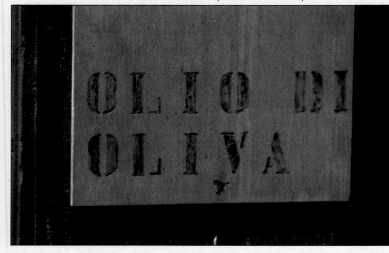

pig's head in gelatin is today's headcheese. At one time aspic jelly was used a great deal, but now it seldom appears except at buffets. In fact, aspic was so important on the Renaissance table that Francesco Berni, a fifteenth-century Tuscan poet, was moved to write seventy-three lines in praise of it.

A clear, flavorful stock was once considered the prince of antipasti. It was said to open the stomach and to prepare it for what was yet to come. *Crostini* and slices of cured meats followed, and they are still the mainstay of Tuscan antipasti, even though plain stock is seldom served today.

On the coast, however, *antipasto di mare* (seafood antipasto) reigns supreme. Clams, both large and small, are sautéed in their shells with oil, garlic and a pinch of chili and served hot. *Crostini* are spread with a mixture of warm seafood. Then there are stuffed mussels and clams, as well as cold shrimp in an olive oil, vinegar and parsley dressing.

Crostini have assumed the role that aspic played during the Renaissance. When Tuscans say *crostini,* by definition they mean chicken liver pâté on rounds of bread. All other *crostini*—and there are many others—are usually described by their color.

At first glance, all chicken liver *crostini* appear to be exactly alike. After all, the basic ingredient is always the same. Nevertheless, if you make a tour of Tuscan restaurants, you will never find precisely the same *crostini* served in two different places. Some cooks add onion,

Previous pages, front: Zucchini Flowers Stuffed with Sausage (page 40), Marinated Shrimp (page 38), Fried Sage Leaves (page 40). Rear: Chicken Liver Toasts (page 37), Anchovies with Oil, Garlic and Chili (page 43).

others do not. Some flavor them with bay leaves, others are horrified at the mere idea. An occasional cook even breaks the golden rule of Tuscan food and uses butter instead of olive oil. Even the bread and wine vary. Some toast the bread, some fry it, some moisten it with stock, some serve it warm, some serve it cold. There are chefs who flavor the pâté with white wine and those who swear by red, and yet others who flame it with cognac. One thing is certain, however: whatever the subtle changes may be, in a Tuscan restaurant *crostini* are everpresent.

Cured meats are another essential to a plate of mixed antipasti. They range from Tuscan ham, drier and more strongly flavored than the famous Parma and San Daniele hams, to coarse-grained Tuscan salami, from *biroldo,* a blood sausage, to *finocchiona,* a large, fairly fresh salami seasoned with fennel seed. The most celebrated *finocchiona* comes from Colonnata in the Apuan Alps, where it is left to dry in the marble caves.

All over Tuscany, fried dough is served with antipasti. The sizes of the dough pieces and the names vary, but essentially bread dough is fried in good olive oil, which makes it crisp and full of flavor. In Versilia it is called *panzerotti;* in Lucca, *pane fritto;* and in Prato, *figattole.*

Another popular antipasto is *panzanella,* a very simple dish that probably originated in farmhouse kitchens when the farmers' wives moistened stale bread and mixed it with whatever salad ingredients were available from the kitchen garden. The *pan lavato* ("washed bread") mentioned by Boccaccio was very similar. In the sixteenth century, the painter Bronzino was inspired to write a poem about *panzanella:* "He who would fly over the stars should dip his bread and eat it until . . . "

Panzanella, like *crostini,* boasts a hundred different versions. Moistened bread, tomato and onion are the essential ingredients, but there are those who add cucumber and celery and others who toss in greens. The

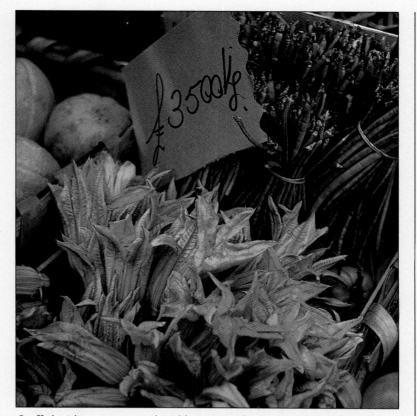

Stuffed with sausage, zucchini blossoms make a savory antipasto. The flowers are available in Tuscan markets throughout the summer.

simplest version is probably the best, however.

Crostini and cured meats are the everyday antipasti, but on special occasions there are additions. Eggs are stuffed in a variety of ways and are always delicious. Then there are the vegetables, either pickled in the local wine vinegar or preserved in the magnificent olive oil of the region. *Porcini* mushrooms in extra virgin oil are a delight to the most jaded palate, and onions and carrots in white vinegar whet the dullest appetite.

A display of the freshest cheeses and meats lures customers to this market stall at Pisa's Piazza Vettovaglie.

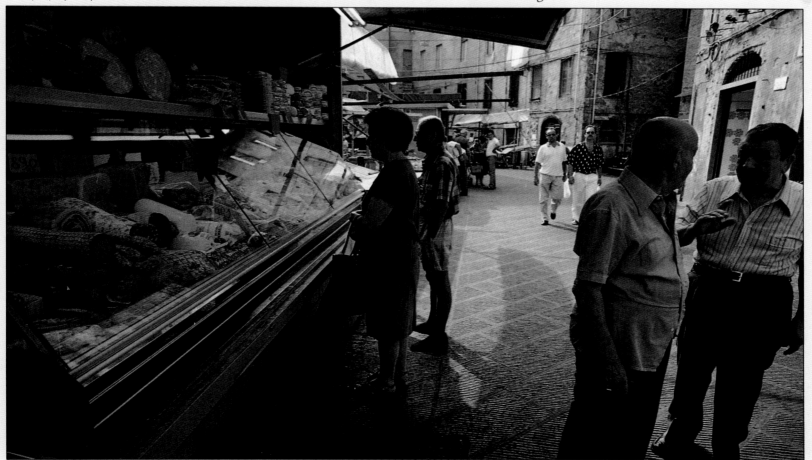

CROSTINI DI CACCIA
Game Toasts

Tuscans are keen hunters, and each province has its own game dishes. In the Maremma, the area around Grosseto, wild boars are in abundance; excellent ham and sausages are made from their meat. If you are not lucky enough to find wild boar's liver, calf's liver may be used instead.

2 slices dried *porcini* mushrooms
6 oz (200 g) wild boar's liver or calf's liver
2 tablespoons extra virgin olive oil
2 oz (60 g) *pancetta,* chopped
¼ cup (2 fl oz/60 ml) dry red wine
1 plum (egg) tomato, peeled and chopped
1 teaspoon fennel seed
1 teaspoon juniper berries
salt
1 tablespoon unsalted butter, at room temperature
12 slices coarse country bread or French baguette

♠ In a small bowl, soak the mushroom slices in warm water to cover for 30 minutes. Drain and squeeze out any excess moisture. Meanwhile, preheat an oven to 350°F (180°C). Cut the liver into 2-in (5-cm) slices about ¼ in (6 mm) thick.
♠ In a skillet over high heat, warm the olive oil. Add the liver and *pancetta* and cook, stirring, until the liver changes color, about 5 minutes.
♠ Add the wine, tomato, fennel seed, juniper berries, mushrooms and salt to taste. Reduce the heat to moderate and cook until the liquid evaporates, about 5 minutes.
♠ Remove from the heat and put the liver mixture through the fine disc of a food mill. Alternatively, place the mixture in a food processor and mix until fairly smooth; be careful not to overprocess. Add the butter and blend in with a fork just until combined.
♠ Just before serving, toast the bread slices in the oven until golden. Remove the bread and, while it is still hot, spread the liver mixture on it. Arrange the toasts on a platter and serve immediately.

SERVES 6

CROSTINI DI TONNO
Tuna Fish Toasts

In Florence tuna fish preserved in oil, mixed with white beans and finely sliced onion, is a popular summer salad. This recipe, in which tuna is served on country bread, becomes a delicious appetizer when accompanied with a glass of cold white wine.

1 can (6 oz/180g) tuna fish in olive oil, drained
¼ cup (2 oz/60 g) unsalted butter, softened
1 tablespoon chopped flat-leaf (Italian) parsley
1 tablespoon chopped yellow onion
1 teaspoon fresh lemon juice
pinch of white pepper
12 slices coarse country bread or French baguette

♠ Preheat an oven to 350°F (180°C). Flake the tuna and place it in a bowl. Add the butter, parsley, onion and lemon juice and, using a fork, mash them into the tuna until thoroughly combined. Add the pepper and mix well.
♠ Toast the bread slices in the oven until golden. Remove the toast and, while it is still hot, spread the tuna mixture on it.
♠ Arrange the toasts on a platter and serve.

SERVES 6

CROSTINI DI PESCE
Seafood Toasts

The secret to the success of this recipe lies in the quality of the seafood, which must be small, tender and very fresh. Scallops may be substituted for the cuttlefish if you prefer them.

1 small cuttlefish or squid or 6 sea scallops
6 mussels
6 clams
6 headless shrimp (prawns)
3 tablespoons extra virgin olive oil
2 garlic cloves, chopped
pinch of ground dried chili
¼ cup (2 fl oz/60 ml) dry white wine
1 plum (egg) tomato, peeled and chopped
salt
12 slices French baguette
1 tablespoon finely chopped fresh flat-leaf (Italian) parsley

♠ Preheat an oven to 350°F (180°C).
♠ Pull the tentacles from the cuttlefish (or squid) body. Discard the entrails, ink sac and cartilage from the body. Cut the tentacles off at the point just above the eyes and discard the head. Rinse the body and tentacles under cold running water. Set aside.
♠ Remove the mussel and clam meats from their shells. Peel and devein the shrimp.
♠ Heat the olive oil in a large skillet over moderate heat. Add the cuttlefish (or scallops), mussels, clams, shrimp, garlic and chili and cook, stirring, for 2 minutes. Add the wine and tomato and season to taste with salt. Cook until the liquid evaporates, about 3 minutes. Remove from the heat.
♠ Scoop the seafood mixture from the skillet onto a cutting surface. Chop the mixture fairly finely. Return it to the skillet off the heat.
♠ Just before serving, toast the bread slices in the oven until golden. At the same time, gently reheat the seafood mixture. Add the parsley and stir well.
♠ Remove the bread and, while it is still hot, spread the mixture on it. Arrange the toasts on a warm platter and serve immediately.

SERVES 6

CROSTINI DI POLENTA
Deep-Fried Polenta

Leftover polenta is generally used for frying. The cold polenta is cut into thick slices, deep-fried in olive oil and served immediately. When a lighter version is required, the polenta slices are brushed on both sides with a little oil and baked in a 350°F (180°C) oven until just golden, about 20 minutes.

3½ cups (30 fl oz/900 ml) water
1¾ cups (7 oz/210 g) coarse-grained cornmeal
salt
5 cups (40 fl oz/1.2 l) extra virgin olive oil

♠ In a deep saucepan, bring the water to a boil and add a little salt. Slowly add the cornmeal in a thin, steady stream, stirring constantly. Cook for about 40 minutes over low heat, stirring constantly with a wooden spoon. The polenta should be quite thick and pull away easily from the sides of the pan.
♠ Dampen the bottom and sides of a large, shallow bowl with cold water and pour the polenta into the bowl. Smooth the surface with a wet knife and let cool completely.

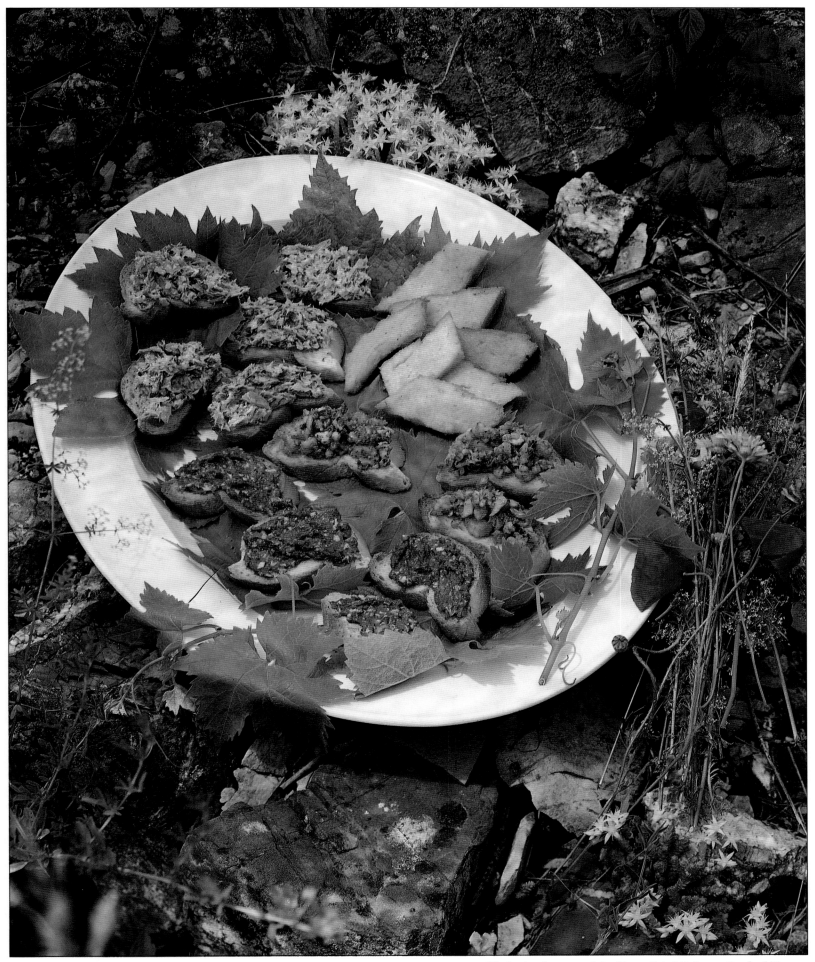

Clockwise from top right: Deep-Fried Polenta, Seafood Toasts,
Game Toasts and Tuna Fish Toasts

🍂 Unmold the cooled polenta by inverting the bowl onto a cutting board. Cut the polenta into slices about ⅜ in (1 cm) thick. Then cut the slices into rectangles about 2 in (5 cm) by 4 in (10 cm). If you prefer rounds, cut the polenta slices with the rim of a glass measuring 2 or 2½ in (5 or 6 cm) in diameter.
🍂 In a deep, heavy skillet, heat the olive oil to 350°F (180°C). A few at a time, slip the polenta pieces into the oil without crowding the pan. Fry until golden, about 10 minutes. With a slotted spoon, remove the polenta pieces to absorbent paper towels to drain briefly. Continue frying the remaining polenta pieces in the same manner.
🍂 Transfer the polenta to a warm plate and serve very hot.

SERVES 6

33

Elder Flower Flat Bread

SCHIACCIATA AL SAMBUCO

Elder Flower Flat Bread

The slight sweetness of elder flowers gives this flat bread a delightful taste. It is baked in the summertime, when the blossoms are abundant. If fresh elder flowers are unavailable, fresh rosemary leaves, in the same quantity, may be substituted.

⅔ cup (5 fl oz/160 ml) lukewarm water (105° to 115°F/42° to 46°C)

1 oz (30 g) fresh cake yeast or 2 packages (1 scant tablespoon each) active dry yeast

2½ cups (10 oz/300 g) all-purpose (plain) flour

pinch of salt

½ cup (3 oz/90 g) fresh, pesticide-free stemmed elder flowers or fresh rosemary leaves

2 tablespoons extra virgin olive oil

❧ Place the lukewarm water in a bowl. Sprinkle the yeast on top of the water and let stand until dissolved and foamy, about 10 minutes.

❧ Heap the flour on a work surface and make a well in the center. Pour the dissolved yeast into the well along with the salt and elder flowers. With a fork, gradually whisk in the flour until all the liquid is absorbed and a soft dough forms. On a lightly floured surface, knead the dough until it is soft and elastic, at least 10 minutes. Shape into a ball.

❧ Transfer the dough ball to a lightly floured bowl and cover with plastic wrap. Let rise at room temperature until doubled in bulk, about 1 hour.

❧ Turn the risen dough out onto a floured work surface. Punch down the dough and knead again briefly. With the palms of your hands, flatten the dough into a round about 9 in (23 cm) in diameter and ⅜ in (1 cm) thick. Sprinkle a 9-in (23-cm) cake pan with flour. Place the dough in the pan and let rise at room temperature for 20 minutes. Meanwhile, preheat an oven to 400°F (200°C).

❧ With a fingertip make several shallow indentations in the surface of the dough. Sprinkle the dough with the olive oil. Bake until the bread begins to turn golden, about 30 minutes.

❧ Remove from the oven, let cool for a few minutes and turn out of the pan onto a wire rack to cool.

❧ Cut into wedges and serve at room temperature.

SERVES 6

Siena

UOVA SODE AL DRAGONCELLO

Stuffed Eggs with Tarragon

In Siena the antipasto generally served is a plate of crostini *and cured meats, such as fennel-flavored salami and thick slices of salty Chiantigiano ham. Occasionally, extra delicacies like these eggs are added. Stuffed eggs are also served in Tuscany as a* piatto di mezzo *(see recipe for* uova sode alla maremmana, *page 107).*

6 eggs
2 tablespoons finely chopped fresh tarragon or flat-leaf
   (Italian) parsley
2 tablespoons extra virgin olive oil

1 tablespoon capers in wine vinegar, drained and chopped
2 tablespoons canned tuna fish in olive oil, drained
salt and freshly ground black pepper

♣ Place the eggs in a saucepan and add cold water to cover barely. Bring the water to a boil. When it reaches a boil, cook for 8 minutes from that moment. Remove the eggs from the pan and let cool to room temperature before shelling.
♣ Shell the eggs, cut them in half lengthwise and remove the yolks. Place the yolks in a mixing bowl. Cut a very thin slice off the rounded base of each egg white so that the egg half will stand upright. Set the whites aside.
♣ Add the tarragon, olive oil, capers and tuna to the egg yolks. Mash the ingredients together with a fork to form a smooth mixture. Season to taste with salt and pepper.
♣ Spoon the yolk mixture into the reserved egg white halves. Arrange on a plate and serve.

MAKES 12 STUFFED EGGS; SERVES 6

Stuffed Eggs with Tarragon

INTINTINO CON LA SALVIA
Bread Dipped in Sizzling Oil and Sage

This very different version of panunto *comes from Arezzo. Sage leaves are fried in olive oil and then bread is dipped into the flavored oil while it still sizzles. The best way to serve this dish is to place the pot on a burner in the middle of the dining table so that the oil stays very hot. Provide each guest with a long-handled fork for spearing and dipping the bread.*

1 cup (8 fl oz/240 ml) extra virgin olive oil
10 large fresh sage leaves
1 garlic clove
6 slices coarse country bread, sliced into finger-sized strips
salt

♣ Pour the olive oil into a pot, preferably made of flameproof earthenware, and warm over moderate heat to 325°F (165°C). Add the sage leaves and garlic and cook until the leaves are crisp, about 1 minute, or until the temperature reaches 350°F (180°C).

♣ Spear the bread onto the prongs of a long-handled fork and immerse the bread in the hot oil until the bread is golden, about 3 minutes.

♣ Lift the bread out of the oil, allowing any excess oil to drip back into the pot. Season the bread with a little salt and eat immediately.

SERVES 6

CROSTINI DI FEGATINI
Chicken Liver Toasts

These are the most traditional Tuscan crostini. *The pâté is often served on toasted country bread slightly moistened with stock. In the local trattorias,* crostini *are a must with the antipasti, which nearly always include a slice of* sopressata *(a cured meat made of pig's head) and a slice of* finocchiona *(a salami laced with fennel seed).*

13 oz (400 g) chicken livers
2 tablespoons extra virgin olive oil
2 garlic cloves
6 bay leaves
salt and freshly ground black pepper
¼ cup (2 fl oz/60 ml) dry white wine
1 cup (8 fl oz/240 ml) light chicken stock (recipe on page 73)
1 tablespoon capers in salt
4 canned flat anchovy fillets in olive oil, drained
2 tablespoons unsalted butter
12 slices coarse country bread or French baguette

♣ Remove and discard any fat and connective tissue from the chicken livers. Slice the livers into fairly large pieces.

♣ In a skillet over high heat, warm the olive oil. Add the garlic, bay leaves and chicken liver pieces. Season very lightly with salt and pepper. Stirring frequently, cook over high heat until the mixture starts sticking to the skillet, about 5 minutes.

♣ Add the wine, scrape the browned bits from the bottom of the skillet and cook over high heat until the wine evaporates, about 2 minutes. Add ¼ cup (2 fl oz/60 ml) of the stock, lower the heat to medium and cook for 5 minutes. Remove from the heat.

♣ Remove and discard the bay leaves. Put the liver mixture through the fine disc of a food mill, collecting the mixture in a small pan.

♣ Rinse the capers in cold water to remove the salt. Place the capers and anchovies on a cutting board and chop together finely. Add the caper-anchovy mixture to the liver mixture along with the butter.

♣ Place the pan over low heat and cook, stirring constantly, until the ingredients are well blended and smooth, just a few minutes. Do not allow the mixture to boil. Transfer the mixture to a bowl and let cool, stirring occasionally.

♣ Meanwhile, preheat an oven to 350°F (180°C). Toast the bread slices in the oven until golden. Remove the bread and, while they are still hot, dip each slice quickly into the remaining ¾ cup (6 fl oz/180 ml) stock. Spread the toasts with the liver mixture and serve.

SERVES 6   *Photograph pages 28–29*

BOCCONCINI DI CARCIOFI
Deep-Fried Baby Artichokes

Small purple artichokes are ideal for this recipe. On the Chianti hills they ripen in late spring and are often eaten raw with olive oil and salt. They are so small that each one is only a mouthful.

juice of 1 lemon
18 small purple artichokes
5 cups (40 fl oz/1.2 l) extra virgin olive oil for frying
salt

♣ Fill a large bowl with water and add the lemon juice. Remove the tough outer leaves and cut away the sharp leaf points from the tops of the artichokes. Cut the stalks off. As each artichoke is trimmed, drop it into the water to prevent discoloration.

♣ In a deep, heavy skillet, heat the oil to 350°F (180°C).

♣ Drain the artichokes and dry them well with absorbent paper towels. A few at a time, slip the artichokes into the hot oil and fry until golden, about 5 minutes. With a slotted spoon, remove the artichokes to drain briefly on absorbent paper towels. Continue frying the remaining artichokes in the same manner.

♣ Transfer the artichokes to a warm plate and sprinkle with salt to taste. Serve very hot.

SERVES 6   *Photograph pages 8–9*

SEDANI IN PINZIMONIO
Dipped Celery

During the winter months, white celery hearts dipped in newly pressed olive oil are particularly crunchy and delicious. Every vegetable garden near Florence has rows of celery plants; each plant has been carefully wrapped and buried in the ground to keep it white and very tender. The stalks are used for cooking and the hearts are eaten raw.

1 cup (8 fl oz/240 ml) extra virgin olive oil
salt and freshly ground black pepper
6 white celery hearts

♣ Divide the olive oil among 6 little bowls. Season each portion with just a touch of salt and pepper.

♣ Trim the celery hearts as needed and arrange them on a serving plate. Provide each diner with a bowl of the seasoned oil in which to dip the celery.

SERVES 6   *Photograph pages 8–9*

Bread Dipped in Sizzling Oil and Sage

FIGATTOLE

Anchovies Fried in Dough

Until a few years ago, Florence was full of friggitorie, shops where food was fried and sold piping hot from the pan. Customers waited to buy little fried fish from the Arno, meatballs and a variety of vegetables, and then usually consumed them on the spot. Sadly these shops have almost all disappeared and, with them, the custom of popping in for a quick snack and a glass of wine.

10 oz (300 g) risen bread dough (any favorite white bread recipe)
9 canned flat anchovy fillets in olive oil, drained
5 cups (40 fl oz/1.2 l) extra virgin olive oil for frying

🌢 On a floured surface, roll out the dough 3/16 in (.5 cm) thick. Cut into 18 rectangles about 2 in (5 cm) by 4 in (10 cm). Cut the anchovy fillets in half crosswise. Place half an anchovy fillet lengthwise on the center of each rectangle. Fold each rectangle in half to form a square and press the edges firmly together to seal.

🌢 In a deep, heavy skillet, heat the olive oil to 350°F (180°C). A few at a time, slip the squares into the hot oil without crowding the pan. Fry until puffy and golden, about 3 minutes.

🌢 With a slotted spoon, remove the squares to absorbent paper towels to drain briefly. Continue frying the remaining squares in the same manner.

🌢 Transfer the squares to a warm plate and serve very hot.

MAKES 18 SQUARES; SERVES 6

GAMBERETTI ALL'AGRO

Marinated Shrimp

The best shrimp are caught close to rocks, and the tiny gray variety is a specialty of Livorno. Headless medium-sized shrimp can be used if small ones are not available. The delicate shellfish may be left to marinate in a cool place for several hours, but should not be refrigerated, as they lose their flavor at low temperatures.

4 cups (32 fl oz/1 l) water
salt
2 lb (900 g) small shrimp (prawns) in the shell
juice of 2 lemons
white pepper
2 tablespoons chopped fresh flat-leaf (Italian) parsley
¼ cup (2 fl oz/60 ml) extra virgin olive oil

🌢 In a saucepan, bring the water to a boil and add a little salt. Add the shrimp and cover the saucepan immediately. When the water returns to a boil, allow the shrimp to cook for only 2 minutes. Drain the shrimp and cool under running water.

🌢 Peel the shrimp, being careful not to tear the bodies. Put the peeled shrimp into a bowl, pour the lemon juice over them and season to taste with salt and pepper.

🌢 Marinate in a cool place for 2–6 hours, turning gently from time to time.

🌢 Drain the shrimp. Arrange them on a serving dish. Sprinkle with the parsley, drizzle with the olive oil and serve.

SERVES 6   *Photograph pages 28–29*

Anchovies Fried in Dough

Livorno

GAMBERETTI ALLA SALVIA
Fried Shrimp with Sage

Fried shrimp have always been served in Livorno on the feast of San Giuseppe in March. In early spring the shrimp are very small and are cooked whole with young sage leaves. For this recipe use the smallest shrimp you can find.

1 lb (450 g) very small shrimp (prawns) in the shell, with or
  without heads
½ cup (4 fl oz/120 ml) extra virgin olive oil
10 fresh sage leaves
salt and freshly ground black pepper

♣ Rinse the shrimp under cold running water and pat them dry with absorbent paper towels; set aside.
♣ In a heavy skillet over moderate heat, warm the olive oil. Add the sage leaves and cook for 2 minutes. Add the shrimp, cover the skillet and cook for 2 minutes. Remove the lid, season to taste with salt and pepper and lower the heat. Cook, uncovered, for 2 minutes.
♣ Transfer the shrimp mixture to a warm platter and serve immediately.

SERVES 6

Siena

FIORI DI ZUCCA RIPIENI DI SALSICCIA
Zucchini Flowers Stuffed with Sausage

Zucchini flowers are prepared in a slightly different way in every Tuscan town. They can be served as an antipasto or as a vegetable accompanying a meat or fish dish (see fiori di zucca *recipe, page 198). In Siena they are particularly tasty, as they are stuffed with sausages made in the Chianti region, which are famous for being lean and full of flavor. Be sure to buy flowers that are still closed.*

3 tablespoons extra virgin olive oil
30 unopened zucchini (courgette) flowers
8 oz (240 g) sweet Italian sausages
1 egg
½ cup (2 oz/60 g) freshly grated Parmesan cheese
1 garlic clove, chopped
salt and freshly ground black pepper

♣ Preheat an oven to 350°F (180°C). Brush a 20-by-12-in (50-by-30-cm) baking dish with half of the olive oil.
♣ With a small, sharp knife, make a small incision in the side of each flower and remove the pistil. Cut off the stalk.
♣ Skin the sausages and crumble the meat into a mixing bowl. Add the egg, Parmesan and garlic; mix well. Carefully open the incision in each flower and insert a little of the sausage mixture. Squeeze the opening closed.
♣ Arrange the stuffed flowers in the prepared baking dish in rows. Season to taste with salt and pepper and sprinkle with the remaining olive oil.
♣ Cover the dish with aluminum foil and bake until the flowers and their stuffing are cooked and sizzling hot, about 15 minutes.
♣ Arrange the flowers on a warm serving dish and serve very hot.

SERVES 6   *Photograph pages 28–29*

Lucca

FOGLIE DI SALVIA FRITTE
Fried Sage Leaves

Sage bushes are grown all over Tuscany, where they are valued as much for their scent and decorativeness in the garden as they are for their contributions in the kitchen. Sage is used to flavor roasts, soups and sauces. When the leaves are large, they are delicious fried in a light batter.

1 egg
¼ cup (2 fl oz/60 ml) water
pinch of salt
½ cup (2 oz/60 g) all-purpose (plain) flour
1 tablespoon extra virgin olive oil, plus 5 cups (40 fl oz/1.2 l)
  for frying
18 large fresh sage leaves

♣ In a small bowl, beat together the egg, water and salt until well blended. Pour the flour into a bowl.
♣ Gradually add the egg mixture and then the 1 tablespoon olive oil to the flour, whisking constantly to keep lumps from forming. Whisk until the batter is the consistency of thick cream.
♣ In a deep, heavy skillet, heat the frying oil to 350°F (180°C). Dip each sage leaf into the batter and immediately drop it into the hot oil; do not crowd the pan. Fry until lightly golden, about 3 minutes.
♣ With a slotted spoon, remove the leaves to absorbent paper towels to drain briefly. Continue coating and frying the remaining sage leaves in the same manner.
♣ Transfer the leaves to a warm plate and serve very hot.

SERVES 6   *Photograph pages 28–29*

Arezzo

FRITTURA DI MELANZANE
Fried Eggplant

Eggplants are at their best in summer and autumn. During the season local restaurants serve various eggplant preparations that are generally associated with southern Italy. The dishes are said to have been introduced by Neapolitans who came to work in the tanneries near Arezzo in the nineteenth century.

3 Asian (slender) eggplants (aubergines), about 1¼ lb (600 g)
  total, cut crosswise into slices ⅜ in (1 cm) thick
1½ cups (6 oz/180 g) all-purpose (plain) flour
5 cups (40 fl oz/1.2 l) extra virgin olive oil for frying
salt and freshly ground black pepper

♣ Dredge the eggplant slices in the flour and shake off any excess.
♣ In a deep, heavy skillet, heat the oil to 350°F (180°C). A few slices at a time, slip the eggplant slices into the hot oil; do not crowd the pan. Fry until golden on both sides, about 3 minutes.
♣ With a slotted spoon, remove the eggplant slices to absorbent paper towels to drain briefly. Continue frying the remaining eggplant slices in the same manner. Season to taste with salt and pepper.
♣ Arrange the eggplant slices on a warm platter and serve piping hot.

SERVES 6

Fried Eggplant (rear) and Fried Shrimp with Sage (front)

Wild Boar Sausages Wrapped in Pastry

Grosseto

SALSICCIE DI CINGHIALE IN CROSTA

Wild Boar Sausages Wrapped in Pastry

In the Maremma hunters generally stop for a lunch of wild boar sausages cooked on an open fire. They also toast bread, douse it with olive oil and wash it down with good red wine. In local trattorias these sausages, either fresh or dried, are nearly always on the menu.

1¼ cups (5 oz/150 g) all-purpose (plain) flour
⅓ cup (3 oz/90 g) unsalted butter
pinch of salt
1 tablespoon water
12 small fresh wild boar sausages or sweet Italian sausages
  (about 1 lb/450 g)
3 tablespoons extra virgin olive oil
1 tablespoon red wine vinegar

♣ Heap the flour on a board. Using your fingertips, work in small pieces of the butter until all the flour has been absorbed by the butter. Add the salt and water and shape the pastry dough quickly into a ball. Wrap the dough ball in plastic wrap and refrigerate it for about 1 hour.
♣ The sausages should be about 2 in (5 cm) in length and a bit narrower than that. If necessary, cut larger sausages to about that size.
♣ In a skillet over moderate heat, warm 2 tablespoons of the olive oil. Add the sausages and cook them until they begin to brown, about 5 minutes. Pour in the vinegar and continue cooking until it evaporates, about 1 minute. Remove from the heat and let the sausages cool to room temperature.
♣ Preheat an oven to 350°F (180°C). Brush a 20-by-12-in (50-by-30-cm) baking dish with the remaining 1 tablespoon oil.
♣ On a lightly floured work surface, gently roll out the pastry about ⅟₁₆ in (2 mm) thick. Cut the pastry into 12 squares, each measuring about 2⅜ in (6 cm). Place a sausage on each square. Roll the pastry around the sausage and fold in the ends to enclose the sausage completely. Seal the seams with a little water.
♣ Arrange the wrapped sausages in the prepared baking dish and bake until golden, about 20 minutes. Serve very hot.

SERVES 6

Livorno

ACCIUGHE ALL'AGLIO E PEPERONCINO

Anchovies with Oil, Garlic and Chili

Anchovies preserved in salt are much tastier than those packed in oil. Before using them, however, they must be well rinsed under cold running water and then dried thoroughly.

1¼ lb (600 g) anchovies in salt
½ cup (4 fl oz/120 ml) extra virgin olive oil
3 garlic cloves, finely chopped
2 tablespoons chopped fresh flat-leaf (Italian) parsley
pinch of ground dried chili

♣ Rinse the anchovies under cold running water and pat dry with absorbent paper towels. Slit them open lengthwise along the belly, keeping the fillets intact. Remove and discard the bones.
♣ Arrange the fillets on a slightly concave serving plate. Pour the oil over the fillets and sprinkle with the garlic, parsley and chili.
♣ Let stand at room temperature for about 2 hours before serving.

SERVES 6   *Photograph pages 28–29*

Chick-pea Flat Bread

Garlic Toasts

CECINA

Chick-pea Flat Bread

This flat, savory bread made with chick-pea flour is slightly salty and is sometimes seasoned with rosemary. It makes an excellent antipasto with a glass of the dry Montecarlo white wine produced near Lucca. Cecina is sometimes served instead of regular bread; when cut into small cubes and added to vegetable stock, it gives a great lift to a simple dish. Chick-pea flour is available in health food stores.

4 tablespoons (2 fl oz/60 ml) extra virgin olive oil
2½ cups (10 oz/300 g) chick-pea (garbanzo) flour
3½ cups (30 fl oz/900 ml) water
generous pinch of salt
1 tablespoon chopped fresh rosemary

♣ Preheat an oven to 350°F (170°C). Oil a 9-in (23-cm) cake pan with 1 tablespoon of the olive oil.
♣ Pour the flour into a large bowl. Gradually add the water to the flour, whisking constantly to keep lumps from forming. Add the salt, rosemary and the remaining 3 tablespoons olive oil. Whisk until the batter is smooth. Pour the batter into the prepared pan. Bake until golden, about 40 minutes.
♣ Remove the bread from the oven and let cool for a few minutes. Remove from the pan and cut into slices. Serve hot.

MAKES 1 ROUND LOAF; SERVES 6

PANUNTO

Garlic Toasts

Recently panunto, *sometimes called* fettunta, bruschetta *or* fegolotta, *has become fashionable in restaurants all over the world. In Tuscany, however, it has always been everyone's favorite snack. When I was a child and went on holiday to the seashore in Versilia, my companions and I loved to ride our bicycles into the hinterland, where the farmers' wives offered us this variation on a classic.*

6 large slices coarse country bread
2 garlic cloves
1 ripe tomato, cut in half
6 tablespoons (3 fl oz/90 ml) extra virgin olive oil
salt

♣ Prepare a fire in a charcoal grill or preheat an oven to 350°F (180°C).
♣ Toast the bread slices on the grill or in the oven until golden. Remove the bread and, while it is still hot, rub one side of each slice with the garlic and then with a cut side of the tomato. Sprinkle each slice with 1 tablespoon of the olive oil and season to taste with salt.
♣ Arrange the toasts on a platter and serve immediately.

SERVES 6

SIENA

SIENA

I f one declares Florence the heart of Tuscany's culture, then Siena is the heart of its magic. With its narrow streets, distinctive *contrade* (neighborhoods), tall palaces and sculpted, almost Nordic air, Siena is a city of mystery and contrast. The most striking contrast is visible when the mad, colorful excitement of the Palio is set amidst these severe surroundings. Every July and August for the last several hundred years, the entire city has thrown itself with a vengeance into the oldest and most dangerous horse race in the world. To the Sienese the Palio race is only incidentally a tourist attraction. It is instead their very life, something that explodes twice a year in the Piazza del Campo, the most beautiful setting in Italy.

The city of Siena is only the beginning, though. Many of the loveliest places in all of Tuscany are set, like so many jewels in a crown, in the province of Siena. They range from Etruscan Volterra with its alabaster to San Gimignano and its towers, from the mystical Abbey of Monte Oliveto Maggiore to the mysterious Abbey of San Galgano.

The Sienese are reserved but fiery, something especially apparent on the two days of the Palio. They love life, and therefore good food. Dante described them as great eaters, and they have good reason to be, living in the oldest part of Tuscany, the former land of the Etruscans. Some of the recipes of those ancient peoples, such as fish from the lake at Chiusi cooked in an earthenware pan, are still used. When Chiusi was Etruscan and called Chamars,

Left: An abandoned farmhouse near Bagno Vignoni seems to blend into the surrounding countryside. Even in the most remote areas of Tuscany lie subtle reminders of man's presence on the land. Previous pages: Members of the Pantera contrada *(district) celebrate their horse's victory at Siena's famed Palio race, held every July 2 and August 16.*

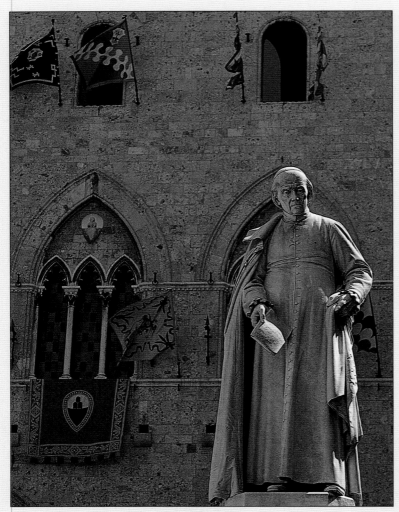

Around every corner in Siena is a small piece of the city's tumultuous history. This statue in Piazza Salimbeni honors Sallustio Antonio Bandini (1677–1760), a famous political economist from Siena.

the entrails of these same fish were used by soothsayers to peer into the future.

The Siena countryside has long been known for its excellent produce. In a nineteenth-century book on the region, an eminent scientist wrote, "The food available in Siena makes one's stay a very happy one . . . the dishes prepared here, all authentic specialities, are envied by experts from all over the world."

The meat, for example, enjoys great fame. True Florentine T-bone steaks are cut from Chianina beef, a breed raised in the Val di Chiana, an area stretching from Arezzo to Chiusi and Montepulciano. The beef from these cattle was first enjoyed by the Etruscans and later by the Romans. In fact, for the last two thousand years these cattle have been constantly bred to improve their extraordinary meat, which, while tender, is not too fatty.

Even Sienese poultry has a particular flavor. Hens raised in confinement have never become popular in this area. Chickens still wander around pecking in large open runs, feeding on grain and leftovers from country kitchens. They are certainly much tougher than supermarket chickens, which disintegrate at a touch, but their flavor is wonderful.

Local farmers husband their animals not only for their meat but also for their milk, and the best Tuscan cheeses are made in the province of Siena. There is good grazing land in the rather wild, uncultivated areas, and a long history of cheesemaking from sheep's milk. In the 1950s, when farmers all over Italy started to leave the land, Sardinian shepherds moved in. Together with the few Tuscans who kept their flocks, these Sardinians have managed to preserve the traditions. Even today Sienese

pecorino, raveggiolo, cacciotte, marzolino and ricotta are made in the same way as they were centuries ago.

The countryside is still home to many varieties of game. Wild boar root about in the holly forests and scrub. Pheasant are shot and stuffed with chopped meat and liver, and wild duck are very popular. Hare are cooked in a sweet and strong sauce made with local biscuits called *cavallucci.*

The whole of Tuscany is renowned for its cured meats, but the very best come from the province of Siena because of the high quality of the local meat. *Finocchiona,* a large salami flavored with fennel seed, is produced here, and so is *capocollo* (made from the upper neck meat of the pig), *soppressata* (headcheese), dried wild boar sausages and *scriccioli* (crisply fried pork fat).

Siena is the Tuscan city with the longest tradition of cake- and biscuitmaking, and honey goes into many of the recipes because it is particularly good here. Sienese sweetmeats were born in the Middle Ages and have a strong Arab influence. *Cavallucci, beriguocoli, ricciarelli* and *panforte* have been appreciated beyond the city walls for many years. Together with the Piazza del Campo, *panforte* (a flat fruitcake) is almost the city's symbol. Centuries ago it was made in the monasteries, but early in the last century *panforte* began to be produced commercially. As though to prove that despite its austere facade Siena is the sweetest city in Tuscany, there are many other desserts produced here, such as *budinone di riso* (a rice pudding), *cenci* (very lightly fried biscuits whose name means "rags"), *copata* (invented in a monastery) and the classic *castagnaccio* (a cake made with chestnut flour).

The Sienese use more herbs in their cooking than do other Tuscan cooks. There are no dishes here without a little sage, calamint, basil, rosemary, mint or thyme. Sometimes recipes that are otherwise very simple are made important by the herbs, so much so that during the last century a famous Italian statesman was moved to say, "It is a poor man's kitchen fit to be served to a king." A corner of every Sienese garden is devoted to the cultivation of herbs, and in towns they are grown in pots

A young boy in the Palio parade. To visitors the Palio may look like just a raucous horse race, but to the Sienese it is a sacred tradition. A local proverb says "He who has not seen the Palio does not know Siena."

The skyline of San Gimignano was once crowded with 72 towers, built by two warring families who tried to outdo one another by building higher and higher structures. Today only 15 towers remain.

decorating the windowsills. At the best restaurants and trattorias in the province, such as La Bottega del Trento at Castelnuovo Berardenga, the restaurant at Badia a Coltibuono, L'Antica Trattoria in Colle di Val d'Elsa, La Chiusa in Montefollonico, and Mugolone in Siena, herbs contribute to the dishes in a hundred different ways.

In addition to these local herbs, a French plant, tarragon, has been adopted by the Sienese. Legend has it that tarragon was first brought to Siena by Charlemagne's troops in the eighth century. During the Middle Ages it was considered a medicinal plant, but now tarragon, used both fresh and dried, even seasons the local salamis.

As though Siena's beautiful buildings, museums, atmosphere and cuisine were not enough, there are yet two other features that make the province of unparalleled importance. They are its wine and its olive oil. The oil is certainly not only the best and most fragrant in all Tuscany, but it also has the lowest acid content. Recent internationally recognized medical studies have confirmed that olive oil is good for the health. But even as long ago as the fourteenth century, this fragrant oil was already defined in Italy as "essential to human life."

The Sienese countryside is home to yet another nectar—wine. In this small area some of the most famous Italian wines are produced. It is not by mere chance that the Enoteca Italica Permanente, the most prestigious promotional center for the great Italian vintages, is situated at the Fortezza Medicea in Siena. Brunello di Montalcino, Vino Nobile di Montepulciano, Vin Santo and Vernaccia di San Gimignano are just a few of the famous local wines.

But, above all, there is Chianti. The area called Chianti, which lies between Florence and Siena, is an old land

rich in treasures from every historical period: hilltop villages, towers, Renaissance villas, imposing monasteries, small parish churches and vineyards. The 170,000 acres that yield the famed Chianti Classico correspond more or less to those proclaimed by the Grand Duke of Tuscany in 1716. This was the first time in the long history of winemaking that a legal document defined an area in which a particular wine could be produced, and it would be another two hundred years before such an initiative would again be taken anywhere else in the world.

Wine has been made for centuries in Chianti, and documents related to winemaking dated 1037 were found in the archives at Badia a Coltibuono. Chianti Classico, depending on its age, goes perfectly with Tuscan food. When it is young and fresh it should be served with antipasti, soups and fried foods. Between two and five years old, it goes well with white meat and young cheese. A robust, well-aged wine is ideal with roast or braised meat, game and well-aged cheese.

One of the most famous dessert wines in Italy, Vin Santo, was born in Chianti and then spread through the rest of Tuscany. Its praises were sung by poets such as Cecco Angiolieri and Boccaccio, and indeed a fine Vin Santo is the pride of its producer, be he prince or peasant. Always made in the same way, it is aged in small sealed casks called *caratelli*. Vin Santo is said by some to have received its name because it is the wine that every priest would like to have on his altar. It is such a superb wine that, around 1760, Pope Clement wrote a glowing letter of thanks to a friend who had sent him a present of some bottles: "Dear Son, as long as you continue to send this Vin Santo, your Pope will always thrive."

I Primi

Bread has been a basic ingredient in Tuscan soups for centuries.

I PRIMI

While antipasti, meat and game dishes, and the brilliant use of the spit for roasting all originated in the kitchens of the Tuscan courts, church prelates and merchants, first courses have far humbler beginnings.

The various soups, *acquecotte, ribollite* and *pappe,* which, in their infinite interpretations are the most traditional first courses in Tuscany, were originally the staple diet of poor families. Their basic ingredient was, and still is, bread. In early times these bread soups were at best occasionally enriched with a little lard or wild herbs. *Zuppa di pane* (bread soup) was distributed to the poor by monks who soaked stale bread and made it into a pap. Sometimes they pounded the bread with garlic and leeks to give it more flavor and nourishment.

It could almost be said that the basis of Tuscan first courses is still bread enriched with beans, black cabbage, leafy greens and other vegetables, plus, of course, olive oil. Each area has its own bread soup, and each claims that its version is the most authentic and, naturally, the most delicious. *Acquacotta,* literally "cooked water," is a good example, although nowadays it is more than just boiled herbs and water. The actual number of varieties of this soup is still a mystery. It is made in Siena, the Maremma, Grosseto and Arezzo, but, as with so many recipes, there are no two houses where it is prepared in the same way, let alone two areas.

Another very old tradition in the mountains of Tuscany is to mix vegetables with polenta. Although

called by various names, this dish is substantially the same everywhere. In the Garfagnana it is called *infarinata* and is excellent sliced and fried. In Versilia it is *intruglia,* meaning "mixture," and in Lunigiana it is *incatenata,* or "chained." In Tuscany cornmeal is made into gnocchi,

Pasta for sale at Siena's Manganelli shop. The hundred-year-old establishment sells spices, candies, wines and other groceries.

Previous pages: Meat Soup (left, page 71) and Cornmeal and Vegetable Soup (right, page 66).

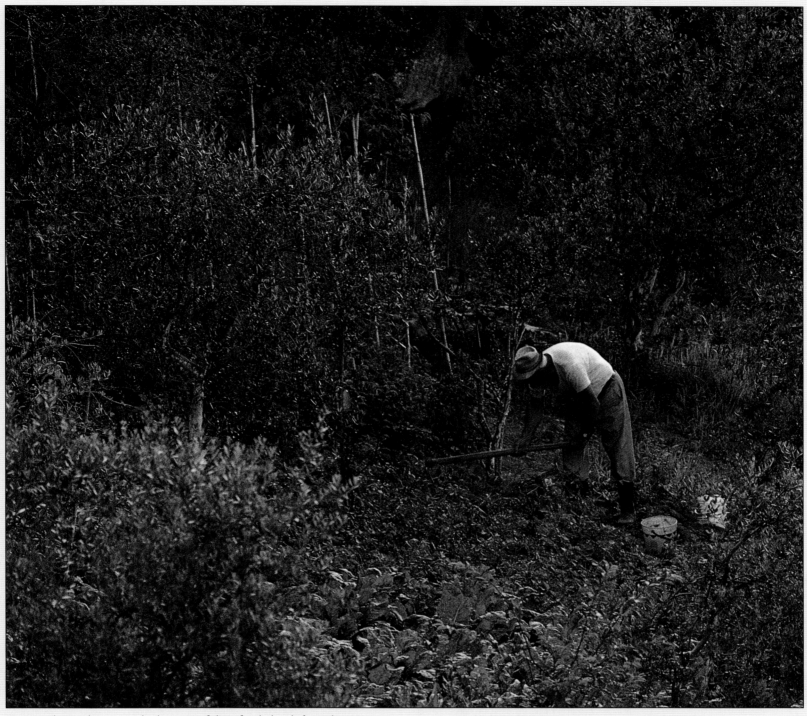

Tuscans have always made the most of their fertile land, from the vast, sweeping vineyards to the tiniest kitchen garden.

which, without varying much from place to place, are called different things ranging from puffs to billiard balls. Basically, fairly thick polenta is rolled into gnocchi and smothered with meat sauce.

In the mountains there are also several first courses prepared with chestnuts, such as *tortelli* stuffed with a mixture of ricotta and chestnuts, or *manifregoli,* a polenta made with chestnut flour and cold milk. For hundreds of years these dishes, together with *incaciata,* a polenta prepared with chestnut flour and dressed with olive oil and sheep's milk cheese, were the usual fare of the marble cutters in the Apuan Alps.

In the Garfagnana spelt continued to be an essential part of the diet long after it had been abandoned in other regions. Now, after centuries, this reddish-tinged grain is becoming fashionable all over Italy, and not only with the health-conscious.

Although soups are considered the highlights of Tuscan first courses, it does not mean that there are no excellent pastas. *Pappardelle alla lepre,* wide ribbons of fresh pasta with hare sauce, is said to be Etruscan in

origin. Purists still leave tomatoes out of the sauce, because it was cooked without them for several hundred years before tomatoes were brought from the New World. There are also Tuscan *maccheroni,* a word which causes a great deal of confusion even to Italians. In the rest of Italy, *maccheroni* is short with a hole in the middle, but in Lucchesia it is about three inches wide, flat and made with egg. Just to add to the confusion, the same pasta is sometimes called *tacconi.*

Some stuffed pastas are also of Tuscan origin. *Tordelli,* stuffed with meat, chard and ricotta, originated in Versilia. Then there are *tortelli* filled with a mixture of potato and chopped bacon, a very economical dish from the hills of Mugello.

Tuscan cuisine even includes a few risottos. This method of preparing rice is not originally Tuscan, but the risottos were developed to use local ingredients. Perhaps the best one of all is black rice with cuttlefish and chard from Livorno.

And finally, at the coast, there is a long list of fish soups and pasta sauces that are well worth trying.

Arezzo

MINESTRA DI CECI E BACCALÀ
Chick-pea and Salt Cod Soup

Friday is by custom fish day in Italy, so on Thursdays salt cod is already soaking in the markets of inland Tuscany. If you buy unsoaked salt cod, it should be soaked in water to cover for a day to soften it and rid it of the salt.

7 oz (210 g) salt cod
1½ cups (10 oz/300 g) dried chick-peas (garbanzos)
3 tablespoons extra virgin olive oil
1 small yellow onion, chopped
8 cups (64 fl oz/2 l) water
10 oz (300 g) plum (egg) tomatoes, peeled and diced

❧ Soak the salt cod in water to cover in the refrigerator for 24 hours, changing the water 3 or 4 times. Drain.
❧ Meanwhile, in a bowl, soak the chick-peas in water to cover for 12 hours. Drain and set aside.
❧ Remove and discard the skin and bones from the salt cod. Chop the cod into bite-sized pieces. In a deep saucepan over low heat, warm the olive oil. Add the onion and salt cod and fry gently, stirring frequently, until the onion is translucent, about 5 minutes. Add the water, tomatoes and chick-peas and stir well. Bring to a boil, cover, lower the heat and simmer gently until the chick-peas are very tender, about 2 hours. Remember not to add any salt.
❧ Pour into a tureen and serve very hot.

SERVES 6

Chick-pea and Salt Cod Soup

Lucca

MINESTRONE DI RISO E CASTAGNE
Chestnut and Rice Soup

Nearly all Tuscan soups are made with at least some beans. In autumn, however, when chestnuts are at the height of their season, they often replace beans in the soup pot.

10 oz (300 g) chestnuts
3 tablespoons extra virgin olive oil
1 small yellow onion, chopped
2 carrots, peeled and chopped
2 celery stalks, trimmed and chopped
1 potato, peeled and coarsely diced
8 cups (64 fl oz/2 l) light chicken stock (recipe on page 73)
2 bay leaves
1 cup (7 oz/210 g) Arborio rice
salt

❧ With a small, sharp knife, make an X on the flat face of each chestnut. Bring a medium saucepan of water to a rolling boil and add the chestnuts. Boil for about 5 minutes, then drain. While the chestnuts are still hot, remove both the hard outer shell and the furry inner skin. (The chestnuts are more difficult to peel if they cool completely.) Chop the chestnuts coarsely and set aside.
❧ In a deep saucepan over low heat, warm the olive oil. Add the onion and fry gently, stirring frequently, until translucent, about 5 minutes. Add the carrots, celery and potato and stir well. Add the chestnuts, stock and bay leaves and bring slowly to a boil. Reduce the heat to a simmer, cover and cook for 1¾ hours.
❧ Add the rice and boil gently for exactly 15 minutes. Season to taste with salt.
❧ Remove and discard the bay leaves and pour the soup into a tureen. Serve immediately.

SERVES 6

Lucca

INFARINATA
Polenta with Vegetables

In the Garfagnana, the mountainous region near Lucca, polenta is served with beans, sausages or small pieces of fried whole-wheat bread. One of the simplest dishes, however, is this polenta flavored with vegetables and olive oil.

5 cups (40 fl oz/1.2 l) water
salt
2½ cups (10 oz/300 g) coarse-grained cornmeal
1 lb (450 g) mixed vegetables, such as carrots, celery, yellow onions and broccoli raab, diced
⅓ cup (3 fl oz/90 ml) extra virgin olive oil

❧ In a deep saucepan, bring the water and salt to a boil. Slowly add the cornmeal in a thin, steady stream, stirring constantly. Add the vegetables and cook over low heat for about 40 minutes, stirring constantly. The polenta is ready when it starts pulling away easily from the sides of the pan.
❧ Dampen the inside of a deep bowl with water. Pour in the polenta and smooth the surface with a wet knife. Cover and let rest for about 10 minutes.
❧ Invert the bowl to unmold the polenta onto a cutting surface. Cut the polenta into slices about ⅜ in (1 cm) thick and arrange on a serving plate. Sprinkle with the olive oil. Serve hot.

SERVES 6

Polenta with Vegetables (top) and Chestnut and Rice Soup (bottom)

Firenze

TAGLIERINI IN BRODO

Thin Noodles in Broth

Some Tuscan cooks scorn pasta machines, saying that it is quicker to make dough by hand, roll it out with a rolling pin and slice it with a knife, but of course pasta machines are widely used.

1¾ cups (7 oz/210 g) all-purpose (plain) flour
2 eggs
2 tablespoons extra virgin olive oil
7 oz (210 g) chicken livers, trimmed and chopped
2 bay leaves
½ cup (4 fl oz/120 ml) dry white wine
6 cups (48 fl oz/1.5 l) light chicken stock (recipe on page 73)
salt

🐦 Heap the flour in a mound on a work surface. Make a well in the center and break the eggs into it. Beat the eggs lightly with a fork, then gradually work the flour into the eggs until a loose ball of dough forms. Knead the dough on a lightly floured surface until soft, smooth and elastic, about 5 minutes. Using a pasta machine, roll out the dough very thinly. Allow to stand for a few minutes, then, using the narrow cutter on the machine, cut the dough into long, thin strips about 1/16 in (2 mm) wide. Roll the noodles into nests about 2 in (5 cm) in diameter and place on a clean cloth. Sprinkle very lightly with flour.
🐦 In a large skillet over moderate heat, warm the olive oil. Add the chicken livers and bay leaves and cook, stirring frequently, until the livers start to brown. Pour in the wine, stir well and simmer until the wine evaporates, about 5 minutes. Meanwhile, in a saucepan, bring the stock to a boil. Season to taste with salt. Add the noodles and boil them for exactly 2 minutes.
🐦 Remove and discard the bay leaves. With a slotted spoon, transfer the chicken livers to the noodles and stock. Pour the soup into a tureen immediately.

SERVES 6

Lucca

ZUPPA DI FARRO

Spelt Soup

This farmhouse soup can be refined by making it with capon stock instead of water. Farmers' wives generally leave it to cook gently on the corner of a wood-burning stove; the fire gradually dies out during the night and by morning the soup is perfectly cooked. If you have a way of cooking very, very slowly, there is no need to soak the spelt.

2½ cups (14 oz/420 g) spelt
3 tablespoons extra virgin olive oil
½ yellow onion, chopped
2 garlic cloves, chopped
1 fresh rosemary sprig, chopped
10 oz (300 g) plum (egg) tomatoes, peeled and diced
pinch of fennel seed
8 cups (64 fl oz/2 l) light capon or chicken stock (recipe on page 73)

🐦 In a bowl, soak the spelt in water to cover for 12 hours. Drain the spelt and set aside.
🐦 In a large saucepan over low heat, warm the olive oil. Add the onion, garlic and rosemary and fry gently, stirring frequently, until the onion is translucent, about 5 minutes. Add the spelt, tomatoes, fennel seed and stock and bring slowly to a boil. Lower the heat, cover and simmer gently for 2 hours.
🐦 Pour into a tureen and serve very hot.

SERVES 6

Spelt Soup (left) and Thin Noodles in Broth (right)

Top to bottom: Cabbage Soup, Ribollita, and Cabbage with Bread and Oil

ZUPPA DI CAVOLO

Cabbage Soup

A kitchen garden in Tuscany always has at least one row of black cabbages. They are never eaten until after the first frosts, when they are much tastier and more tender, and they are an important ingredient in the preparation of a variety of soups. If unavailable, Savoy cabbage may be used as a substitute.

1⅛ cups (7 oz/210 g) dried *cannellini* beans
2 lb (1 kg) black cabbage or Savoy cabbage
4 tablespoons (2 fl oz/60 ml) extra virgin olive oil
1 yellow onion, chopped
2 garlic cloves, chopped, plus 2 whole garlic cloves
1 carrot, peeled and chopped
1 celery stalk, trimmed and chopped
3 plum (egg) tomatoes, peeled and chopped
8 cups (64 fl oz/2 l) light vegetable stock (recipe on page 73)
1 tablespoon fresh thyme leaves
salt
6 slices coarse country bread
freshly ground black pepper

🦂 In a bowl, soak the beans in water to cover for 12 hours. Drain and set aside.

🦂 Remove and discard the hard stalks from the cabbage leaves. Slice the leaves roughly; set aside.

🦂 In a deep saucepan over moderate heat, warm 2 tablespoons of the olive oil. Add the onion and chopped garlic and fry gently, stirring frequently, until translucent, about 5 minutes. Add the carrot, celery, tomatoes and cabbage. Stir and then let cook until the vegetables wilt, about 10 minutes. Add 1¼ cups (10 fl oz/300 ml) of the stock; season with thyme and salt to taste.

🦂 Cover and slowly bring to a boil. Boil gently for 30 minutes, stirring frequently. Add the remaining stock and the beans. Stir well and continue to cook, covered, for 1½ hours, stirring occasionally.

🦂 Meanwhile, preheat an oven to 350°F (180°C). Toast the bread in the oven until golden. Rub the toast on one side with the whole garlic cloves and place it in the bottom of a soup tureen, garlic side up.

🦂 Pour the soup over the toast. Adjust seasoning with salt. Sprinkle with pepper and drizzle with the remaining 2 tablespoons olive oil. Serve piping hot.

SERVES 6

ACQUACOTTA MAREMMANA

Egg and Vegetable Soup

The vegetables vary with the seasons and an egg is broken over the bread in this richer version of the famed Sienese soup of the same name. This is a favorite of the Maremma cowherds.

⅓ cup (3 fl oz/90 ml) extra virgin olive oil
12 fresh sage leaves
1 cup (4 oz/120 g) shelled broad (fava) beans
1 carrot, peeled and diced
1 celery stalk, trimmed and diced
4 oz (120 g) Swiss chard (silverbeet), trimmed and chopped
1 yellow onion, sliced
6 cups (48 fl oz/1.5 l) water
salt and freshly ground black pepper
6 slices coarse country bread
6 eggs

❧ In a medium saucepan over low heat, warm the olive oil. Add the sage and fry gently, stirring frequently, until the sage is golden. Add the broad beans, carrot, celery, Swiss chard and onion and stir until they wilt, about 5 minutes. Pour in the water and bring to a boil. Reduce the heat to low and simmer for 30 minutes. Season to taste with salt and pepper.

❧ Meanwhile, preheat an oven to 350°F (180°C). Toast the bread in the oven until golden. Put a slice of toast into each of 6 individual soup bowls. Break 1 egg onto each piece of toast.

❧ Ladle some of the piping hot soup into each bowl and serve immediately.

SERVES 6

RIBOLLITA

Twice-Cooked Soup

Ribollita, *Tuscany's most famous bread soup, is so-called because it is always reboiled before being served the first time and is often saved for the next day and boiled yet again. Although officially a soup,* ribollita *is often thick enough to eat with a fork.*

1⅛ cups (7 oz/210 g) dried *cannellini* beans
1¼ lb (600 g) black cabbage or Savoy cabbage
9 tablespoons (4½ fl oz/150 ml) extra virgin olive oil
2 yellow onions, sliced
1 tablespoon tomato paste
3 ripe plum (egg) tomatoes, peeled and chopped
3 celery stalks, diced
3 carrots, peeled and diced
8 cups (64 fl oz/2 l) water
1 tablespoon fresh thyme leaves
salt and freshly ground black pepper
6 slices coarse country bread
2 garlic cloves

❧ In a bowl, soak the beans in water to cover for 12 hours. Drain the beans and set aside.

❧ Remove and discard the hard stalks from the cabbage leaves. Slice the leaves roughly; set aside.

❧ In a deep saucepan over moderately low heat, warm 3 tablespoons of the olive oil. Add three fourths of the onion and fry gently until translucent, about 5 minutes. Add the tomato paste, tomatoes, celery and carrots. Cook, stirring frequently, for 5 minutes. Add the cabbage and pour in the water. Add the beans and thyme. Season to taste with salt and pepper and

bring to a boil. Reduce the heat to low, cover and simmer for about 2 hours.

❧ Meanwhile, preheat an oven to 350°F (180°C). Toast the bread in the oven until golden. Rub the toast on one side with the garlic and place it in the bottom of a deep bowl, garlic side up. Pour the soup over the toast and let stand until completely cool.

❧ Before serving, return the soup and the toasted bread to the cooking pot. Bring to a boil and pour into a tureen. Taste and adjust the seasoning. Sprinkle the soup with the remaining onion and the remaining 6 tablespoons olive oil. Serve immediately.

SERVES 6

CAVOLO CON LE FETTE

Cabbage with Bread and Oil

This is a simple country dish that is much in vogue in Chianti in December, when the olive oil has just been pressed and is still quite sharp. Black cabbage is widely eaten in Tuscany and, as the name suggests, the leaves are very dark, long and curly. Savoy cabbage may be used instead.

2 lb (1 kg) black cabbage or Savoy cabbage
8 cups (64 fl oz/2 l) water
6 slices coarse country bread
2 garlic cloves
salt and freshly ground black pepper
6 tablespoons (3 fl oz/90 ml) extra virgin olive oil

❧ Remove and discard the hard stalks from the cabbage leaves. In a large saucepan, bring the water to a boil and salt lightly. Add the leaves and cook until tender, about 30 minutes.

❧ Meanwhile, preheat an oven to 350°F (180°C). Toast the bread in the oven until golden. Rub the toast on one side with the garlic and place 1 slice on each of 6 individual serving dishes, garlic side up; keep warm.

❧ Drain the cabbage well and arrange the leaves on the toast. Season to taste with salt and pepper and sprinkle each serving with 1 tablespoon of the olive oil. Serve immediately.

SERVES 6

Egg and Vegetable Soup

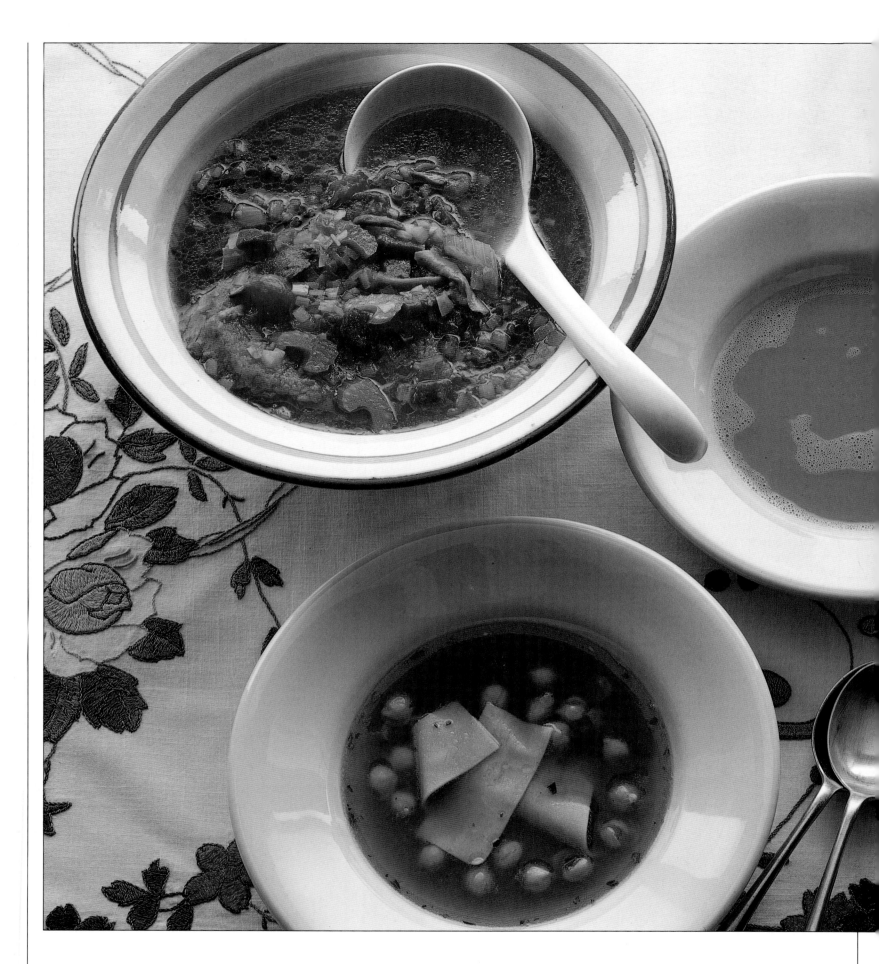

ACQUACOTTA ALLA SENESE

Bread Soup, Siena Style

Literally "cooked water," this was once a very humble soup made out of a little tomato, onion and celery boiled in water and poured over toasted bread. Nowadays cooks use their imaginations to add to it in various ways.

3 oz (90 g) fresh *porcini* mushrooms or button mushrooms
3 tablespoons extra virgin olive oil
3 oz (90 g) sweet Italian sausages, skinned and crumbled
1 large yellow onion, chopped
1 celery stalk, chopped
10 oz (300 g) plum (egg) tomatoes, peeled and chopped
6 cups (48 fl oz/1.5 l) water
salt and freshly ground black pepper
6 slices coarse country bread

🌢 Clean the mushrooms by rubbing them with a dampened cloth; do not wash them. Trim the mushroom stems, then

Left to right: Siena-Style Bread Soup, Chick-pea Soup and Chianti Soup

slice the mushrooms; set aside.

♣ In a large, deep pot over low heat, warm the olive oil. Add the sausage and onion and fry gently, stirring frequently, until the onion is translucent, about 5 minutes. Add the celery, mushrooms, tomatoes and water. Bring to a boil and season to taste with salt and pepper. Allow the soup to boil for about 15 minutes.

♣ Meanwhile, preheat an oven to 350°F (180°C). Toast the bread in the oven until golden. Place in the bottom of a soup tureen. Pour the boiling soup over the toast slices and serve immediately.

SERVES 6

Siena

MINESTRA DI CECI
Chick-pea Soup

Fresh pasta plays an important role in many Tuscan soups. It is usually cut by hand into fairly wide short strips.

1½ cups (10 oz/300 g) dried chick-peas (garbanzos)
4 tablespoons (2 fl oz/60 ml) extra virgin olive oil
1 tablespoon chopped fresh rosemary
3 garlic cloves, chopped
8 cups (64 fl oz/2 l) light meat stock (recipe on page 73)
salt and freshly ground black pepper
1¾ cups (7 oz/210 g) all-purpose (plain) flour
2 eggs

♣ In a bowl, soak the chick-peas in cold water to cover for 12 hours. Drain and set aside.

♣ In a large, deep saucepan over low heat, warm 1 tablespoon of the olive oil. Add the rosemary and garlic and fry gently for 2 minutes. Add the chick-peas and stock, bring to a boil, reduce the heat to low, and simmer gently for 2 hours. Season to taste with salt and pepper.

♣ Meanwhile, heap the flour in a mound on a work surface. Make a well in the center and break the eggs into it. Beat the eggs lightly with a fork, then gradually work the flour into the eggs until a loose ball of dough forms. Knead the dough on a lightly floured surface until soft, smooth and elastic, about 5 minutes. Using a pasta machine, roll out the dough very thinly. Allow to stand for a few minutes, then, using a long, sharp knife, cut the dough into strips ¾ in (2 cm) wide by 4 in (10 cm) long. Set the noodles aside on a clean cloth.

♣ Remove half of the chick-peas from the saucepan and purée them. Return the purée to the soup. Bring the soup to a boil and add the pasta. Cook for exactly 2 minutes.

♣ Pour the soup into a soup tureen. Sprinkle with the remaining 3 tablespoons olive oil and season with a little pepper. Serve immediately.

SERVES 6

Siena

BRODO AL CHIANTI
Chianti Soup

A good piece of meat, which is used later for making croquettes or stuffings, generally goes into the pot when preparing the stock for this classic soup. If the meat is fatty, the stock must be left to cool and the fat removed from the surface before the stock can be used.

8 cups (64 fl oz/2 l) Chianti Classico or other good red wine
3 whole cloves
1 cinnamon stick
4 cups (32 fl oz/1 l) light meat stock (recipe on page 73)
salt and freshly ground black pepper
3 egg yolks

♣ Pour the wine into a saucepan, add the cloves and cinnamon and bring to a boil. Reduce the heat to low and simmer for about 15 minutes.

♣ In another saucepan, bring the stock to a boil. Season to taste with salt and pepper.

♣ Place the egg yolks in the bottom of a soup tureen and whisk until well blended. Slowly add the stock, stirring well. Pour the wine through a fine sieve into the tureen. Stir and serve very hot.

SERVES 6

GARMUGIA

Spring Vegetable Soup

This soup is made with fresh spring vegetables. Swiss chard (silverbeet), celery and zucchini (courgettes) may be substituted for those vegetables that are listed, but the soup will not be nearly as tasty.

2 yellow onions
juice of 1 lemon
2 globe artichokes
1¼ lb (600 g) asparagus, trimmed
3 oz (90 g) sweet Italian sausages
2 tablespoons extra virgin olive oil
3 oz (90 g) ground (minced) veal
3 oz (90 g) shelled broad (fava) beans (about ¾ cup)
¾ cup (3 oz/90 g) shelled green peas
8 cups (64 fl oz/2 l) light chicken stock (recipe on page 73)
salt and freshly ground black pepper

❧ Chop half of 1 onion and thinly slice the remaining 1½ onions; set aside.
❧ Fill a large bowl with water and add the lemon juice. Cut the stalks off the artichokes. Remove the tough outer leaves and cut away any sharp leaf points from the tops. Pull the leaves apart gently and, with a spoon, scoop out and discard the prickly choke. Thinly slice the artichokes lengthwise, dropping them as you do into the water to prevent discoloration.
❧ Cut the asparagus into ½-in (1-cm) pieces. Skin the sausage and crumble the meat.
❧ In a deep saucepan over low heat, warm the olive oil. Add the chopped onion and cook gently, stirring frequently, until translucent, about 5 minutes. Add the veal and sausage and cook and stir for 2 minutes. Add the sliced onion, artichokes,

broad beans, peas and asparagus. Cook, stirring, for 10 minutes. Pour in the stock and bring to a gentle boil. Cover and simmer for 2 hours.
❧ Taste and adjust seasoning with salt and pepper. Pour into a soup tureen and serve.

SERVES 6

ZUPPA DI PORRI E BACCALÀ

Salt Cod and Leek Soup

Sailors seem to prefer salt cod to fresh fish, perhaps because it is tasty and nutritious and keeps forever.

5 oz (150 g) salt cod
1 lb (450 g) leeks
2 tablespoons extra virgin olive oil
10 oz (300 g) plum (egg) tomatoes, peeled and chopped
6 cups (48 fl oz/1.5 l) water
6 slices coarse country bread

❧ Soak the salt cod in water to cover in the refrigerator for 24 hours, changing the water 3 or 4 times. Drain. Remove and discard the skin and bones from the salt cod. Cut the cod into bite-sized pieces; set aside.
❧ Cut off and discard the green tops and roots from the leeks. Wash the leeks well to rid them of all dirt and slice them finely.
❧ In a deep saucepan over low heat, warm the oil. Add the leeks and cook gently, stirring frequently. When they begin to turn golden, add the tomatoes and stir well. Pour in the water and bring to a boil over high heat. Add the fish, lower the heat, cover and simmer for 30 minutes.
❧ Meanwhile, preheat an oven to 350°F (180°C). Toast the bread in the oven until golden. Put a slice of toast in each of 6 individual soup bowls. Ladle some of the hot soup into each bowl and serve at once.

SERVES 6

BRODO DI FAGIANO

Pheasant Broth

Pheasant must be aged before being cooked, and traditionally this is done by hanging it in a cool, breezy place until the body detaches from the head. The pheasant must, however, be well protected from flying insects that would render it inedible.

1 pheasant
3 qt (3 l) water
1 carrot, peeled and chopped
1 celery stalk, trimmed and chopped
1 yellow onion, chopped
3 bay leaves
1 teaspoon black peppercorns
salt
½ cup (4 fl oz/120 ml) Vin Santo or white dessert wine

❧ Place the pheasant in a deep saucepan. Add the water, carrot, celery, onion, bay leaves and peppercorns and bring to a boil. Lower the heat, cover with the lid ajar and simmer for 4 hours, at which time the liquid should be reduced to about 6 cups (48 fl oz/1.5 l).
❧ Strain the liquid and return it to the saucepan. (The meat from the pheasant can be reserved for making a pâté.) Place over high heat and bring to a boil. Add salt to taste and the Vin Santo.
❧ Serve immediately.

SERVES 6

Salt Cod and Leek Soup (bottom) and Pheasant Broth (top)

GNOCCHI DEL CASENTINO
Casentine Gnocchi

The Casentino mountains are among the highest in Tuscany. They are home to many monasteries, including the Camaldoli Hermitage and La Verna, where the monks are renowned not only for their liqueurs, but also for their recipes using wild greens gathered on the nearby mountainside.

2½ lb (1.2 kg) mixed wild greens (such as dandelion, chicory [curly endive] or nettles) or spinach, trimmed
1¼ cups (10 oz/300 g) ricotta
1 egg
1⅓ cups (5 oz/150 g) freshly grated Parmesan cheese
pinch of freshly grated nutmeg
salt and freshly ground black pepper
⅔ cup (3 oz/90 g) all-purpose (plain) flour
⅓ cup (3 oz/90 g) unsalted butter

❧ In a large saucepan, cook the greens in a little boiling water until tender. Drain thoroughly, wrap in a cloth and squeeze until the greens are very dry. Chop finely and place in a bowl.
❧ Add the ricotta, egg, ⅔ cup (3 oz/90 g) of the Parmesan and nutmeg to the greens. Season to taste with salt and pepper.
❧ Sprinkle your hands with some of the flour and roll the greens mixture into balls about 1¼ in (3 cm) in diameter. Dredge the balls lightly in the remaining flour.
❧ Bring at least 6 qt (6 l) salted water to a boil in a shallow saucepan. Drop the gnocchi, a few at a time, into the water. As soon as they rise to the surface, remove them with a slotted spoon, draining well. Arrange on a warm serving dish and keep warm. Continue cooking the remaining gnocchi in the same manner.
❧ Meanwhile, melt the butter in a small saucepan. Sprinkle the gnocchi with the remaining Parmesan and the melted butter. Serve hot.

SERVES 6

BORDATINO
Cornmeal and Vegetable Soup

Bordatino is a coarse striped cloth used for making aprons and kitchen towels. This hearty country soup was probably named after that sturdy fabric because it is thick and yellow colored.

2 lb (1 kg) black cabbage or Savoy cabbage
⅓ cup (3 fl oz/90 ml) extra virgin olive oil
1 yellow onion, chopped
3 garlic cloves, chopped
8 cups (64 fl oz/2 l) water
salt and freshly ground black pepper
1¾ cups (7 oz/210 g) coarse-grained cornmeal

❧ Remove and discard the hard stalks from the cabbage leaves. Slice the leaves roughly; set aside.
❧ In a deep saucepan over low heat, warm the olive oil. Add the onion and garlic and fry gently, stirring frequently, until translucent, about 5 minutes. Add the cabbage and cook, stirring, until it wilts.
❧ Add the water, season to taste with salt and pepper and bring to a boil. Add the cornmeal in a thin, steady stream, stirring constantly. Lower the heat, cover and simmer for about 40 minutes, stirring from time to time.
❧ Pour the soup into a tureen and serve very hot.

SERVES 6   *Photograph pages 52–53*

CREMA DI POLLO
Creamed Chicken Soup

It is essential to use a chicken with very little fat, preferably free-range, for this delicate soup made from an ancient recipe. If all you can find is a fatty chicken, remove all the visible fat before cooking.

1 chicken, about 2½ lb (1.2 kg), with gizzard and liver
6 whole cloves
1 yellow onion
2 bay leaves
1 celery stalk, trimmed and chopped
8 cups (64 fl oz/2 l) light chicken stock (recipe on page 73)
salt

❧ Remove the gizzard and liver from the chicken. Stick the cloves into the onion and wrap it in a small piece of cheese-cloth (muslin) together with the gizzard, bay leaves and celery. Tie the cheesecloth bag closed and place the chicken and cheesecloth bag in a deep, heavy pot. Pour the stock into the pot and bring to a boil. Lower the heat, cover and simmer gently for about 2 hours.
❧ Remove the chicken and cheesecloth bag from the pot and discard the bag. Skin the chicken and then bone it, keeping the meat from half of the chicken breast intact. Cut the reserved breast meat into julienne strips and set aside. Put all of the remaining chicken meat through the fine disc of a food mill or purée it in a food processor.
❧ Add the puréed chicken to the stock with salt to taste. Bring to a boil, stirring to combine well. Add the julienned chicken and heat through.
❧ Pour the soup into a tureen and serve.

SERVES 6

MINESTRA DI CASTAGNE
Chestnut Soup

There are sweet chestnut trees all over the rural areas of Arezzo, and on autumn weekends whole families drive out to the country-side to gather chestnuts, leaving behind the prickly husks. Chest-nuts that are not immediately roasted over the fire are often made into this delicious soup.

2 lb (900 g) chestnuts
2 tablespoons extra virgin olive oil
3 bay leaves
6 cups (48 fl oz/1.5 l) light meat stock (recipe on page 73)
1 teaspoon dried mint
salt and freshly ground black pepper

❧ With a small, sharp knife, make an X on the flat face of each chestnut. Bring a large saucepan of water to a rolling boil and add the chestnuts. Boil for about 5 minutes, then drain. While the chestnuts are still hot, remove both the hard outer shell and the furry inner skin. (The chestnuts are more difficult to peel if they cool completely.) Chop the chestnuts coarsely and set aside.
❧ In a deep saucepan over low heat, warm the olive oil. Add the chestnuts and bay leaves and fry gently, stirring fre-quently, about 5 minutes. Pour in the stock, sprinkle with the mint and simmer for about 30 minutes.
❧ Remove and discard the bay leaves and season to taste with salt and pepper. Serve piping hot.

SERVES 6

*Top to bottom: Chestnut Soup, Casentine Gnocchi
and Creamed Chicken Soup*

Arezzo

ZUPPA FRANTOIANA

Olive Press Soup

This soup is so-called because it is generally made in December, when the olives have just been pressed in the frantoio *(olive press) and the oil is still very sharp. Another important ingredient is the bread, which should not only be coarse-textured but also fairly hard.*

1½ cups (10 oz/300 g) dried cranberry (borlotti) beans
1 large yellow onion
1 lb (450 g) black cabbage or Savoy cabbage
¾ cup (6 fl oz/180 ml) extra virgin olive oil
1 carrot, peeled and diced
1 zucchini (courgette), trimmed and diced
1 celery stalk, trimmed and diced
1 large boiling potato, peeled and diced
2 plum (egg) tomatoes, peeled and chopped
8 cups (64 fl oz/2 l) water
1 tablespoon fresh thyme leaves
1 teaspoon fennel seed
salt
12 slices coarse country bread
2 whole garlic cloves

In a large bowl, soak the beans in water to cover for 12 hours. Drain the beans and put them in a deep saucepan. Add water to cover by 1 in (2.5 cm) and slowly bring to a boil. Lower the heat, cover and simmer for 1 hour.

Drain the beans and put them through the fine disc of a food mill or purée them in a food processor. Set aside.

While the beans are cooking, cut the onion in half. Chop one half of the onion and slice the other half. Remove and discard the hard stalks from the cabbage leaves. Shred the leaves and set aside.

In a deep saucepan over low heat, warm half of the olive oil. Add the chopped onion and fry gently, stirring occasionally, until translucent, about 5 minutes. Add the carrot, zucchini, celery, potato, tomatoes, cabbage and the sliced onion. Stir well and cook for 5 minutes. Add the puréed beans, the water, thyme and fennel seed. Season to taste with salt, cover and simmer over low heat for 2 hours.

Meanwhile, preheat an oven to 350°F (180°C). Toast the bread in the oven until golden. Rub the toast with the garlic cloves and place a layer of toast in the bottom of a soup tureen. Drizzle half of the remaining olive oil over the toast and then ladle in half of the vegetables and stock. Top with the remaining toast. Drizzle with the remaining olive oil and pour in the rest of the soup. Serve very hot.

SERVES 6

Olive Press Soup

Lamb Soup

ZUPPA D'AGNELLO

Lamb Soup

Great flocks of sheep are raised in the countryside of Grosseto, where the shepherds are famous for the excellent pecorino, sheep's milk cheese, *they make. Because the flavor is much more delicate, lamb is slaughtered when it weighs little more than 20 lb (10 kg).*

3 tablespoons extra virgin olive oil
1 small yellow onion, chopped
1 carrot, peeled and chopped
1 celery stalk, trimmed and chopped
1 tablespoon chopped fresh flat-leaf (Italian) parsley
3 garlic cloves, chopped

10 oz (300 g) ground (minced) lamb
10 oz (300 g) plum (egg) tomatoes, peeled and chopped
6 cups (48 fl oz/1.5 l) light meat stock (recipe on page 73)
salt and freshly ground black pepper
6 slices coarse country bread

🐑 In a deep saucepan over moderate heat, warm the olive oil. Add the onion, carrot, celery, parsley and garlic and fry gently, stirring frequently, for 5 minutes. Add the lamb, mix in well and cook, stirring occasionally to blend the flavors, for 5 minutes. Add the tomatoes and stir well. Pour in the stock, season to taste with salt and pepper and bring to a boil. Reduce the heat, cover with the lid ajar and simmer gently for 1 hour.
🐑 Meanwhile, preheat an oven to 350°F (180°C). Toast the bread in the oven until golden. Place in the bottom of a soup tureen. Ladle the soup into the tureen and serve very hot.

SERVES 6

Left to right: White Bean Soup, Bean and Rice Soup, and Tripe Soup

ZUPPA DI FAGIOLI

White Bean Soup

A ham bone is traditionally used to flavor this soup. In every Tuscan kitchen there is a locally produced, pleasantly salty ham that family members slice whenever they are hungry.

1½ cups (10 oz/300 g) dried *cannellini* beans
half of a ham bone or 3 oz (90 g) *pancetta,* in one piece
3 garlic cloves, chopped, plus 2 whole garlic cloves
6 fresh sage leaves
6 tablespoons (3 fl oz/90 ml) extra virgin olive oil
2 celery stalks, chopped
4 plum (egg) tomatoes, peeled and chopped
8 cups (64 fl oz/2 l) light meat stock (recipe on page 73)
salt and freshly ground black pepper
6 slices coarse country bread

🖎 In a bowl, soak the beans in water to cover for 12 hours. Drain and set aside.
🖎 Combine the ham bone (or *pancetta*), chopped garlic and

70

sage in a deep saucepan. Add 3 tablespoons of the olive oil and cook over low heat until the garlic is golden. Add the celery, tomatoes, beans and stock and bring to a slow boil. Reduce the heat to low and simmer gently until the beans are tender, about 2 hours.

🐾 Remove the ham bone (or *pancetta*) and season the soup to taste with salt and pepper. Remove half of the beans from the saucepan and purée them. Return the purée to the pot and bring the soup to a simmer.

🐾 Meanwhile, preheat an oven to 350°F (180°C). Toast the bread in the oven until golden. Rub the toast on one side with the whole garlic cloves and place in the bottom of a soup tureen, garlic side up. Drizzle the remaining 3 tablespoons olive oil over the toast and then sprinkle with a little pepper.

🐾 Pour the soup into the tureen and serve immediately.

SERVES 6

Firenze

MINESTRA DI RISO E CANNELLINI

Bean and Rice Soup

The most popular local beans in Tuscany are cannellini, *which are small, white and very tender. They are at their best in late summer, when they are sold fresh in all the markets. Dried beans must be soaked in cold water to cover for at least 12 hours before cooking; fresh beans will cook in 1½ hours without soaking.*

1¼ cups (8 oz/240 g) dried *cannellini* beans
1 tablespoon extra virgin olive oil
2 oz (60 g) *pancetta,* chopped
1 fresh rosemary sprig, chopped
1 small yellow onion, chopped
8 cups (64 fl oz/2 l) light meat stock (recipe on page 73)
1 cup (7 oz/210 g) Arborio rice
salt and freshly ground black pepper

🐾 In a bowl, soak the beans in water to cover for 12 hours. Drain and set aside.

🐾 In a soup pot over low heat, warm the olive oil. Add the *pancetta,* rosemary and onion and cook, stirring occasionally, for 5 minutes. Add the beans and stock and bring to a simmer. Cover and simmer gently until the beans are just tender, about 1½ hours.

🐾 Add the rice and season to taste with salt and pepper. Cook for another 17 minutes.

🐾 Pour into a soup tureen and serve immediately.

SERVES 6

Firenze

MINESTRA DI TRIPPA

Tripe Soup

Before being sold, tripe is skinned and boiled for three or four hours, depending on whether it is veal or beef. Ruminants have three stomachs, which means that the texture of the tripe you purchase will vary accordingly. Honeycomb tripe is the best type to use for this hearty soup.

3 tablespoons extra virgin olive oil
1 yellow onion, chopped
3 oz (90 g) *pancetta,* chopped

---

1 lb (480 g) honeycomb tripe, cut into narrow strips
1 celery stalk, trimmed and chopped
1 carrot, peeled and chopped
6 fresh sage leaves
1 tablespoon fresh thyme leaves
1 bay leaf
1 lb (480 g) Swiss chard (silverbeet), torn into pieces
3 plum (egg) tomatoes, peeled and chopped
2 tablespoons tomato paste
6 cups (48 fl oz/1.5 l) water
salt and freshly ground black pepper

🐾 In a soup pot over low heat, warm the olive oil. Add the onion and *pancetta* and fry gently until the onion is translucent, about 5 minutes. Add the tripe and cook for 5 minutes, stirring frequently.

🐾 Add the celery, carrot, sage, thyme, bay leaf, Swiss chard, tomatoes and tomato paste. Cook for 5 minutes, stirring from time to time. Pour in the water, cover and simmer over low heat until the tripe is tender, about 1 hour.

🐾 Season to taste with salt and pepper. Pour into a soup tureen and serve hot.

SERVES 6

Arezzo

ZUPPA DI CARNE

Meat Soup

The Aretines are great meat-eaters, and the cattle raised in the Chiana valley are famous all over Italy for their meat, particularly the T-bone steaks. Aretines are also very fond of bread, so much so that they often put it in soup when other Italians would use pasta or rice.

2 tablespoons extra virgin olive oil
6 oz (180 g) lean beef
6 oz (180 g) lean veal
6 oz (180 g) lean pork
2 oz (60 g) *pancetta,* chopped
1 fresh rosemary sprig, chopped
6 fresh sage leaves
1 small yellow onion, chopped
1 lb (450 g) plum (egg) tomatoes, peeled and chopped
1 celery stalk, trimmed and chopped
1 bay leaf
pinch of ground dried chili
salt
6 cups (48 fl oz/1.2 l) light meat stock (recipe on page 73)
6 slices coarse country bread

🐾 In a deep saucepan over moderate heat, warm the olive oil. Add the meats, *pancetta,* rosemary and sage and cook, stirring frequently, until the meat browns, about 10 minutes. Add the onion, tomatoes, celery, bay leaf and chili. Season to taste with salt, cover and lower the heat. Simmer for 2 hours, gradually adding about half of the stock to prevent the sauce from sticking to the bottom of the pan.

🐾 Remove the meat from the pan and chop fairly finely. Return the meat to the pan and, if necessary, add a little more stock to thin the sauce; it should be quite thin.

🐾 Meanwhile, preheat an oven to 350°F (180°C).

🐾 Heat the remaining stock in a saucepan on the stovetop until very hot. Toast the bread in the oven until golden. One by one, dip the toast slices in the stock, place in individual soup dishes and top each slice with part of the meat sauce. Pour the hot stock over the meat sauce and serve immediately.

SERVES 6　　　　　　　　　　*Photograph pages 52–53*

Livorno

SBURRITA
Salt Cod and Mint Soup

Although this Livornese soup is simple and inexpensive to make, it is full of flavor and the herbs infuse it with fragrance. Traditionally it is seasoned with calamint, which grows wild around Livorno, but spearmint or fresh thyme can be substituted.

7 oz (210 g) salt cod
10 garlic cloves, chopped
1 large handful of fresh mint leaves
pinch of ground dried chili
6 cups (48 fl oz/1.5 l) water
6 slices coarse country bread

🌿 Soak the salt cod in water to cover in the refrigerator for 24 hours, changing the water 3 or 4 times. Drain. Remove and discard the skin and bones from the salt cod. Chop the cod into bite-sized pieces; set aside.

🌿 Combine the garlic, mint and chili in a medium saucepan. Add the water and bring to a boil over high heat. Cook for 10 minutes. Add the cod, reduce the heat to low and cook, uncovered, for 20 minutes.

🌿 Meanwhile, preheat an oven to 350°F (180°C). Toast the bread in the oven until golden. Place the toast in the bottom of a soup tureen. Ladle the fish pieces and the stock over the toast. Serve immediately.

SERVES 6

Lucca

ZUPPA LOMBARDA
Lombard Soup

Lombard soup is a strange name for a strictly Tuscan soup that has never been heard of in Lombardy. Legend has it that it was named after a group of workmen from Lombardy who went to Lucca in the early nineteenth century and very much appreciated the dish, but other Tuscan provinces claim the soup as well.

1½ cups (10 oz/300 g) dried *cannellini* beans
9 tablespoons (4½ fl oz/150 ml) extra virgin olive oil
12 fresh sage leaves
6 cups (48 fl oz/1.5 l) water
6 slices coarse country bread
salt and freshly ground black pepper

🌿 In a bowl, soak the beans in water to cover for 12 hours.

🌿 Preheat an oven to 325°F (160°C).

🌿 Drain the beans and place them in a heavy ovenproof pot with 3 tablespoons of the olive oil, the sage and water. Cover and bring very slowly to a gentle boil on the stovetop. Transfer the pot to the oven and cook for about 3 hours.

🌿 Just before the soup is ready, toast the bread in the oven until golden. Put a slice of toast in each of 6 individual soup bowls. Sprinkle 1 tablespoon of the remaining olive oil over each slice and then season with a little salt and pepper.

🌿 Ladle the bean soup over the toast and serve immediately.

SERVES 6

Salt Cod and Mint Soup

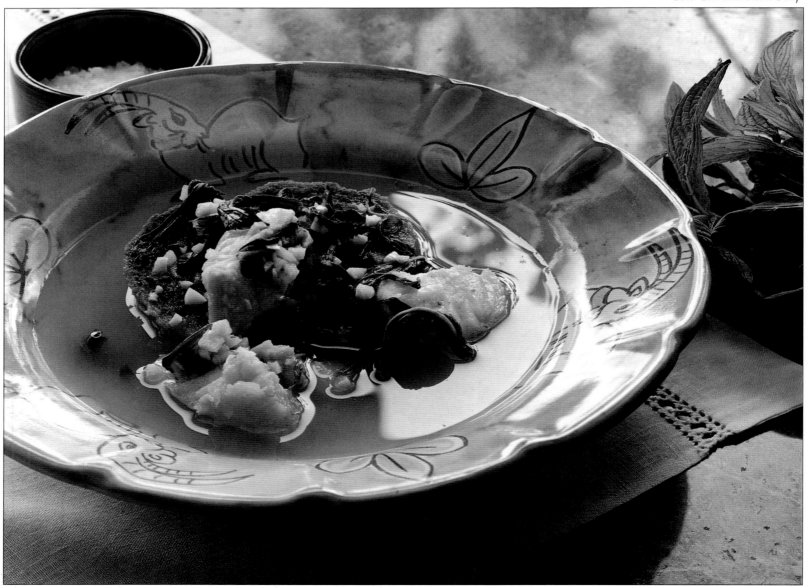

Lucca

Brodo Leggero di Carne o Pollo

Light Meat or Chicken Stock

Tuscan stock is very light but flavorful because the taste of the vegetables and herbs comes through. If you like, add thyme, basil, sage or any other herb you might choose, or a tomato. When light stock is called for in various recipes in this book, this is the stock required. The cooked beef can be used for making croquettes, while the chicken can be shredded for a salad. You can use this recipe to make a light vegetable stock by omitting the chicken or beef and adding slightly more vegetables.

1 beef brisket or whole chicken, about 2 lb (900 g)
2 celery stalks, sliced
1 small yellow onion, sliced
2 carrots, sliced
1 zucchini (courgette), trimmed and sliced
1 handful of flat-leaf (Italian) parsley
1 bay leaf
1 teaspoon black peppercorns
3 qt (3 l) cold water
salt and freshly ground black pepper

❧ Place the beef or chicken in a deep pot with all of the vegetables, the parsley, bay leaf and peppercorns. Add the water and bring to a boil. Lower the heat, skim off any foam that forms on the surface, cover with the lid ajar and simmer gently until the liquid has been reduced by half, about 2 hours.
❧ Strain the stock, let cool to room temperature and refrigerate to solidify the fat on the surface.
❧ Lift off the fat and reheat the stock. Season to taste with salt and pepper. Pour into soup cups and serve or use in recipes as directed. Any leftover stock should be frozen in ice-cube trays and the cubes stored in plastic bags for ease of use.

MAKES ABOUT 6 CUPS (48 FL OZ/1.5 L); SERVES 6

Light Chicken Stock (left) and Lombard Soup (right)

Firenze

Pappardelle alla Lepre

Wide Noodles with Hare Sauce

Pappardelle, the most Tuscan of pastas, are sometimes cut with a serrated wheel to make them more decorative. The hare should be cooked in its own blood, but if the blood is not available, the same quantity of rich beef stock may be substituted.

SAUCE
1¼ lb (600 g) piece of hare or rabbit
3 tablespoons extra virgin olive oil
2 oz (60 g) *prosciutto,* chopped
2 small yellow onions, chopped
2 celery stalks, trimmed and chopped
2 carrots, peeled and chopped
1 tablespoon all-purpose (plain) flour
small pinch of freshly grated nutmeg
1 whole clove
salt and freshly ground black pepper
1¼ cups (10 fl oz/300 ml) dry red wine
⅓ cup (3 fl oz/90 ml) hare's blood or rich beef stock
NOODLES
2½ cups (10 oz/300 g) all-purpose (plain) flour
3 eggs

½ cup (2 oz/60 g) freshly grated Parmesan cheese

❧ To prepare the sauce: cut the hare into medium-sized pieces. In a heavy pot over low heat, warm the olive oil. Add the *prosciutto* and onion and fry gently for 5 minutes. Add the celery, carrot and hare pieces. Fry over moderate heat, stirring from time to time, until the hare colors, about 5 minutes. Sprinkle with the flour and nutmeg. Add the clove and season to taste with salt and pepper.
❧ Pour about one third of the wine and the blood (or beef stock) into the pot. Stir well, scraping up any small browned bits stuck on the bottom of the pot. Lower the heat, cover the pot and cook slowly for about 1½ hours. Gradually add the remaining red wine throughout this cooking period.
❧ Bone the hare and chop the meat coarsely. Return the meat to the pot, adding a little water if the sauce seems too dry. Keep warm.
❧ To prepare the noodles: heap the flour in a mound on a work surface. Make a well in the center and break the eggs into it. With a fork, gradually work the flour into the eggs until a loose ball of dough forms. Knead the dough on a lightly floured surface until soft, smooth and elastic, about 5 minutes. Using a pasta machine, roll out the dough very thinly. Allow to stand for a few minutes, then, using a long, sharp knife, cut into strips 1¼ in (3 cm) wide and 4 in (10 cm) long.
❧ In a saucepan, bring at least 6 qt (6 l) salted water to a boil. Add the noodles and boil them for exactly 2 minutes. Drain and tip onto a warm serving platter.
❧ Spoon the sauce over the noodles and toss. Sprinkle with the Parmesan and serve immediately.

SERVES 6   *Photograph page 4*

Lucca

RISOTTO CON LE BIETE
Swiss Chard Risotto

In the springtime Swiss chard is very tender and the entire leaf may be used. Later in the season, the white ribs become tough and should be removed for this recipe, and the quantity of chard must be doubled.

6 slices dried *porcini* mushrooms
1 small yellow onion
2 canned flat anchovy fillets in olive oil, drained
6 cups (48 fl oz/1.5 l) light meat stock (recipe on page 73)
6 tablespoons (3 fl oz/90 ml) extra virgin olive oil
3 cups (1¼ lb/600 g) Arborio rice
1¼ lb (600 g) Swiss chard (silverbeet), trimmed and sliced
1 tablespoon chopped fresh flat-leaf (Italian) parsley
¾ cup (3 oz/90 g) freshly grated Parmesan cheese
salt and freshly ground black pepper

�٭ In a small bowl, soak the mushrooms in warm water to cover for 30 minutes. Drain and squeeze out any excess moisture. Combine the mushrooms, onion and anchovy fillets on a cutting surface and chop together.

🌭 In a saucepan, bring the stock to a boil, then reduce the heat to maintain a very slow simmer. Meanwhile, in a saucepan over low heat, warm 4 tablespoons of the olive oil. Add the anchovy mixture and fry gently, stirring frequently, about 5 minutes. Add the rice, stir well and allow the flavors to blend for a few minutes. Add the Swiss chard and mushroom mixture. Add a ladleful of the warm stock to the rice so that it is just covered with liquid; stir well. As the liquid is absorbed, add a little more stock, stirring after each addition. The rice should never be allowed to become dry. It should constantly be just covered with liquid. Exactly 15 minutes after you began adding the stock, remove the saucepan from the heat and stir in the remaining 2 tablespoons oil, the parsley and Parmesan. Season to taste with salt and pepper. Cover and let stand for precisely 2 minutes. The rice should be tender but firm and the risotto should flow without being runny. (You may not have needed all of the stock. Any leftover stock may be refrigerated or frozen for another use.)

🌭 Pour the risotto onto a large platter and serve immediately.

SERVES 6

Grosseto

TOPINI AL CINGHIALE
Gnocchi with Wild Boar Sauce

In this recipe wild boar is used only to flavor the sauce. The meat itself is served as a separate course or together with the gnocchi for a buffet. Gnocchi are called topini, *or "little mice," in Tuscany because their shape resembles the tiny animals.*

SAUCE
2½ lb (1.2 kg) boneless wild boar, preferably cut from the
    leg
1½ cups (12 fl oz/400 ml) dry red wine
1 tablespoon juniper berries
2 bay leaves
6 fresh sage leaves
3 tablespoons extra virgin olive oil
1 small yellow onion, chopped
1 carrot, peeled and chopped
1 celery stalk, trimmed and chopped
1¼ lb (600 g) plum (egg) tomatoes, peeled and chopped
salt and freshly ground black pepper

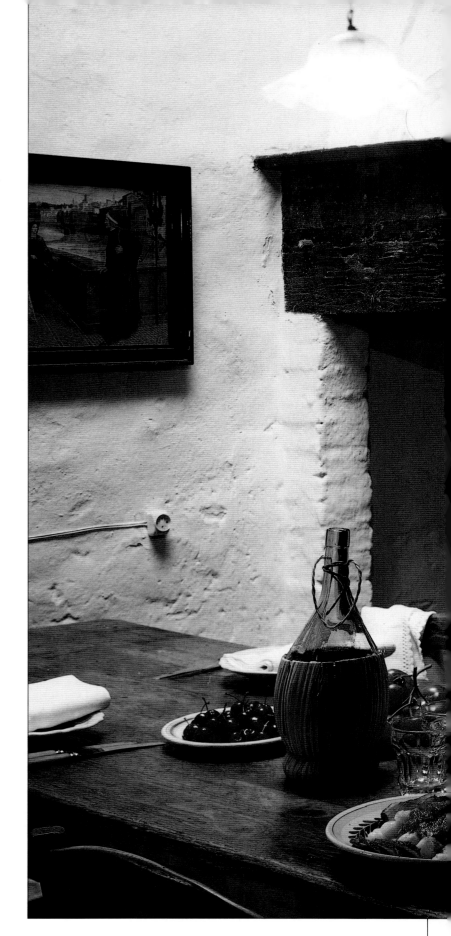

GNOCCHI
2½ lb (1.2 kg) baking potatoes
1¾ cups (7 oz/210 g) all-purpose (plain) flour
2 egg yolks

🌭 To prepare the sauce: in a glass or ceramic vessel, combine the wild boar, wine, juniper berries, bay leaves and sage. Marinate the boar in a cool place for 12 hours.

🌭 Drain the meat and pat it dry with absorbent paper towels. Strain the marinade, reserving the liquid and seasonings separately; set aside.

🌭 In a flameproof casserole over moderate heat, warm the olive oil. Add the meat and cook until browned on all sides, about 10 minutes. Add the onion, carrot and celery and cook, stirring, over low heat for 2 minutes. Add the tomatoes and the seasonings from the marinade and continue cooking over

Gnocchi with Wild Boar Sauce (left) and Swiss Chard Risotto (right)

low heat for about 50 minutes. When the liquid from the tomatoes has evaporated, add 1 cup of the marinade liquid. Cook the boar for about 3 hours, gradually adding the remaining marinade so that the sauce never sticks to the pan. When the sauce is ready, season to taste with salt and pepper. Remove the boar and keep it and the sauce warm.

🐗 Meanwhile, prepare the gnocchi: steam the potatoes in their skins until tender, about 30 minutes. Remove the potatoes from the steamer and peel them. Place in a bowl and mash while still hot.

🐗 Add half of the flour and the egg yolks and work them very quickly into the potatoes until the mixture forms a firm, smooth dough.

🐗 Flour the palms of your hands and a work surface with some of the remaining flour. Using the palms of your hands and the surface, roll the dough into cylinders about ¾ in (2 cm) in diameter. Cut the cylinders into pieces about 1⅛ in (3 cm) long. Roll each piece over the prongs of a fork, pressing it in the center lightly with your thumb. As the gnocchi are made, place them on another lightly floured surface.

🐗 Bring at least 6 qt (6 l) salted water to a boil in a shallow saucepan. Drop the gnocchi, a few at a time, into the water. As soon as they rise to the surface, remove them with a slotted spoon, draining well. Arrange on a warm serving dish. Continue cooking the remaining gnocchi in the same manner.

🐗 As soon as all the gnocchi are ready, ladle the hot sauce over them. Slice the wild boar and arrange it around the edges of the dish. Serve immediately.

SERVES 6

Firenze

RISOTTO AL SUGO DI CARNE

Risotto with Meat Sauce

Florentines are very fond of meat sauce, which is also served on noodles, lasagna and timbales. Their meat sauce is made with more tomato than the Bolognese version.

6 slices dried *porcini* mushrooms
3 tablespoons extra virgin olive oil
1 tablespoon chopped yellow onion
2 oz (60 g) *pancetta,* chopped
2 tablespoons chopped fresh sage
2 tablespoons chopped fresh rosemary
5 oz (150 g) ground (minced) beef
5 oz (150 g) ground (minced) veal
3 oz (90 g) chicken livers, trimmed and chopped
1¼ lb (600 g) plum (egg) tomatoes, peeled and chopped
salt and freshly ground black pepper
4 cups (32 fl oz/1 l) light meat stock (recipe on page 73)
2½ cups (1 lb/480 g) Arborio rice
1 cup (8 fl oz/240 ml) dry white wine
¾ cup (3 oz/90 g) freshly grated Parmesan cheese

❧ In a small bowl, soak the mushroom slices in warm water to cover for 30 minutes. Drain well and squeeze out any excess moisture. Chop the mushrooms and set aside.

❧ In a heavy saucepan over low heat, warm the olive oil. Add the onion, *pancetta,* sage and rosemary and fry gently until just golden, about 5 minutes. Add the mushrooms, beef, veal and livers and stir to break up the meat. Increase the heat to moderate and cook for 5 minutes, stirring from time to time. Add the tomatoes and season to taste with salt and pepper. Reduce the heat to low, cover and simmer until the liquid evaporates, about 50 minutes.

❧ In a saucepan, bring the stock to a boil, then reduce the heat to maintain a very slow simmer. Meanwhile, pour the rice into

the meat sauce and stir a few minutes over moderate heat to blend the flavors. Add a ladleful of the warm stock and a little of the wine to the rice so that it is just covered with liquid; stir well. As the liquid is absorbed, add a little more stock and some of the wine, stirring after each addition. The rice should never be allowed to become dry. It should constantly be just covered with liquid. Exactly 15 minutes after you began adding the stock, remove the pan from the heat and stir in the Parmesan. Cover and let stand for precisely 2 minutes. The rice should be tender but firm and the risotto should flow without being runny. (You may not have needed to add all of the stock. Any leftover stock may be refrigerated or frozen for another use.)

❧ Pour the risotto onto a large platter and serve immediately.

SERVES 6

Grosseto

RISOTTO CON LE BECCACCE

Risotto with Woodcock Sauce

The hinterland of Grosseto is sparsely populated, still unpolluted and rich in game, so there is a great deal of hunting. If woodcocks are not available, other small birds such as partridge and pigeons (squab) may be used for this sauce. The woodcocks should be dressed with the liver and gizzard left inside.

1 oz (30 g) black truffle, finely chopped (optional)
1 tablespoon juniper berries, chopped
2 woodcocks, about 10 oz (300 g) each, with liver and gizzard inside
2 tablespoons extra virgin olive oil
2 oz (60 g) *pancetta,* chopped
1 tablespoon chopped yellow onion
salt and freshly ground black pepper
⅞ cup (7 fl oz/210 ml) good red wine
6 cups (48 fl oz/1.5 l) light meat stock (recipe on page 73)
3 cups (1¼ lb/600 g) Arborio rice

❧ Place the truffle and juniper berries inside the woodcocks but do not truss them.

❧ In a shallow saucepan over moderate heat, warm the olive oil and *pancetta.* Add the onion and fry gently until beginning to soften, about 3 minutes. Place the birds on the *pancetta* and onion and cook gently until golden. Season to taste with salt and pepper and add half of the wine. Cover and cook over low heat for about 1 hour, gradually adding the rest of the wine to keep the cooking juices moist.

❧ In a saucepan, bring the stock to a boil, then reduce the heat to maintain a very slow simmer.

❧ Meanwhile, bone the birds, retrieving the gizzard and liver. Chop the meat, gizzard and liver and place in a medium saucepan.

❧ Add the cooking juices and warm over moderate heat. Add the rice and cook, stirring, for 2 minutes. Add a ladleful of the warm stock to the rice so that it is covered with liquid; stir well. As the liquid is absorbed, add a little more stock, stirring after each addition. The rice should never be allowed to become dry. It should constantly be just covered with liquid. Exactly 15 minutes after you began adding the stock, remove the saucepan from the heat. Season to taste with salt and pepper. Stir well, cover and let stand for precisely 2 minutes. The rice should be tender but firm and the risotto should flow without being runny. (You may not have needed all of the stock. Any leftover stock may be refrigerated or frozen for another use.)

❧ Pour the risotto onto a large warm platter and serve immediately.

SERVES 6

Risotto with Meat Sauce

Spaghetti with Sea Urchin Sauce (left) and Risotto with Woodcock Sauce (right)

SPAGHETTI AI RICCI DI MARE

Spaghetti with Sea Urchin Sauce

There are beautiful beaches and maritime pinewoods around Grosseto, and at the foot of Monte Argentario lie Porto Ercole and Porto Santo Stefano, fashionable sailing resorts where it is still possible to pick off sea urchins from the rocks. If sea urchins are too expensive, you may substitute mussels.

30 sea urchins or mussels in the shell or 6 oz (180 g) sea
   urchin meat
⅓ cup (3 fl oz/90 ml) extra virgin olive oil
3 garlic cloves, chopped
small piece of dried chili
1¼ lb (600 g) plum (egg) tomatoes, peeled and chopped
salt
1¼ lb (600 g) spaghetti
1 tablespoon chopped fresh flat-leaf (Italian) parsley

🦐 Holding each sea urchin gently in a gloved hand, cut the urchin in half with a pair of kitchen scissors. Empty the contents into a bowl and set aside.

🦐 If using mussels, scrub and debeard them. Place the mussels in a shallow saucepan, cover and place over moderate heat until the shells open, about 5 minutes. Pluck the mussels out of their shells, discarding any that did not open. Set aside.

🦐 In a large skillet over low heat, warm the olive oil. Add the garlic and chili and fry gently until the garlic begins to change color, about 3 minutes.

🦐 Add the tomatoes, season to taste with salt and simmer uncovered until the liquid is almost evaporated, about 50 minutes.

🦐 Meanwhile, in a saucepan, bring at least 6 qt (6 l) salted water to a boil. Add the spaghetti and cook until almost *al dente*, about 5 minutes. Drain and transfer to the skillet with the tomato sauce. Add the sea urchins or mussels, stir gently and let the flavors blend over low heat for 2 minutes. Sprinkle with the parsley.

🦐 Transfer the spaghetti to a warm platter and serve immediately.

SERVES 6

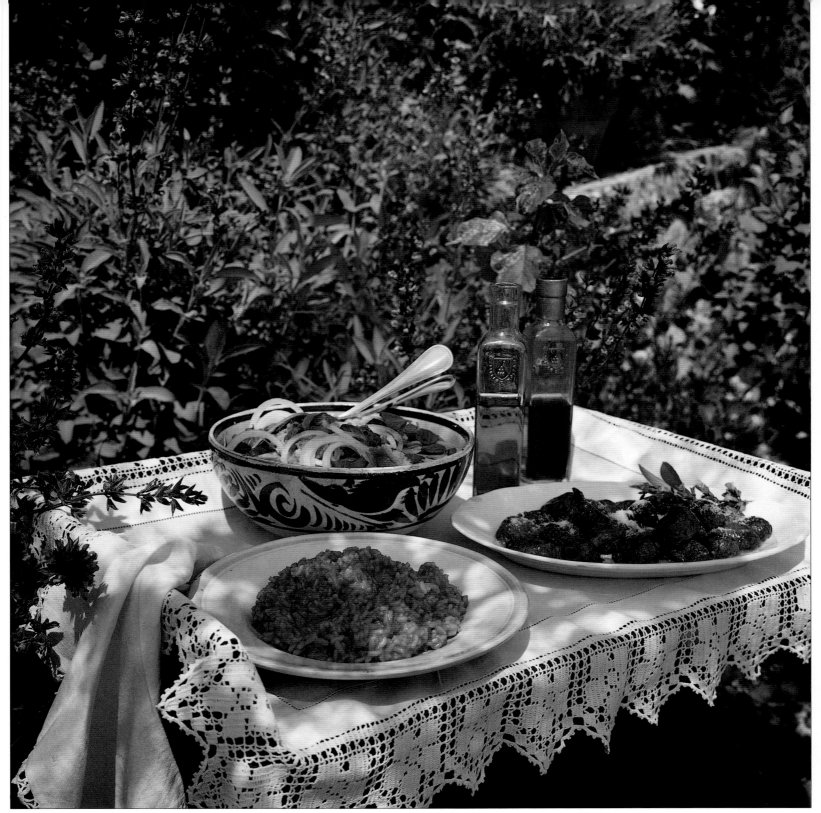

Risotto with Chianti (front), Naked Ravioli (right) and Bread and Tomato Salad (rear)

RAVIOLI IGNUDI

Naked Ravioli

These ravioli are called naked because they are not covered with the usual fresh pasta. In Florence they are generally made with Swiss chard, but spinach may be substituted. Sometimes a little finely ground roast meat or mortadella *is added to the mixture.*

10 oz (300 g) ricotta
2 lb (900 g) Swiss chard (silverbeet), leaves only
3 oz (90 g) *mortadella,* very finely chopped
1⅓ cups (5 oz/150 g) freshly grated Parmesan cheese
½ teaspoon freshly grated nutmeg
2 egg yolks, lightly beaten
⅔ cup (3 oz/90 g) all-purpose (plain) flour
⅓ cup (3 oz/90 g) unsalted butter
8 whole fresh sage leaves
salt

❧ To prevent the ricotta from lumping, press it through a sieve into a mixing bowl or whisk it well. Set aside.

❧ Bring a large saucepan filled with salted water to a boil, add the Swiss chard and boil until tender, about 5 minutes. Drain thoroughly, wrap in a cloth and squeeze until the chard is very dry. Chop very finely.

❧ Gradually combine the Swiss chard with the ricotta. Add the *mortadella,* about two thirds of the Parmesan, the nutmeg and egg yolks. Mix thoroughly. Scoop up a small quantity of the mixture with a spoon and, with well-floured hands, form it into an oval about 1¼ in (3 cm) wide. Dredge the oval lightly with some of the flour and set aside. Form ovals with the remaining ricotta mixture in the same manner.

❧ In a large saucepan, bring at least 6 qt (6 l) lightly salted water to a boil. Meanwhile, in a small pan, melt the butter with the sage leaves and keep warm.

❧ When the water reaches a rapid boil, add the ravioli, a few at a time, and cook until they rise to the surface. Remove the ravioli with a slotted spoon, draining well, and arrange them on a warm serving dish; keep warm. Continue cooking the remaining ravioli in the same manner.

❧ Dust the ravioli with the remaining Parmesan, sprinkle with the melted butter and sage and serve.

SERVES 6

Firenze

PANMOLLE
Bread and Tomato Salad

Panmolle, or panzanella as it is also called, is very much a summer salad. It is essential to use coarse-textured bread, excellent extra virgin olive oil and sun-ripened tomatoes for this recipe.

10 oz (300 g) coarse country bread
3 ripe tomatoes, diced
1 yellow onion, thinly sliced
1 cup loosely packed fresh basil leaves, torn into pieces
salt
2 tablespoons red wine vinegar
⅓ cup (3 fl oz/90 ml) extra virgin olive oil
freshly ground black pepper

🌿 Slice the bread and then break the slices into 2-in (5-cm) pieces. Place the pieces in a bowl, add water to cover completely and soak for about 5 minutes.

🌿 Drain the bread pieces and squeeze out all excess moisture. Crumble the bread into a salad bowl. Add the tomatoes, onion and basil. Toss all the ingredients together with the bread.

🌿 In a small bowl, dissolve salt to taste in the vinegar and sprinkle it over the bread mixture. Pour in the olive oil, add pepper to taste and toss well.

🌿 Serve immediately at room temperature.

SERVES 6

Siena

RISOTTO AL CHIANTI
Risotto with Chianti

This risotto should be made with a fairly old Chianti Riserva, which will give it an excellent wine flavor without being too sharp. The wine must be added in small quantities to prevent a sudden drop in temperature while the rice is cooking.

6 cups (48 fl oz/1.5 l) light meat stock (recipe on page 73)
4 tablespoons (2 oz/60 g) unsalted butter
3 tablespoons extra virgin olive oil
1 small yellow onion, finely chopped
3 cups (1¼ lb/600 g) Arborio rice
1½ cups (12 fl oz/360 ml) Chianti Riserva or other good red wine
1⅓ cups (5 oz/150 g) freshly grated Parmesan cheese
salt and freshly ground black pepper

🌿 In a saucepan, bring the stock to a boil, then reduce the heat to maintain a very slow simmer.

🌿 Meanwhile, in a saucepan over moderate heat, melt the butter with the olive oil. Add the onion and fry gently, stirring occasionally, until translucent, about 5 minutes. Add the rice, stir well and allow the flavors to blend for a few minutes. Add a little of the wine and enough warm stock to cover the rice; stir well. As the liquid is absorbed, add a little more stock and some of the wine every minute or so, stirring after each addition. The rice should never be allowed to become dry. It should constantly be just covered with liquid. Exactly 15 minutes after you began adding the stock, remove the saucepan from the heat, stir in the Parmesan and season to taste with salt and pepper. Cover and let stand for precisely 2 minutes. The rice should be tender but firm and the risotto should flow without being runny. (You may not have needed to add all of the stock. Any leftover stock may be refrigerated or frozen for another use.)

🌿 Pour the risotto onto a large serving platter and serve immediately.

SERVES 6

Grosseto

RISOTTO COI CARCIOFI
Artichoke Risotto

The best artichokes in Tuscany are grown around Grosseto. They are at their peak in May when they are small and purple and need almost no trimming. If ordinary globe artichokes are used, keep only the heart; the leaves can be used to make a soup.

juice of 1 lemon
6 small artichokes or 6 globe artichoke hearts
6 cups (48 fl oz/1.5 l) light meat stock (recipe on page 73)
⅓ cup (3 fl oz/90 ml) extra virgin olive oil
2 oz (60 g) *pancetta,* chopped
3 cups (1¼ lb/600 g) Arborio rice
salt and freshly ground black pepper

🌿 Fill a large bowl with water and add the lemon juice. Remove the tough outer leaves and cut away the sharp leaf points from the tops of the small artichokes. Cut the stalks off. Thinly slice the artichokes, dropping them as you do so into the water to prevent discoloration. When all of the artichokes have been cut, drain them and pat dry with absorbent paper towels. If you are using globe artichokes, see the above note.

🌿 In a saucepan, bring the stock to a boil, then reduce the heat to maintain a very slow simmer. Meanwhile, in a saucepan over low heat, warm the olive oil and *pancetta.* Add the sliced artichokes and fry gently for about 5 minutes. Add the rice and cook, stirring, for 2 minutes. Add a ladleful of the warm stock to the rice, so that it is just covered with liquid; stir well.

🌿 As the liquid is absorbed, add a little more stock, stirring after each addition. The rice should never be allowed to become dry. It should constantly be just covered with liquid. Exactly 15 minutes after you began adding the stock, remove the saucepan from the heat. Stir well, season to taste with salt and pepper, cover and let stand for precisely 2 minutes. The rice should be tender but firm and the risotto should flow without being runny. (You may not have needed all of the stock. Any leftover stock may be refrigerated or frozen for another use.) Pour the risotto onto a large warm platter and serve immediately.

SERVES 6

Artichoke Risotto

Risotto with Spring Greens

RISOTTO ALL'ERBE

Risotto with Spring Greens

In springtime the Tuscan countryside is blanketed in wildflowers and many edible plants. The farmers' wives gather dandelions, arugula (rocket) and chicory (curly endive) for salads, soups and pasta stuffings. Sometimes these plants are boiled briefly and dressed with oil and lemon, or they are used for a delicious risotto.

8 cups (64 fl oz/2 l) light meat stock (recipe on page 73)
⅓ cup (3 fl oz/90 ml) extra virgin olive oil
1 yellow onion, finely chopped
1¼ lb (600 g) spring greens (see note above), Swiss chard (silverbeet) or spinach, trimmed and chopped
3 cups (1¼ lb/600 g) Arborio rice
1⅓ cups (5 oz/150 g) freshly grated Parmesan cheese
salt and freshly ground black pepper

🐾 In a saucepan, bring the stock to a boil, then reduce the heat to maintain a very slow simmer. Meanwhile, in a heavy saucepan over low heat, warm the olive oil. Add the onion and greens and fry gently, stirring frequently, about 5 minutes. Add the rice, stir well and allow the flavors to blend for a few minutes. Add a ladleful of the warm stock to the rice so that it is just covered with liquid; stir well. As the liquid is absorbed, add a little more stock, stirring after each addition. The rice should never be allowed to become dry. It should constantly be just covered with liquid. Exactly 15 minutes after you began adding the stock, remove the saucepan from the heat, stir in the Parmesan and season to taste with salt and pepper. Cover and let stand for precisely 2 minutes. The rice should be tender but firm and the risotto should flow without being runny. (You may not have needed all of the stock. Any leftover stock may be refrigerated or frozen for another use.)
🐾 Pour the risotto onto a large platter and serve immediately.

SERVES 6

Livorno

RISOTTO ALLA LIVORNESE
Fish Risotto, Livorno Style

In Livorno this risotto is prepared with inexpensive fish such as sea robin (gurnard or grondin), scorpionfish (sculpin), mackerel, dogfish (rock salmon) and salpa. All of them are very tasty, but they also have many bones and are therefore not considered choice.

4 tablespoons (2 fl oz/60 ml) extra virgin olive oil
1 carrot, peeled and chopped
1 celery stalk, trimmed and chopped
2 lb (900 g) mixed fish (see note above), cleaned
10 oz (300 g) plum (egg) tomatoes, peeled and chopped
1 bay leaf
4 cups (32 fl oz/1 l) water
salt
2 garlic cloves, chopped
2¼ cups (1 lb/450 g) Arborio rice
1 tablespoon finely chopped fresh flat-leaf (Italian) parsley

In a heavy pot over low heat, warm 2 tablespoons of the olive oil. Add the carrot, celery and all of the fish. Cook, stirring occasionally, for 10 minutes. Add the tomatoes, bay leaf and water and bring to a boil. Season to taste with salt and cook for 10 minutes.

Pass the tomato-fish mixture carefully through a sieve to eliminate all the fish bones and other inedible parts. Return the strained sauce to the pot and bring back to a boil.

In a separate, shallow saucepan, heat the remaining 2 tablespoons olive oil over moderate heat. Add the garlic and rice and cook, stirring, for 3 minutes. Add a ladleful of the warm sauce to the rice so that it is just covered with liquid; stir well. As the liquid is absorbed, add a little more sauce, stirring after each addition. The rice should never be allowed to become dry. It should constantly be just covered with liquid. Exactly 15 minutes after you began adding the sauce, remove the saucepan from the heat, add the parsley and stir well. Cover and let stand for precisely 2 minutes. The rice should be tender but firm and the risotto should flow without being runny.

Pour the risotto onto a large platter and serve immediately.

SERVES 6

Livorno

SPAGHETTI ALLO SCOGLIO
Spaghetti with Mussel and Mushroom Sauce

This sauce is particularly delicious when it is made with date shell mussels. They embed themselves in rocks, however, making them difficult to gather and therefore quite expensive. Regular mussels may be substituted.

6 slices dried *porcini* mushrooms (optional)
4 lb (1.8 kg) mussels
6 tablespoons (3 fl oz/90 ml) extra virgin olive oil
½ yellow onion, chopped
2 garlic cloves, chopped
1 lb (480 g) spaghetti
salt and freshly ground black pepper
1 tablespoon chopped fresh flat-leaf (Italian) parsley

In a small bowl, soak the mushrooms in warm water to cover for 30 minutes.

Meanwhile, scrub and debeard the mussels. Place the mussels in a shallow saucepan, cover and place over moderate heat until the shells open, about 5 minutes. Remove from the heat and pluck the mussels out of their shells, discarding any that did not open. Strain the liquid the mussels released into the saucepan and set aside.

Drain the mushrooms and squeeze out any excess moisture. Chop coarsely and set aside.

In a wide skillet over low heat, warm 3 tablespoons of the olive oil. Add the onion and garlic and fry gently, stirring frequently, until translucent, about 5 minutes. Add the mussels, mushrooms and half of the liquid from the mussels. Cook for 2 minutes.

Meanwhile, in a saucepan, bring at least 6 qt (6 l) salted water to a boil. Add the spaghetti and cook until *al dente,* about 5 minutes. Drain the spaghetti and transfer to the skillet with the sauce. Season to taste with salt and pepper. Cook, stirring, for 2 minutes.

Sprinkle the remaining 3 tablespoons olive oil over the pasta and sauce and transfer to a warm serving bowl. Sprinkle with the parsley. Serve piping hot.

SERVES 6

Spaghetti with Mussel and Mushroom Sauce (left) and Livorno-Style Fish Risotto (right)

Livorno

SPAGHETTI ALLA FORNAIA
Baker's Spaghetti

If you use very fresh walnuts and the inner skin is still pale, it must be removed because it will be bitter. If the skin is brown, it may be left on.

1½ cups (5 oz/150 g) walnuts
3 garlic cloves
½ cup (4 fl oz/120 ml) extra virgin olive oil
3 oz (90 g) fine dry bread crumbs
salt
1 lb (450 g) spaghetti
1 tablespoon chopped fresh flat-leaf (Italian) parsley

❧ Chop the nuts and garlic finely with a knife.
❧ In a skillet over low heat, warm half of the olive oil. Add the nuts, garlic and bread crumbs and fry until the garlic is just golden, about 5 minutes. Season to taste with salt.
❧ Meanwhile, in a saucepan, bring at least 6 qt (6 l) salted water to a boil. Add the spaghetti and cook until *al dente,* about 7 minutes. Drain and tip into a warm serving bowl.
❧ Add the remaining ¼ cup (2 fl oz/60 ml) olive oil and the nut sauce to the spaghetti and toss well. Sprinkle with the parsley and serve immediately.

SERVES 6

Firenze

TAGLIERINI FRITTI
Fried Noodle Nests

Frying is an art in Florence. It is essential to use extra virgin olive oil because it reaches the smoking point at a higher temperature than seed oils and therefore produces less toxins.

2½ cups (10 oz/300 g) all-purpose (plain) flour
3 eggs
2 lb (900 g) plum (egg) tomatoes, peeled and chopped
1 garlic clove, chopped
1 tablespoon granulated sugar
pinch of ground chili
salt
2 tablespoons extra virgin olive oil, plus 4 cups (32 fl oz/1 l) for frying
6 tablespoons (1½ oz/45 g) freshly grated Parmesan cheese

❧ Heap the flour in a mound on a work surface. Make a well in the center and break the eggs into it. Beat the eggs lightly with a fork, then gradually work the flour into the eggs until a loose ball of dough forms. Knead the dough on a lightly floured surface until soft, smooth and elastic, about 5 minutes. Using a pasta machine, roll out the dough very thinly. Allow to stand for a few minutes, then, using the narrow cutter on the machine, cut the dough into long, thin strips about 1/16 in (2 mm) wide. Roll the noodles into nests about 2 in (5 cm) in diameter and place on a clean cloth. Sprinkle very lightly with flour.
❧ Combine the tomatoes, garlic, sugar and chili in a saucepan. Season to taste with salt and cook over low heat until the liquid evaporates, about 50 minutes. Remove from the heat, add the 2 tablespoons olive oil and stir well.
❧ In a large, deep, heavy skillet heat the oil for frying to 350°F (180°C). Add half of the noodle nests and fry, turning gently, until crisp and golden, about 5 minutes. With a slotted spoon, remove to absorbent paper towels to drain; keep warm. Continue frying the remaining nests in the same manner.
❧ Reheat the sauce gently. Arrange the fried nests on a serving platter and sprinkle with a little salt and the Parmesan cheese. Serve immediately. Pass the sauce separately.

SERVES 6   *Photograph page 4*

Baker's Spaghetti

CACCIUCCO ALLA LIVORNESE

Fish Soup, Livorno Style

Although originally from Livorno, this rich soup has been copied all over Italy. It is generally very peppery and made with inexpensive fish, which add to the intense flavor but risk making it bony. A variety of large and small fish and a few shrimp are essential.

4 lb (1.8 kg) mixed fish and shellfish, such as sole, red mullet, sea robin (gurnard or grondin), dogfish (rock salmon) and shrimp (prawns)
3 tablespoons extra virgin olive oil
½ yellow onion, chopped
3 garlic cloves, chopped
2 lb (900 g) plum (egg) tomatoes, peeled and chopped
¾ cup (7 fl oz/210 ml) water
salt and freshly ground black pepper
6 slices coarse country bread
1 tablespoon chopped fresh flat-leaf (Italian) parsley

🐟 Clean the fish and peel the shrimp. Remove the heads and tails from the larger fish and discard, then cut the fish into thick slices. Leave the small fish whole.
🐟 In a shallow saucepan over low heat, warm the olive oil. Add the onion and garlic and fry gently, stirring frequently, until translucent, about 5 minutes. Add the tomatoes and water and simmer uncovered for 10 minutes. Add the fish and season to taste with salt and pepper. Cook at a gentle simmer for about 10 more minutes.
🐟 Meanwhile, preheat an oven to 350°F (180°C). Toast the bread in the oven until golden. Place a slice of toast in each of 6 soup bowls and sprinkle each with a little of the parsley.
🐟 Divide the hot soup and fish pieces evenly among the bowls. Serve immediately.

SERVES 6

Wide Noodles with Wild Boar Sauce

LINGUINE CON GLI SCAMPI

Linguine with Shrimp Sauce

The markets and restaurants in Livorno offer a great variety of shrimp, the best of which are spannocchie, *or imperial prawns, which are usually about 8 in (20 cm) long. They are always sold whole, but if unavailable, headless shrimp may be used instead.*

⅓ cup (3 fl oz/90 ml) extra virgin olive oil
1 small yellow onion, chopped
4 lb (1.8 kg) whole imperial shrimp (prawns) or 10 oz (300 g) headless shrimp, peeled
10 oz (300 g) plum (egg) tomatoes, peeled, chopped and then drained for at least 30 minutes
2 tablespoons Marsala wine
salt
1 lb (450 g) linguine

🐟 In a medium saucepan over low heat, warm the olive oil. Add the onion and fry gently, stirring frequently, until translucent, about 5 minutes. Add the shrimp and cook for 2 minutes for small shrimp and 7 minutes for imperial shrimp. Add the tomatoes, Marsala and a little salt. Cook over moderate heat until the liquid evaporates, about 3 minutes. Keep warm over very low heat.
🐟 Meanwhile, in a saucepan, bring at least 6 qt (6 l) salted water to a boil. Add the linguine and cook until *al dente,* about 6 minutes. Drain and tip onto a warm serving platter.
🐟 Pour the hot sauce directly over the linguine, toss and serve. If you were able to find imperial shrimp, arrange them on top of the linguine.

SERVES 6

PAPPARDELLE AL CINGHIALE

Wide Noodles with Wild Boar Sauce

The Maremma is famous for its wild boar, which appears on nearly every restaurant menu in one form or another. The meat is full of flavor but, as it tends to be tough, it should be marinated before being cooked.

SAUCE
1 lb (450 g) wild boar meat, preferably from the leg
1½ cups (12 fl oz/400 ml) good red wine
½ yellow onion, chopped
1 tablespoon juniper berries
½ teaspoon black peppercorns
2 bay leaves
1 fresh rosemary sprig
3 tablespoons extra virgin olive oil
1 tablespoon all-purpose (plain) flour
10 oz (300 g) plum (egg) tomatoes, peeled and chopped
salt

PASTA
2½ cups (10 oz/300 g) all-purpose (plain) flour
3 eggs

🐟 To prepare the sauce: cut the meat into 1½-in (3-cm) cubes and place them in a deep glass or ceramic bowl. Add the wine, onion, juniper berries, peppercorns, bay leaves and rosemary. Let stand to marinate in a cool place for 12 hours.
🐟 Drain off, strain and reserve the marinade. Dry the meat well with absorbent paper towels. In a shallow saucepan over moderate heat, warm the olive oil. Add the meat and brown on all sides, about 10 minutes.

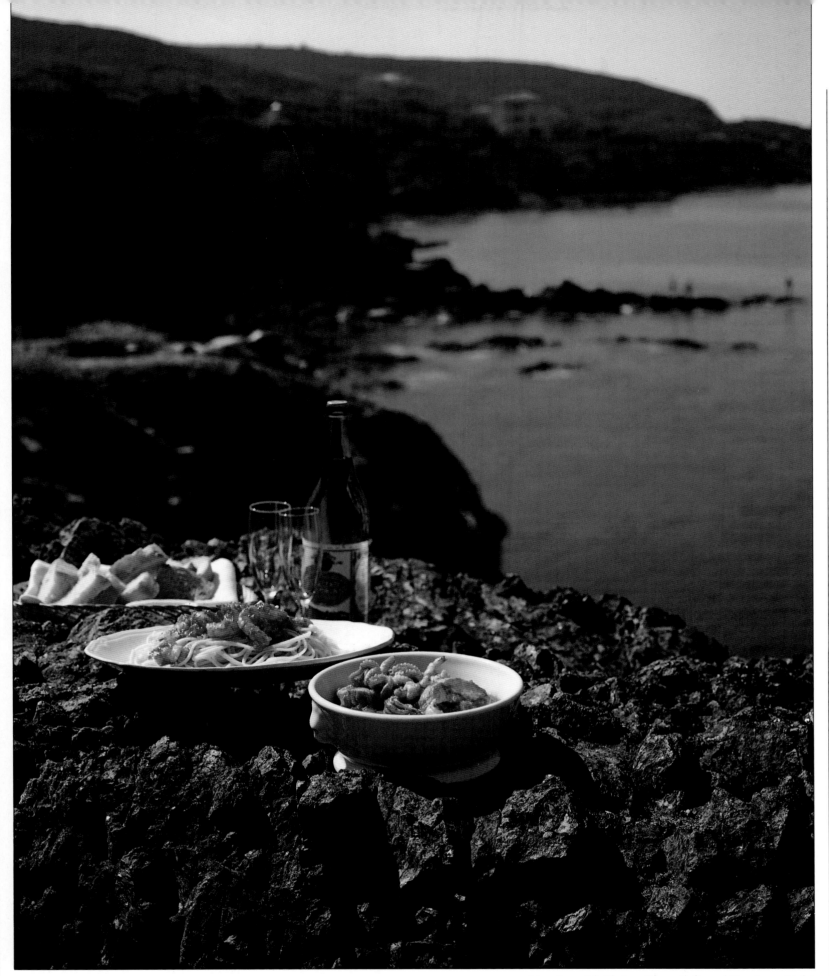

Linguine with Shrimp Sauce (left) and Cacciucco (right)

❧ Sprinkle the meat with the flour and stir well. Add the tomatoes and marinade and stir well, scraping up any browned bits on the pan bottom. Bring to a boil over high heat. Reduce the heat to low, cover and simmer gently until nearly all the liquid has been absorbed, about 2 hours. Remove the meat from the pan with a slotted spoon and chop it finely. Return the chopped meat to the pan, stir well, season with salt and simmer to blend. Set the sauce aside.

❧ To make the noodles: heap the flour in a mound on a work surface. Make a well in the center and break the eggs into it. Beat the eggs lightly with a fork, then gradually work the flour into the eggs until a loose ball of dough forms. Knead the

dough on a lightly floured surface until soft, smooth and elastic. Using a pasta machine, roll out the dough very thinly. Allow to stand for a few minutes, then, using a long, sharp knife, cut into long strips about 1¼ in (3 cm) wide and 4 in (10 cm) long.

❧ In a saucepan, bring at least 6 qt (6 l) salted water to a boil. Add the noodles and boil them for exactly 2 minutes. Drain and tip onto a warm serving dish.

❧ Reheat the sauce. Pour the hot sauce over the noodles, toss and serve immediately.

SERVES 6

Lucca

TAGLIERINI CON PICCIONI

Thin Noodles with Pigeon

Tuscan farmers breed pigeons for the pot, but they leave them free to fly around so that their meat will have plenty of flavor. In this recipe dry linguine are a satisfactory substitute for homemade pasta.

2 pigeons (squab), about 10 oz (300 g) each
3 tablespoons extra virgin olive oil
½ yellow onion, chopped
½ carrot, peeled and chopped
½ celery stalk, trimmed and chopped
10 oz (300 g) plum (egg) tomatoes, peeled and chopped
salt
2½ cups (10 oz/300 g) all-purpose (plain) flour
3 eggs
3 oz (90 g) *prosciutto,* chopped

❧ Cut the pigeons into quarters and set aside.
❧ In a saucepan over low heat, warm the olive oil. Add the onion, carrot and celery and fry gently, stirring frequently, for about 5 minutes. Add the pigeons and, turning occasionally, fry them for about 10 minutes. Stir in the tomatoes, season to taste with salt and cover the pan. Cook for 1 hour, adding a little water if the pan begins to dry.
❧ Meanwhile, heap the flour in a mound on a work surface. Make a well in the center and break the eggs into it. Beat the eggs lightly with a fork, then gradually work the flour into the eggs until a loose ball of dough forms. Knead the dough on a lightly floured surface until soft, smooth and elastic, about 5 minutes. Using a pasta machine, roll out the dough very thinly. Allow to stand for a few minutes, then, using the narrow cutter on the machine, cut into long, thin strips about ¹⁄₁₆ in (2 mm) wide. Roll the noodles into nests about 2 in (5 cm) in diameter and place on a clean cloth. Sprinkle very lightly with flour.
❧ Remove the pigeon pieces from the saucepan, bone them and chop the meat coarsely. Return the meat to the pot and reheat gently with the *prosciutto.*
❧ In a saucepan, bring at least 6 qt (6 l) salted water to a boil. Add the noodles and boil them for exactly 2 minutes. Drain the noodles and tip them onto a warm serving dish. Toss with the sauce and serve.

SERVES 6

Lucca

MINESTRONE DI CAVOLO

Cabbage Soup

This is a very thick soup that is often prepared in quantity, because farm workers take it with them to the fields to have cold for lunch.

1⅛ cups (7 oz/210 g) dried *cannellini* beans
3 oz (90 g) pork fat or *pancetta,* thinly sliced
10 oz (300 g) curly-leaf cabbage
10 oz (300 g) black cabbage or Savoy cabbage
⅓ cup (3 fl oz/90 ml) extra virgin olive oil
2 yellow onions, chopped
2 celery stalks, chopped
1 large potato, peeled and cubed
10 oz (300 g) Swiss chard (silverbeet), sliced
1 tablespoon fresh thyme leaves
salt and freshly ground black pepper
8 cups (64 fl oz/2 l) water

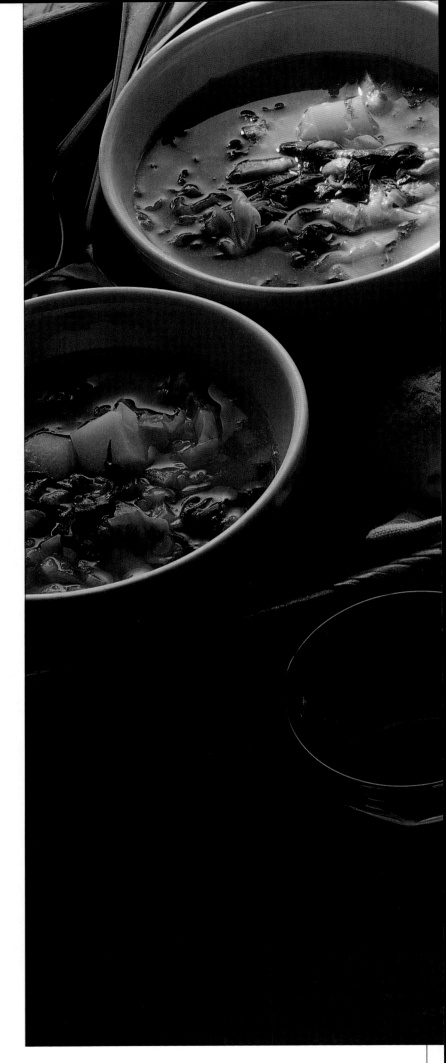

❧ In a bowl, soak the beans in water to cover for 12 hours. Drain the beans and put them into a deep saucepan. Add water to cover by 1 in (2.5 cm) and the pork fat. Slowly bring to a boil. Lower the heat, cover and simmer for 1½ hours.
❧ Remove and discard the hard stalks from both types of cabbage leaves. Slice roughly and set aside.
❧ In another deep saucepan over moderate heat, warm the

Cabbage Soup (left) and Thin Noodles with Pigeon (right)

olive oil. Add the onion and celery and fry gently, stirring frequently, for 5 minutes. Add both types of cabbage, the potato, Swiss chard and thyme and season to taste with salt and pepper.

♣ Drain the beans and add their liquid and the pork fat to the saucepan with the vegetables. Cover and simmer for about 10 minutes, then add the water and bring to a boil. Cover and

boil gently for 2 hours.

♣ Meanwhile, purée half of the beans. When the vegetables have finished cooking, add the whole beans and the purée to the soup and cook for 10 minutes.

♣ Pour the soup into a tureen and serve immediately.

SERVES 6

Gnocchi with Fake Sauce

Arezzo

TOPINI AL SUGO FINTO
Gnocchi with Fake Sauce

Tuscans love ragù *and make infinite varieties of it. To them it is the only "real" sauce, which is why they call this tomato and vegetable sauce* sugo finto, *or "fake sauce."*

SAUCE
3 tablespoons extra virgin olive oil
1 small yellow onion, chopped
1 carrot, peeled and chopped
1 celery stalk, chopped
2 lb (900 g) plum (egg) tomatoes, peeled and chopped
½ cup (4 fl oz/120 ml) dry red wine
salt and freshly ground pepper to taste
1 tablespoon chopped fresh flat-leaf (Italian) parsley

GNOCCHI
2 lb (900 g) baking potatoes
1½ cups (6 oz/180 g) all-purpose (plain) flour
2 egg yolks

🍃 To prepare the sauce: in a saucepan over low heat, warm the olive oil. Add the onion, carrot and celery and fry gently for 5 minutes.

🍃 Add the tomatoes and wine. Stir and season to taste with salt and pepper. Cover and cook until the sauce is thick and the liquid evaporates, about 50 minutes.

🍃 To prepare the gnocchi: steam the potatoes in their skins until tender, about 30 minutes.

🍃 Remove the potatoes from the steamer and peel them. Place in a bowl and mash while still hot. Add half of the flour and the egg yolks and work them very quickly into the potatoes until the mixture forms a firm, smooth dough.

🍃 Flour the palms of your hands and a work surface with some of the remaining flour. Using the palms of your hands and the surface, roll the dough into cylinders about ¾ in (2 cm) in diameter. Cut the cylinders into pieces about 1⅛ in (3 cm) long. Roll each piece over the prongs of a fork, pressing it in the center lightly with your thumb. As the gnocchi are made, place them on another lightly floured surface.

🍃 Bring at least 6 qt (6 l) salted water to a boil in a shallow saucepan. Drop the gnocchi, a few at a time, into the water. As soon as they rise to the surface, remove them with a slotted spoon, draining well. Arrange on a warm serving dish. Continue cooking the remaining gnocchi in the same manner.

🍃 As soon as all the gnocchi are ready, pour the hot sauce over them and sprinkle with the parsley. Serve immediately.

SERVES 6

Firenze

CRESPELLE ALLA RICOTTA
Crêpes with Spinach and Ricotta

In Florence these crêpes are often served instead of lasagna. They are much lighter and have a delicate flavor. On Italian menus alla fiorentina *generally means "with spinach." Crêpes are also tasty filled with cream sauce or meat sauce.*

CRÊPES
2 eggs
⅓ cup (3 fl oz/90 ml) milk
2 tablespoons extra virgin olive oil, plus extra for frying
pinch of salt
¾ cup (3 oz/90g) all-purpose (plain) flour, sifted

FILLING
1¼ lb (600 g) spinach, trimmed
1¼ cups (10 oz/300 g) ricotta

Crêpes with Spinach and Ricotta

3 tablespoons freshly grated Parmesan cheese
1 egg, lightly beaten
pinch of freshly grated nutmeg
salt

SAUCE
1 tablespoon unsalted butter
¼ cup (1 oz/30 g) all-purpose (plain) flour
2 cups (16 fl oz/480 ml) milk
3 tablespoons freshly grated Parmesan cheese
salt and freshly ground black pepper

🍃 To prepare the crêpes: whisk the eggs in a bowl until well blended. Add the milk, the 2 tablespoons olive oil and salt. Gradually mix in the flour. The batter should be smooth and have the consistency of thick cream.

🍃 Brush a 6-in (15-cm) nonstick skillet with oil and place over moderate heat. Pour in just enough batter to create a very thin sheet when the pan is tilted. Cook for 1 minute until the edges lift easily. Turn with a spatula and cook the other side for 30 seconds. Remove the crêpe from the pan to a flat surface to cool. Continue cooking the crêpes in the same manner until the batter is finished. There should be about 18 crêpes in all.

🍃 To prepare the filling: cook the spinach in a little salted boiling water until tender, about 2 minutes. Drain well, pressing out any excess liquid. Finely chop the spinach and place in a mixing bowl. Add the ricotta, Parmesan, egg and nutmeg and mix well. Season to taste with salt.

🍃 Preheat an oven to 350°F (180°C). Spoon a little filling in a line down the center of each crêpe and roll up. Set the crêpes aside, seam side down.

🍃 To prepare the sauce: in a small saucepan over moderate heat, melt the butter. Add the flour, blend in well and cook, stirring constantly, until very smooth, 2–3 minutes. Gradually add the milk, stirring constantly, and cook, continuing to stir, until the sauce has thickened, about 5 minutes. Remove from the heat and stir in the Parmesan. Season to taste with salt and pepper.

🍃 Pour enough sauce into a shallow 12-by-16-in (30-by-40-cm) baking dish to form a thin layer. Arrange the crêpes side by side and seam side down on top of the sauce. Spoon the remaining sauce over the crêpes. Bake until the sauce bubbles slightly and the crêpes are heated through, about 20 minutes.

🍃 Remove from the oven and serve immediately.

SERVES 6

LUCCA

LUCCA

Although Byron and Shelley loved Lucca, and Heine and Montaigne visited often, until a few years ago it was unique among Tuscan cities in that it was practically unknown to tourists. Its three miles of protective walls, all beautifully intact, perhaps saved it from the great floods of tourists who have altered the character of other Tuscan towns, Florence above all.

Today Lucca is very fashionable. Milanese and Britons, Americans and Germans compete to bid small fortunes for the few country houses still for sale. But Lucca has managed to remain unchanged. It could be that the locals have always been reluctant to accept busloads of daytrippers laden with cameras and instead have welcomed visitors who are interested in learning about their city and spending some time there.

The uniqueness of Lucca may not captivate a visitor immediately, but its cuisine most certainly will. Only a few miles from the sea and with mountains behind it, the city and its surroundings enjoy a varied local table. The offerings range from dishes made with spelt (the ancient grain still cultivated on the slopes of the Garfagnana mountains) to a cornucopia of soups made from black cabbage, from succulent poultry and rabbit preparations to delicious creations based on fish fresh from the lakes, streams and sea.

Lucca has maintained its long traditions, and not even the restaurateurs in the city have succumbed to the demands of nouvelle cuisine. The great variety of local

Left: The real life of Italy takes place out on the street, whether it be a lively festa in the village piazza, or a quiet morning spent reading the papers in a sidewalk café. Previous pages: A villa lies nestled in the hills near Barga. This mountainous region of Lucca province is known as the Garfagnana.

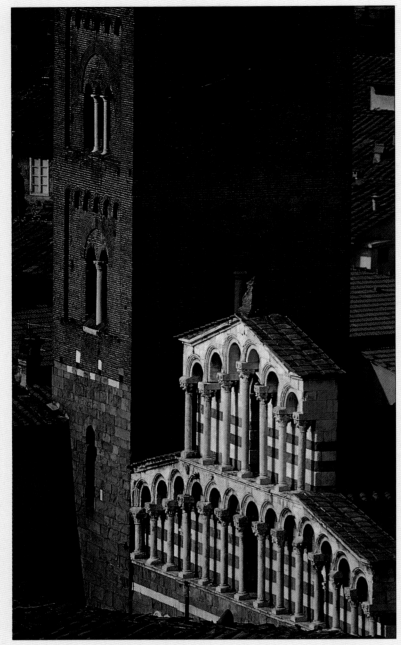

Amidst the red roofs of Lucca lies San Pietro Somaldi, one of the many Romanesque churches built during the city's glory days of the twelfth and thirteenth centuries. This view is from the top of Guinigi Tower.

dishes all share a common denominator: their simplicity and the quality of their ingredients. The olive oil produced near Lucca is among the finest in Italy. Wild herbs are mixed with the produce from the innumerable market gardens, and these, together with farmyard animals like hens and rabbits, are the basic ingredients of most local recipes.

Special flours, such as chick-pea, corn and chestnut, have always played an important role in Lucchese kitchens. In fact, until the end of the last war, chestnut flour was the staple diet of the farmers in the Garfagnana area, where there are still great chestnut woods. Although the flour is now used much less, no self-respecting Lucchese would ever give up roasting chestnuts on the fire or cooking *necci* in iron molds on the embers. *Necci,* which are pancakes made of chestnut flour, were traditionally spread with olive oil and fresh *pecorino* (sheep's milk cheese) or with *biroldo.* Made all over Tuscany, *biroldo* is a pig's blood salami that is a specialty of Lucca, where it is seasoned with pine nuts and raisins.

Restaurant owners in Lucchesia must be given a great deal of credit for having made the real Lucchese cuisine well-known. Sauro Brunicardi, owner of La Mora in Ponte a Moriano, is one of several restaurateurs whose faith in traditional recipes has made them famous throughout the world. His *gran farro* alone merits more than one visit to Lucca.

It is worth devoting a few lines to *farro,* or, as it is called in English, spelt. Although in ancient times this grain was grown so widely that it was even found in the pharaohs' tombs, after the advent of wheat its cultivation was nearly abandoned outside Lucchesia. Recently, however, some health food stores in Europe and North America have begun stocking it. Spelt was grown by the Romans and was, in fact, the staple food of Caesar's legions during their military campaigns. In the Garfagnana there are still several mills that grind *farro* in the same way it was produced centuries ago, and the local cooks use it in soups and cakes. In this region people live very long lives, which they attribute to the fact that they eat so much spelt.

Herbs, from borage and thyme to calamint and rosemary, are also much in evidence. Cesare, a young and enterprising restaurateur whose Ristorante Vipore has one of the most beautiful views of Lucca, bases his recipes on herbs. He has an herb garden behind his restaurant and constantly experiments with new and delicious ways of using them.

As in the rest of Tuscany, very few cakes are made in Lucchesia. The only exception is *bucellato,* a ring-shaped cake that is as much a symbol of Lucca as its walls and the Guinigi Tower. This cake, with its strong aniseed accent, dates back to very early times. Even the ancient Romans had a ring-shaped bread that they called *buccelatum.* During the Middle Ages, vassals took gifts of *bucellato* to their feudal lords, and today it is the traditional present godparents give to their godchildren on confirmation day. It is at its best when eaten with strawberries.

The most popular first courses in Lucchesia are soups, such as *frantoiana,* made with black cabbage; *infarinata,* thickened with cornmeal; or *garmugia,* a delicate blend of young broad (fava) beans, peas, asparagus and tiny artichokes. Mario Tobino, a famous Italian writer who was born in Viareggio, describes the last-named soup thus: "Garmugia, the secret dish of the sixteenth century, was used by the well-to-do in Lucca when recovering from a long illness or affliction or when, to save their souls, they decided to bring comfort to the poor. The finest herbs and chopped meat were left to bubble over the burning embers." Even for one without an infirmity, a spoonful of *garmugia* is grateful to the palate.

The typical pastas from Lucchesia are *maccheroni,* which, despite their name, bear no resemblance to the usual Italian *macccheroni.* They are rather like small lasagna and are generally served with mushroom sauce. Then there are broad *tagliatelle* and *tordelli,* the classic first courses. *Tordelli* are twice the size of the typical Italian *tortellini* from Emilia-Romagna, and their filling is much tastier. *Tordelli* are to Lucca what pizza is to Naples.

Red meat has never played an important part in Lucca's cooking. The farmers were poor and lived off what they had: pork and all its derivatives; chicken and rabbit, either stewed or grilled; and, because all Tuscans are keen hunters, game. Vegetables are another vital ingredient. Not only are they used in numerous soups, but in omelets, savory cakes and molds. They are also cooked with meat and fish. Salt cod with chick-peas and cuttlefish with Swiss chard are two typical examples of Lucchese cookery. Mushrooms are very important too, because even today they spring up in great quantity in the Garfagnana.

Lucchese cuisine also means fish. By the sixteenth century, there was a port in Viareggio, just a few miles from Lucca, but it was not until the beginning of this century that the town became a fashionable bathing resort. Aristocrats and the rich middle classes from central and northern Italy spent and continue to spend their summer holidays in Viareggio and nearby Forte dei Marmi. Beautiful art nouveau houses, such as the Salone Margherita, line the seafront at Viareggio. The fishermen go out to sea at dawn, but regrettably they no longer sail down the Burlamacca canal or from the Darsena, instead using the new port. But they still return at dusk, their boats laden with fish. At restaurants like Tito del Molo, da Roma, the Patriarca, and the Buonamico in Viareggio, and at Pino or Lorenzo in Forte dei Marmi, the fish are prepared in the simple traditional way that leaves the natural flavor intact.

In Lucchesia, however, fish also means fresh-water fish. There are trout from the streams, eels from the Serchio River and fish from Lake Massaciuccoli, which lies in a nature reserve where rare species of migratory birds find shelter. Giacomo Puccini, who had a house at Torre del Lago on the side of the lake near the sea, loved the fish from Lake Massaciuccoli and also enjoyed shooting coot from a boat hidden among the reeds. His villa is now open to the public, and every summer the famous Puccini Festival is held in the adjoining gardens. It is said that Puccini, a pure-blooded Lucchese, chose to build a villa there, not so much for the beautiful lake as for the hunting. When he first went there in 1891, its few inhabitants were all said to be poachers.

At Torre del Lago, Puccini, a man who lived life to the full, founded the Club la Bohème with a group of friends. The club itself was little more than a tavern where he met his friends to play cards, drink wine, eat good food and create new recipes. In this area there are numerous dishes attributed to Puccini, and although doubt is cast on some of these attributions, everyone agrees that he truly did invent coot *alla Puccini*.

The best place from which to admire Lucchesia's breathtaking natural beauty is undoubtedly Torre del Lago. With the sea a mile or so behind it, the town looks up at the Apuan Alps. Even in midsummer the peaks appear to be covered with snow. It is not snow, however, but the famous white Carrara marble. This is the same

Laundry day in the Garfagnana village of Gioviano. The windows of Tuscany frame the small delights of everyday life.

An afternoon of fishing at Torre del Lago, Lake Massaciuccoli. The composer Giacomo Puccini, who built a house here, described the lake as his "supreme joy, paradise, Eden."

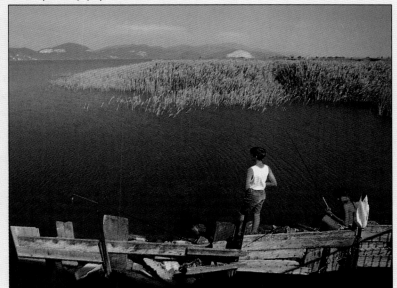

Versilia coast loved by Michelangelo, who, on the peak of Mount Altissimo, had wished to sculpt a statue large enough to be seen from the sea. He never fulfilled his wish, but the sparkling apex of the mountain is still a monument to the great master.

Lucca is one of the few cities where the pleasures of the table could always be indulged, even when other cities in Tuscany, the rest of Italy and Europe were at war. The rich population invariably preferred to pay off their enemies rather than find them armed at their gates. In all their long history, the mighty walls of Lucca have never been used in battle, and only once did they defend the city. That was in 1812, when the nearby Serchio River overflowed. The gates were closed and the water that flooded the surrounding countryside did not spill into the city.

Their philosophy of avoiding conflict left the citizens of Lucca free to devote their attention to silkmaking, banking and to the creation of plaster figurines, which for many years they exported around the world. And, of course, to their excellent table.

I Piatti di Mezzo

A wine shop plaque boasts a black rooster (gallo nero), *the symbol of authentic Chianti Classico.*

I Piatti di Mezzo

In Florence, from the Middle Ages through the Renaissance, there was a meal called *la matta cena,* or "the mad supper." It was rather more than a snack but less than a normal evening meal. From Boccaccio we learn that "mad" really meant improvised, and that a few light dishes were prepared as an excuse to gather friends. Most of the items served were those we now call *piatti di mezzo,* or "middle dishes"—frittatas, vegetable loaves and molds. Nowadays they all make excellent luncheon

Vendors prepare for another day of selling at Florence's indoor San Lorenzo market.

dishes, although at formal dinners, as the name suggests, they are served as entrées between the first and main courses.

Torta di verdura (vegetable loaf) is fairly common throughout Tuscany, but perhaps the best version is prepared in Lunigiana, where it is called *scarpazza* and is made with leeks, zucchini and wild salad plants that vary with the seasons. Borage and chicory are typical ingredients. A different kind of vegetable loaf is made in Versilia and the Garfagnana, where ricotta and sheep's milk cheese are also used and occasionally lard or bacon. An excellent fourteenth-century version that has chicken livers among its ingredients is still very popular.

There is a long tradition of stuffing either whole cabbages or cabbage leaves. Evidence of this legacy can be found in a cookbook published in 1885 by Arezzo chef Giobatta Magi, who points out that her cabbage recipe is very old. In fourteenth-century Florence, *la porrata,* a leek dish, was offered to the population outside the Basilica of San Lorenzo on the feast of St. Lawrence.

Vegetables mixed with cream sauce are the basis of a grand assortment of molds in which cooks can indulge their whims. The most classic molds are made with spinach, green beans, peas or cardoons. They are baked in a ring shape and, after being turned out, the hole in the center is filled with chicken liver and sage or with the famous Florentine *cibreo,* made with cockscombs and other delicacies.

Previous pages, front to rear: Snails with Sausage and Tomato Sauce (page 102), Green Pea and Ham Frittata (page 112) and Chicken Liver Frittata (page 104).

Another interesting *piatto di mezzo* is stuffed celery. It is the great specialty of Prato, where it is prepared in the most traditional way. The celery stalks are filled with chicken liver and chopped meat, but here too there are numerous interpretations, including the addition of dried mushrooms and ham. Although the stuffed celery in Lunigiana is not as renowned as that of Prato, it is equally delicious.

It is, however, the infinite variety of the frittata that reigns supreme over the *piatti di mezzo*. Whether mixed with onions or zucchini, artichokes or herbs, cauliflower or asparagus, sausage or potato, these open-faced omelets are always a pleasure to eat. Frittatas are also a great disguise for leftovers such as boiled meat and spaghetti. In Versilia the well-known dish called *miglieccio* is actually a frittata made from leftover minestrone. Local housewives are said to make too much minestrone so that they will have enough for *miglieccio* the next day. Then there is *frittata con gli zoccoli,* which translates as "frittata with clogs." The clogs are actually pieces of fried bacon, which leads one to believe that in the past bacon was much tougher. This particular dish is sometimes folded rather than cooked on both sides in the classic Italian manner. At one time these folded omelets were called *pesce d'uova,* or "egg fish."

Tuscans maintain that making frittatas is a fine art. Until the advent of nonstick pans, they were always fried in heavy iron skillets that were never washed. For a Tuscan, a frittata cannot even be considered seriously unless it stands nobly high, is golden on both sides, and is lusciously soft at the center. Any meats and vegetables used must be absolutely cold before being stirred into the eggs, or the eggs would start cooking and spoil the entire operation.

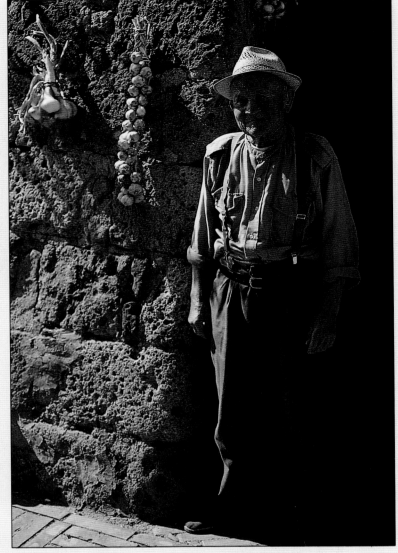

A shopkeeper stands proudly by his produce in the medieval village of Sovana.

Zucchinis are a popular choice for the recipes known as piatti di mezzo—*frittatas, vegetable loaves and vegetable molds.*

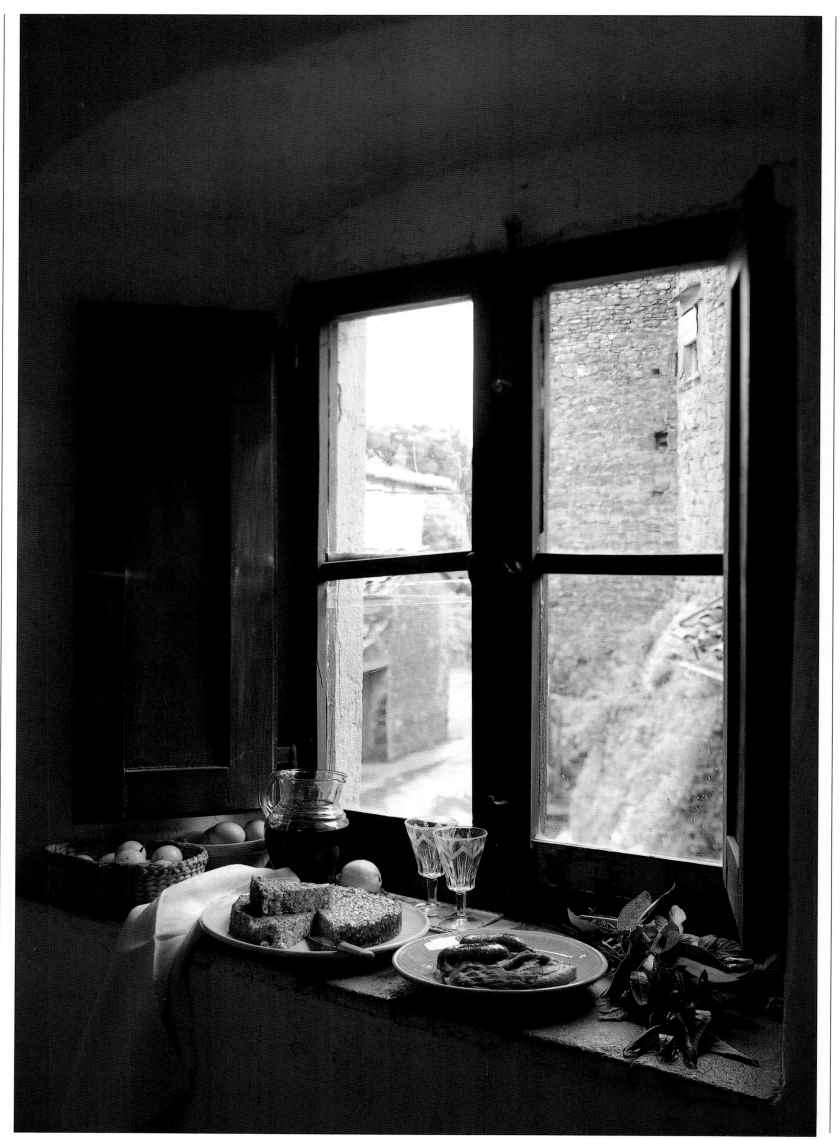

Savory Spelt Cake (left) and Chestnut Flour Polenta (right)

100

Whitebait Omelet

POLENTA DI NECCIO
Chestnut Flour Polenta

Because there are so many chestnut woods around Lucca, there are dozens of recipes calling for chestnut flour. The local cooks are particularly proud of their necci, chestnut pancakes made in a mold and cooked over an open fire. Chestnut flour is available in health food stores and specialty food markets. This polenta is excellent served with fried pancetta, sausages or stewed pork.

5 cups (40 fl oz/1.2 l) water
salt
2½ cups (10 oz/300 g) chestnut flour
3 tablespoons extra virgin olive oil
½ cup (2 oz/60 g) freshly grated *pecorino* cheese or Parmesan cheese

❧ In a large saucepan, bring the water to a boil and add a little salt. Lower the heat to a simmer. Whisking constantly, slowly add the flour in a thin, steady stream. Return the mixture to a boil and cook, stirring from time to time, until done, about 40 minutes. The polenta is ready when it starts pulling away easily from the sides of the pan.
❧ Pour the polenta onto a warm platter. Sprinkle the surface with the olive oil and cheese. Serve very hot.

SERVES 6

TORTINO DI BIANCHETTI
Whitebait Omelet

Bianchetti are tiny whitebait, actually sardines and anchovies caught when they are only ¾ in (2 cm) long. Their season is very short and they are considered a great delicacy.

3 eggs
14 oz (420 g) small whitebait
salt and freshly ground black pepper
1 teaspoon freshly grated lemon zest
1 tablespoon extra virgin olive oil

❧ In a mixing bowl, whisk the eggs until well blended. Add the whitebait with a touch of salt and pepper and the lemon zest. Mix carefully as the whitebait break very easily.
❧ Warm the oil in an 8-in (20-cm) nonstick skillet over moderate heat. Pour in the egg mixture. Cook, occasionally moving the egg with a wooden spoon, until the egg sets and only the surface is runny, about 5 minutes. Turn the omelet out onto a plate, browned side up. Slide the omelet back into the skillet and cook the other side for 1 minute.
❧ Turn the omelet out onto a serving plate. Serve immediately.

SERVES 6

TORTA DI FARRO
Savory Spelt Cake

Spelt is very popular in Lucchesia, where it has been eaten since Etruscan times. It is excellent in soups and with meat dishes and is available in health food stores.

1¾ cups (10 oz/300 g) spelt
3 eggs
10 oz (300 g) ricotta
1 handful of fresh borage leaves, chopped
salt and fresh ground black pepper
extra virgin olive oil for brushing pan

❧ In a bowl, soak the spelt in water to cover overnight.
❧ Drain the spelt and transfer to a saucepan. Add water to cover and cook over low heat, stirring occasionally, until the water is absorbed, about 1 hour.
❧ Preheat an oven to 350°F (180°C).
❧ Place the spelt in a mixing bowl Add the eggs, ricotta, borage and salt and pepper to taste.
❧ Brush a round 9-in (23-cm) cake pan with olive oil. Spoon the spelt mixture into the prepared pan, forming a layer about 1 in (2.5 cm) deep. Bake until the cake is just golden, about 45 minutes.
❧ Remove the pan from the oven and let cool a few minutes. Run a thin, sharp knife blade around the edge of the pan to loosen the cake, then remove the cake to a serving dish. Serve warm but not hot.

SERVES 6

Firenze

TORTINO DI CARCIOFI
Artichoke Omelet

The difference between an artichoke omelet served in Florence and those made elsewhere is that the Florentine version is never cooked in an oven or turned, and the artichokes are fried before being mixed with the egg.

juice of 1 lemon
6 globe artichokes
¾ cup (3 oz/90 g) all-purpose (plain) flour
4 cups (32 fl oz/1 l) extra virgin olive oil for frying
6 eggs
salt and freshly ground black pepper

🌢 Fill a large bowl with water and add the lemon juice. Cut the stalks off the artichokes. Remove the tough outer leaves and cut away the sharp leaf points from the tops. Cut the artichokes into quarters and remove and discard the furry chokes. Immediately drop them into the bowl of water to prevent discoloration. When all of the artichokes have been cut, drain them and pat dry with absorbent paper towels.
🌢 Dredge the artichoke quarters in the flour and shake off any excess.
🌢 Meanwhile, reserve 1 tablespoon of the olive oil and pour the remainder into a deep, heavy skillet. Heat the oil in the skillet to 350°F (180°C). A few at a time, slip the artichoke quarters into the hot oil without crowding the pan. Fry until golden, about 5 minutes. With a slotted spoon, remove the artichokes to absorbent paper towels to drain. Let cool completely.
🌢 In a bowl, whisk the eggs until well blended and season to taste with salt and pepper.
🌢 In a 9-in (23-cm) nonstick skillet, warm the 1 tablespoon olive oil over moderate heat. Pour the eggs into the skillet and arrange the artichoke quarters on top. Cook, occasionally moving the egg with a wooden spoon, until the egg thickens and sets, about 5 minutes.
🌢 Slide the omelet onto a serving plate and serve hot.

SERVES 6

Lucca

TORTA DI CECI
Chick-pea Cake

Around Lucca and in the Garfagnana mountains, flat breads made of unusual flours such as chick-pea, chestnut and cornmeal are often served instead of ordinary bread.

2½ cups (10 oz/300 g) chick-pea (garbanzo) flour
3½ cups (28 fl oz/900 ml) water
salt and freshly ground black pepper
¼ cup (2 fl oz/60 ml) extra virgin olive oil

🌢 Pour the flour into a large bowl. Gradually add the water to the flour, whisking constantly to keep lumps from forming. You should have a smooth, runny batter. Season to taste with salt and pepper and let stand for at least 3 hours. With a slotted spoon, skim the froth that forms on the surface.
🌢 Preheat an oven to 350°F (180°C). Pour the olive oil into a shallow ovenproof pan, then pour in the batter, making a layer about ¼ in (6 mm) deep. Bake until just golden on top, about 30 minutes.
🌢 Remove from the oven pan and cut into serving pieces. Serve piping hot.

SERVES 6

Arezzo

CHIOCCIOLE ALLA SALSICCIA
Snails with Sausage and Tomato Sauce

Snails are considered a great delicacy around Arezzo. They require a lot of preparation, however, because they must be cleaned thoroughly before being cooked. After a rainfall women go out to gather snails in covered baskets. They leave the snails in their new woven homes and feed them with three handfuls of flour and a few stalks of mint, which flushes out the impurities and improves their flavor. After about a week the snails are rinsed several times in cold water. They are then sprinkled with half a quart (500 ml) of vinegar and a handful of salt and moved around frequently. After half an hour they are again rinsed in cold water until they stop frothing. At this point they are ready to be cooked. But of course you can also buy good quality shelled snails in cans at specialty markets.

2 tablespoons extra virgin olive oil
1 small yellow onion, chopped
3 oz (90 g) sweet Italian sausages, skinned and crumbled
36 snails, without shells, prepared for cooking
½ cup (4 fl oz/120 ml) dry white wine
juice of 1 lemon
7 oz (210 g) plum (egg) tomatoes, peeled and chopped
salt and freshly ground black pepper

🌢 In a large skillet over low heat, warm the olive oil. Add the onion and sausage and cook over low heat, stirring frequently, for about 5 minutes.
🌢 Add the snails, wine, lemon juice, tomatoes and salt and pepper to taste. Cook, stirring frequently, for 20 minutes.
🌢 Arrange the snails on a platter and pour the sauce over them. Serve piping hot.

SERVES 6   *Photograph pages 96–97*

Firenze

SALVIATA
Baked Omelet with Sage

In the spring when the sage is young and tender, Tuscan cooks prepare this simple omelet. In Florence, salviata is traditionally cooked in a brown earthenware dish so that the omelet forms a crust on top but stays deliciously soft at the center, but any ovenproof dish will do.

10 eggs
pinch of salt
2 tablespoons all-purpose (plain) flour
¼ cup (2 fl oz/60 ml) milk
12 fresh sage leaves
1 tablespoon extra virgin olive oil

🌢 Preheat an oven to 350°F (180°C). Combine the eggs and salt in a large bowl. Whisk the eggs until well blended. Whisking constantly, gradually add the flour through a sieve to prevent lumps from forming. Whisk in the milk. Tear the sage leaves into pieces with your fingers and add them to the mixture.
🌢 Brush an ovenproof earthenware dish that measures about 8 by 12 in (20 by 30 cm) with the oil. Pour in the egg mixture. Bake until the omelet has formed a golden crust but is still soft at the center, about 20 minutes. Serve hot from the dish.

SERVES 6

Top to bottom: Baked Omelet with Sage, Chick-pea Cake and Artichoke Omelet

Stuffed Turkey Neck

PANE FRITTO ALLA SALSICCIA

Fried Bread Dipped in Egg with Sausage

The Maremma is a land of hunters and strong flavors. After a day out, hunters fry bread in large skillets over open fires and spread it with air-cured wild boar sausages.

3 eggs
salt and freshly ground black pepper
6 slices coarse country bread
4 cups (32 fl oz/1 l) extra virgin olive oil for frying
13 oz (390 g) air-cured wild boar sausages or other spicy
    sausages

🐾 In a shallow bowl, whisk the eggs until well blended. Season to taste with salt and pepper. Soak the bread slices in the beaten egg.

🐾 Meanwhile, in a deep skillet, heat the olive oil to 350°F (180°C).

🐾 Slip the bread, 2 or 3 slices at a time, into the hot oil and fry until just golden, about 3 minutes. With a slotted spoon, remove to absorbent paper towels to drain. Continue frying the remaining bread slices in the same manner. Skin the sausages and spread the meat on the hot fried bread. Serve while the bread is still hot.

SERVES 6

COLLO DI TACCHINO RIPIENO

Stuffed Turkey Neck

Occasionally chicken livers instead of sausage meat are used in this stuffing for turkey neck. This dish is served at room temperature with mayonnaise, pickled onions and gherkins.

8 slices dried *porcini* mushrooms
4 oz (120 g) crustless coarse country bread
1 cup (8 fl oz/240 ml) milk
1 turkey neck (about 1¼ lb/600 g)
7 oz (210 g) sweet Italian sausages, skinned and crumbled
3 oz (90 g) ground (minced) turkey breast
1 egg
1 tablespoon chopped fresh flat-leaf (Italian) parsley
salt and freshly ground black pepper

🐾 In a bowl, soak the mushrooms in warm water to cover for 30 minutes. At the same time, in a separate bowl, soak the bread in the milk for 30 minutes. Drain the mushrooms and squeeze out any excess moisture. Chop the mushrooms and place in a mixing bowl.

🐾 Squeeze all the milk out of the bread and add the bread to the bowl as well.

🐾 Meanwhile, keeping the skin intact, remove the skin from the neck. To do this, very gently turn the skin inside out while carefully detaching it from the bone. When the skin is completely detached turn the skin right side out again.

🐾 Add the sausage, turkey breast, egg and parsley to the bowl. Season to taste with salt and pepper and mix thoroughly.

🐾 Stuff the turkey neck with the sausage mixture. Sew up both ends with kitchen thread. Prick the skin with a needle in several places.

🐾 Bring a large saucepan filled with salted water to a gentle boil. Add the turkey neck, reduce the heat to low and simmer uncovered for 1 hour.

🐾 Drain the turkey neck and let cool completely. Cut into slices about ⅜ in (1 cm) thick and serve at room temperature.

SERVES 6

FRITTATA DI FEGATINI DI POLLO

Chicken Liver Frittata

The Sienese use lamb's liver for this dish during the spring months, but the rest of the year they make it with chicken livers, which are just as delicious.

10 oz (300 g) chicken livers
3 tablespoons extra virgin olive oil
1 handful of fresh sage leaves
6 eggs
salt and freshly ground black pepper

🐾 Remove and discard any fat and connective tissue from the chicken livers. Slice them into fairly large pieces.

🐾 In a skillet over moderate heat, warm 2 tablespoons of the olive oil.

🐾 Add the sage and chicken livers and cook until the livers are firm but still pink in the center, about 2 minutes. Remove from the heat and cool to room temperature.

🐾 In a medium bowl, whisk the eggs until well blended. Season to taste with salt and pepper and mix in the chicken livers.

🐾 Heat the remaining 1 tablespoon olive oil in a 9-in (23-cm) nonstick skillet over moderate heat. Pour in the egg mixture. Cook, occasionally moving the egg with a wooden spoon, until the egg sets and only the surface is slightly runny, about 5 minutes.

🐾 Turn the frittata out onto a plate, browned side up. Slide the frittata back into the skillet and cook the other side for 1 minute.

🐾 Turn the frittata out onto a serving plate. Serve hot.

SERVES 6   *Photograph pages 96–97*

Grosseto

CROSTONI DI UOVA ALLA CACCIATORA

Hunters' Eggs

These eggs are traditionally prepared for excursions to Monte Amiata, a tall mountain with an enormous cross on its summit. The area abounds in game and wild mushrooms.

12 slices dried *porcini* mushrooms
6 tablespoons (3 fl oz/90 ml) extra virgin olive oil, plus
   5 cups (40 fl oz/1.2 l) for frying
1 small yellow onion, chopped
1 lb (450 g) plum (egg) tomatoes, peeled and chopped
small piece of dried chili
salt
6 slices coarse country bread
6 eggs

🐾 Soak the mushrooms in warm water to cover for 30 minutes. Drain and squeeze out any excess moisture; set aside.

🐾 In a saucepan over moderate heat, warm 3 tablespoons of the olive oil. Add the onion and fry gently, stirring frequently, until translucent, about 5 minutes. Add the tomatoes, chili, mushrooms and salt to taste. Simmer over low heat until the liquid evaporates, about 30 minutes.

🐾 In a deep skillet, pour in the olive oil for frying and heat to 350°F (180°C). Add the bread, 2 or 3 slices at a time, and fry until golden, about 3 minutes. With a slotted spoon, remove to absorbent paper towels to drain; keep warm. Continue frying the remaining bread in the same manner.

🐾 In a large nonstick skillet over moderate heat, warm the remaining 3 tablespoons olive oil. Break the eggs into the skillet and fry sunny side up (without turning).

🐾 Arrange the fried bread on a serving plate. Place an egg on each slice and cover with the tomato sauce. Serve immediately.

SERVES 6

Livorno

PANZANELLA CON SCAMPI

Bread, Tomato and Seafood Salad

Panzanella, a strictly Tuscan dish, acquires a taste of the sea in Livorno, where shrimp and cuttlefish are added to the classic recipe.

13 oz (390 g) coarse country bread
6 oz (180 g) cuttlefish or squid
6 oz (180 g) shrimp (prawns), peeled and deveined
3 salad tomatoes, chopped
1 small yellow onion, very finely chopped
1 handful of fresh basil leaves, torn into pieces
1 tablespoon chopped fresh flat-leaf (Italian) parsley
salt
1 tablespoon white wine vinegar
¼ cup (2 fl oz/60 ml) extra virgin olive oil
1 garlic clove, chopped

🐾 Break the bread into pieces. Place in a bowl, add water to cover and soak for about 10 minutes.

🐾 Meanwhile, pull the tentacles from each cuttlefish (or squid) body. Discard the entrails, ink sac and cartilage from the bodies. Cut the tentacles off at the point just above the eyes and discard the heads. Rinse the bodies and tentacles under cold running water.

🐾 Bring a medium saucepan filled with salted water to a boil. Add the shrimp and cook until they turn pink and are opaque, about 2 minutes. Remove with a slotted spoon and set aside to cool. Add the cuttlefish to the boiling water and cook for 15 minutes. Drain and cool completely. Cut the shrimp and cuttlefish into fairly small pieces and place in a salad bowl.

🐾 Drain the bread and squeeze out any excess moisture. Crumble the bread into the salad bowl. Add the tomatoes, onion, basil and parsley. In a small bowl, dissolve salt to taste in the vinegar. Add the olive oil and garlic; mix well. Sprinkle the dressing over the salad. Toss well. Serve at room temperature.

SERVES 6

Hunters' Eggs

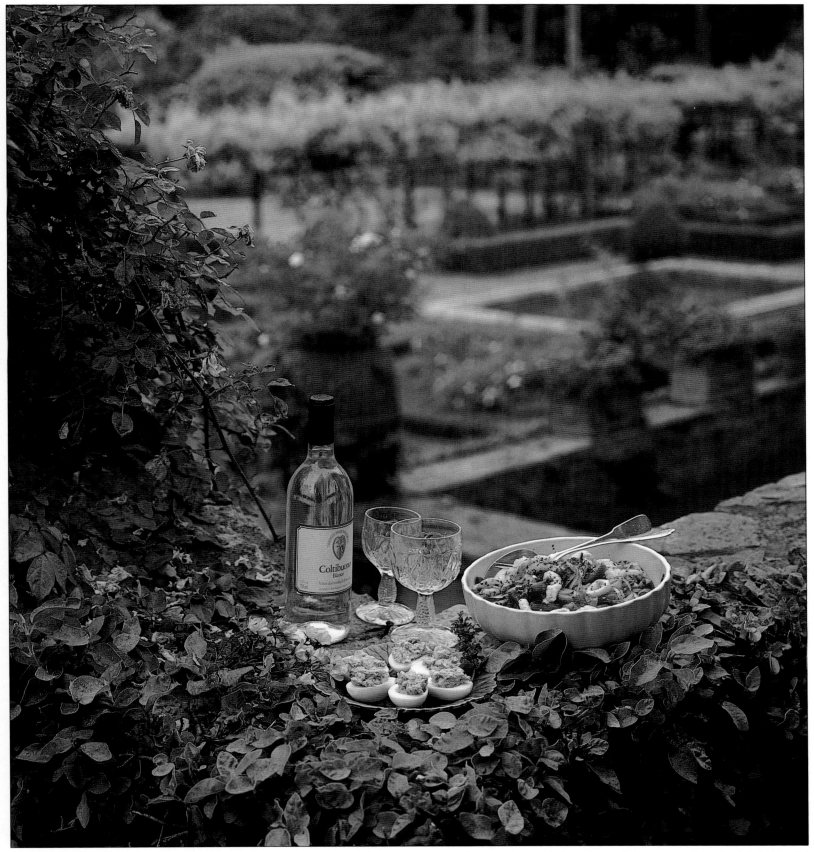

Maremma-Style Stuffed Eggs (left) and Bread, Tomato and Seafood Salad (right)

Grosseto

UOVA SODE ALLA MAREMMANA

Stuffed Eggs, Maremma Style

Wild boar sausages are very strong, so if they are not available, another spicy sausage should be substituted.

6 eggs
7 oz (210 g) air-cured wild boar sausages or other spicy
  sausages, skinned

🐾 Place the eggs in a saucepan and add cold water to cover barely. Bring the water to a boil. When it reaches a boil, cook for 8 minutes from that moment. Remove the eggs from the pan and let cool to room temperature.

🐾 Shell the eggs, cut them in half lengthwise and remove the yolks. Place the yolks in the bowl of a food processor fitted with a metal blade. Cut a very thin slice off the rounded base of each egg white so that the egg half will stand upright. Set the whites aside.

🐾 Add the sausages to the food processor. Process until a creamy mixture forms.

🐾 Spoon the yolk mixture into the reserved egg white halves. Arrange on a plate and serve.

SERVES 6

Arezzo

CROSTONI DI PANE FRITTO
Fried Country Bread

This fried bread is generally eaten plain, but sometimes eggs scrambled with a little tomato and mushroom are served on it.

6 slices coarse country bread, about ⅜ in (1 cm) thick
5 cups (40 fl oz/1.2 l) extra virgin olive oil for frying
salt and freshly ground black pepper

❧ In a deep, heavy skillet, heat the oil to 350°F (180°C). Slip the bread, 2 or 3 pieces at a time, into the hot oil and fry until just golden on both sides, turning once if necessary, about 3 minutes.
❧ With a slotted utensil, remove to absorbent paper towels to drain. Continue frying the remaining bread in the same manner.
❧ Sprinkle the fried bread lightly with salt and pepper. Arrange on a warm platter and serve immediately.
SERVES 6

Grosseto

FRITTATA DI RICOTTA
Ricotta Frittata

The hilly area between Grosseto and Siena is referred to as the Upper Maremma. Flocks of sheep are sent to graze on the hills, and the shepherds' wives produce very good pecorino *cheese and* ricotta.

1¼ cups (10 oz/300 g) ricotta
4 eggs
1 teaspoon fennel seed
salt and freshly ground black pepper
1 tablespoon extra virgin olive oil

❧ Place the ricotta in a mixing bowl. One at a time, add the eggs, stirring well after each addition to prevent lumps from forming. Add the fennel seed and season to taste with salt and pepper.
❧ Heat the oil in an 8½-in (22-cm) nonstick skillet over moderate heat. Pour in the egg mixture and cook, occasionally moving the egg with a wooden spoon, until the egg sets and only the surface is runny, about 5 minutes. Turn the frittata out onto a plate, browned side up. Slide the frittata back into the skillet and cook on the other side for 1 minute.
❧ Turn the frittata out onto a platter. Serve immediately.
SERVES 6

Grosseto

MELANZANE ALLA MAREMMANA
Fried Eggplant Frittata

Along the Maremma coast toward Rome, there were once only eucalyptus trees. Now the land is covered with vast market gardens where tomatoes, peppers and eggplants are grown.

3 Asian (slender) eggplants (aubergines), about 1 lb (450 g) total weight
4 cups (32 fl oz/1 l) extra virgin olive oil for frying
1 cup (4 oz/120 g) all-purpose (plain) flour
3 eggs
3 plum (egg) tomatoes, peeled and chopped
salt and freshly ground pepper

❧ Cut the eggplants crosswise into slices about ⅛ in (3 mm) thick. Reserve 1 tablespoon of the olive oil and pour the remainder into a deep, heavy skillet. Heat the oil in the skillet to 350°F (180°C).
❧ Lightly dredge the eggplant slices in the flour. A few at a

Left to right: Ricotta Frittata, Fried Country Bread and Fried Eggplant Frittata

time, slip the eggplant slices into the hot oil and fry until golden, about 2 minutes. With a slotted spoon, remove to absorbent paper towels to drain. Continue frying the remaining eggplant slices in the same manner. Let cool completely.
🐾 In a mixing bowl, whisk the eggs until well blended. Add the tomatoes and fried eggplant. Season to taste with salt and pepper.
🐾 In a nonstick skillet over moderate heat, warm the 1

tablespoon olive oil. Pour in the egg mixture and cook, occasionally moving the egg with a wooden spoon, until the egg sets and only the surface is runny, about 5 minutes. Turn the frittata out onto a plate, browned side up. Slide the frittata back into the skillet and cook the other side for 1 minute.
🐾 Turn the frittata out onto a platter. Serve immediately.

SERVES 6

Stuffed Mussels on the Half Shell

TORTA DI ERBE

Green Vegetable Tart

This tart is generally made with such wild leaf vegetables as chicory (curly endive), dandelion, St. Peter's grass, nettles and the like, but spinach or Swiss chard may be used instead.

2 lb (900 g) spinach or Swiss chard (silverbeet), trimmed
6 tablespoons (3 fl oz/90 ml) extra virgin olive oil, plus extra for tart pan
2 garlic cloves, chopped
salt and freshly ground black pepper
3 eggs
1¾ cups (7 oz/240 g) all-purpose (plain) flour
½ cup (4 fl oz/120 ml) water

❧ Bring a large saucepan of salted water to a boil. Add the spinach (or Swiss chard) and cook for just a few minutes. Drain well and squeeze out any excess water. Chop and set aside.
❧ In a large skillet over low heat, warm 3 tablespoons of the olive oil. Add the garlic and spinach and season to taste with salt and pepper. Cook, stirring occasionally, for 10 minutes. Remove from the heat and let cool to room temperature. Stir in the eggs.
❧ In a large bowl, combine the flour, the remaining 3 tablespoons olive oil and the water. Mix well until the ingredients come together in a ball. Transfer the ball to a lightly floured surface and knead until it forms a smooth, elastic dough, about 5 minutes.
❧ Preheat the oven to 350°F (180°C). Brush an 8½-in (22-cm) tart pan with a removable bottom with olive oil. On a lightly floured board, roll out the dough with a rolling pin into a round about 10 in (25 cm) in diameter. Carefully transfer it to the prepared pan and press it gently against the bottom and sides of the pan. Trim the dough even with the rim of the tart pan. Spoon the vegetable mixture into the pastry shell and smooth the surface.
❧ Bake the tart until the crust is browned and the center is set, about 40 minutes.
❧ Remove from the oven and let cool slightly. Remove the pan rim and transfer the tart to a serving plate. Serve hot or at room temperature.

SERVES 6

Livorno

COZZE RIPIENE
Stuffed Mussels on the Half Shell

In Livorno the stuffed mussels differ from those of other regions because of the addition of a little sausage meat to the classic mixture of herbs and bread crumbs.

7 oz (210 g) sweet Italian sausages, skinned and crumbled
3 tablespoons fine dry bread crumbs
2 tablespoons chopped fresh flat-leaf (Italian) parsley
2 garlic cloves, chopped
2 plum (egg) tomatoes, peeled and chopped
1 egg
salt
5 lb (2.4 kg) large mussels
2 tablespoons extra virgin olive oil

In a mixing bowl, combine the sausage, 2 tablespoons of the bread crumbs, the parsley, garlic, tomatoes and egg. Season to taste with salt, mix well and set aside.

Scrub and debeard the mussels. Place the mussels in a shallow saucepan, cover and place over moderate heat until the shells open, about 5 minutes. Remove from the heat and discard any mussels that did not open. Open the mussels and discard the top shells. With a small, sharp knife, loosen the mussel meats from the bottom shells and leave them nestled in the shells.

Preheat an oven to 350°F (180°C). Divide the sausage mixture among the mussels, mounding it on top. Sprinkle with the remaining 1 tablespoon bread crumbs and the olive oil.

Arrange the mussels on a flat ovenproof pan. Bake for 15 minutes.

Serve very hot.

SERVES 6

Arezzo

FRITTATA AFFOGATA
Drowned Frittata

Because porcini grow so abundantly in the Casentino mountains, local cooks often add them to the simple tomato sauce in which they "drown" this frittata. They dry the mushrooms for winter by slicing them and threading them onto strings, which are either hung in front of the fire or, on sunny days, stuck on the branches of thorn trees outdoors.

3 tablespoons extra virgin olive oil
1 small carrot, peeled and chopped
1 yellow onion, chopped
½ celery stalk, trimmed and chopped
2 lb (900 g) plum (egg) tomatoes, peeled and chopped
1 tablespoon chopped fresh flat-leaf (Italian) parsley
salt and freshly ground black pepper
8 eggs

In a large skillet over low heat, warm 2 tablespoons of the olive oil. Add the carrot, onion and celery and fry gently, stirring frequently, until the onion is translucent, about 5 minutes. Stir in the tomatoes and parsley. Season to taste with salt and pepper and simmer until the liquid evaporates, about 50 minutes.

In a bowl, whisk the eggs until well blended. Season lightly to taste with salt and pepper. Heat the remaining 1 tablespoon olive oil in an 8-in (20-cm) nonstick skillet over moderate heat. Pour in the egg and cook, occasionally moving the egg with a wooden spoon, until the egg sets and only the surface is runny, about 5 minutes. Turn the frittata out onto a plate, browned side up. Slide the frittata back into the skillet and cook the other side for 1 minute.

Turn the frittata out onto a serving plate. Cover with the tomato sauce and let stand for 2 minutes to allow the flavors to blend. Serve hot.

SERVES 6

Green Vegetable Tart (left) and Drowned Frittata (right)

Siena

SFORMATINI DI FUNGHI
Mushroom Timbales

Mushrooms that are less expensive than prized porcini *can be used for preparing this dish. If you use fresh button mushrooms, however, it is a good idea to add a few soaked dried* porcini *to intensify the flavor.*

1¼ lb (600 g) fresh *porcini* mushrooms
3 tablespoons extra virgin olive oil
1 tablespoon fresh thyme leaves
3 eggs
2 tablespoons all-purpose (plain) flour
¼ cup (2 fl oz/60 ml) milk
2 tablespoons unsalted butter
¾ cup (3 oz/90 g) fine dry bread crumbs

❧ Preheat an oven to 350°F (180°C). Clean the mushrooms by wiping them with a dampened cloth; do not wash them in water. Trim off the ends of the mushroom stems. Thinly slice the mushrooms.
❧ In a medium skillet over moderate heat, warm the olive oil. Add the mushrooms and sauté until tender, about 5 minutes. Add the thyme, stir to combine and set aside to cool completely.
❧ In a bowl, whisk the eggs until well blended. Whisking constantly, gradually add the flour through a sieve to prevent lumps from forming. Whisk in the milk and then stir in the cooled mushrooms.
❧ Butter 6 ramekins each about 4 in (10 cm) in diameter and then coat them evenly with the bread crumbs. Divide the egg mixture evenly among the prepared ramekins. Place the ramekins in a baking dish and pour water into the dish to a depth of 1 in (2.5 cm). Bake in the center of the oven until the custard sets and the tops are golden, about 30 minutes.
❧ Remove the ramekins from the oven. Run a thin, sharp knife blade around the edge of each ramekin and then invert the timbales onto individual serving plates. Serve hot.

SERVES 6

Siena

UOVA TRIPPATE
Omelet Strips with Tomato Sauce

Egg dishes are particularly popular all over Tuscany because new-laid eggs are still available from the farmers. This recipe is so named because it looks like tripe.

3 tablespoons extra virgin olive oil
1 tablespoon chopped yellow onion
4 oz (120 g) *prosciutto,* chopped
1¼ lb (600 g) plum (egg) tomatoes, peeled and chopped
10 eggs
2 tablespoons all-purpose (plain) flour
¼ cup (2 fl oz/60 ml) milk
salt

❧ In a saucepan over moderate heat, warm 2 tablespoons of the olive oil. Add the onion and *prosciutto* and fry gently until the onion is translucent, about 5 minutes. Add the tomatoes and simmer over low heat until the liquid evaporates, about 50 minutes.
❧ In a bowl, whisk the eggs until well blended. Whisking constantly, gradually add the flour through a sieve to prevent lumps from forming. Whisk in the milk and season to taste with salt.

❧ To make the omelets, heat a little of the remaining olive oil in a 7-in (18-cm) nonstick skillet. Add just enough of the egg mixture to the skillet to make a thin sheet, tilting the skillet to spread it evenly. Cook until the egg thickens, about 2 minutes. Turn the omelet over and cook the other side, about 30 seconds. Slide the omelet from the skillet and set aside on a flat surface. Continue making the omelets in the same manner until all the egg mixture is used.
❧ Roll up each omelet in a cylinder and slice into strips about ⅜ in (1 cm) wide. Toss the omelet strips in the tomato sauce and heat for 1 minute. Serve immediately.

SERVES 6

Firenze

MIGLIACCIO
Polenta with Pancetta and Rosemary

This dish is sometimes prepared with chestnut flour and occasionally with millet. At one time a little corn was grown on every Tuscan farm, but now most of it comes from northern Italy.

2 tablespoons extra virgin olive oil
6 oz (180 g) *pancetta,* thinly sliced
5 cups (40 fl oz/1.2 l) water
salt
2⅓ cups (10 oz/300 g) coarse-grained cornmeal
2 tablespoons chopped fresh rosemary

❧ In a skillet over moderate heat, combine the olive oil and *pancetta.* Fry gently until the *pancetta* is crisp, about 5 minutes. Set aside.
❧ In a deep saucepan, bring the water to a boil and add a little salt. Slowly add the cornmeal in a thin, steady stream, stirring constantly. Cook for about 20 minutes over low heat, stirring constantly with a wooden spoon, until the polenta thickens.
❧ Meanwhile, preheat the oven to 350°F (180°C). Line the bottom of an 8-by-12-in (20-by-30-cm) baking dish with half of the *pancetta.*
❧ Cover the *pancetta* with the polenta, smoothing the surface with a wet knife. The polenta should be about 1⅛ in (3 cm) thick. Arrange the remaining *pancetta* on top and sprinkle with the rosemary.
❧ Bake until the top is just golden, about 20 minutes. Serve hot.

SERVES 6

Firenze

FRITTATA DI PISELLI E PROSCIUTTO
Green Pea and Ham Frittata

Despite the fact that Tuscans pick peas when they are very young, they cook them for quite a long time to bring out their flavor.

3 tablespoons extra virgin olive oil
3 oz (90 g) *prosciutto,* chopped
1 small yellow onion, chopped
3 lb (1.3 kg) fresh green peas, shelled
6 eggs
salt and freshly ground black pepper

❧ In a skillet over low heat, warm 2 tablespoons of the olive oil. Add the *prosciutto* and onion and fry gently, stirring fre-

Polenta with Pancetta and Rosemary (left), Mushroom Timbales (right) and Omelet Strips with Tomato Sauce (rear)

quently, until the onion is translucent, about 5 minutes.

❧ Add the peas and then add water just to cover. Simmer over low heat until the water has been absorbed, about 20 minutes. Remove from the heat and let cool to room temperature.

❧ In a bowl, whisk the eggs until well blended, then mix in the cooled peas. Season to taste with salt and pepper.

❧ Heat the remaining 1 tablespoon olive oil in a 9-in (23-cm) nonstick skillet over moderate heat. Pour in the egg mixture.

Cook, occasionally moving the egg with a wooden spoon, until the egg sets and only the surface is runny, about 5 minutes. Turn the frittata out onto a plate, browned side up. Slide the frittata back into the skillet and cook the other side for 1 minute.

❧ Turn the frittata out onto a serving plate. Serve hot.

SERVES 6   *Photograph pages 96–97*

SFORMATO DI FORMAGGIO
Cheese Mold

The house of my friend Signora Titti Nepi has one of the most beautiful views in Siena. This recipe, a favorite of hers, calls for sheep's milk cheese, but Parmesan or Swiss (Gruyère) may be used quite successfully.

¼ cup (2 fl oz/60 ml) extra virgin olive oil
½ cup (2 oz/60 g) all-purpose (plain) flour
2⅓ cups (20 fl oz/600 ml) milk, at room temperature
3 eggs
pinch of freshly grated nutmeg
½ lb (240 g) sheep's milk, Parmesan or Swiss cheese, grated
salt and freshly ground black pepper
2 tablespoons unsalted butter

♣ Preheat an oven to 350°F (180°C). In a medium saucepan over moderate heat, warm the olive oil. Add the flour and cook, stirring continuously, until the flour has absorbed all of the oil, about 2 minutes. Continuing to stir, gradually add the milk and cook until you have a smooth, thick sauce, about 5 minutes. Remove from the heat and let cool to room temperature.

♣ Add the eggs, one at a time, to the sauce, mixing well after each addition. Then mix in the nutmeg and all but 2 tablespoons of the cheese. Season to taste with salt and pepper.

♣ Grease a 5-cup (40-fl oz/1.2-l) mold with the butter and then coat it evenly with the reserved 2 tablespoons cheese. Pour in the cheese mixture.

♣ Place the mold in a baking dish and pour water into the dish to a depth of 1 in (2.5 cm). Bake in the center of the oven until set and the top is golden, about 1 hour.

♣ Remove the mold from the oven. Run a thin, sharp knife blade around the edge of the mold and then invert it onto a serving platter. Serve hot.

SERVES 6

NIDI DI ERBUCCE
Green Nests

In Lucchesia wild leaf vegetables are used often, either combined with other greens or on their own. They are also delicious eaten at room temperature with an oil and lemon dressing or tossed in a pan with oil and garlic and served hot.

2¼ lb (1.2 kg) mixed wild leaf vegetables (such as borage, dandelion or chicory [curly endive]) or spinach, trimmed
4 tablespoons (2 fl oz/60 ml) extra virgin olive oil
salt and freshly ground pepper
6 eggs

♣ Bring a large saucepan filled with salted water to a boil. Add the vegetables and cook for a few minutes. Drain well and let cool. Squeeze out any excess water.

♣ In a large skillet over moderate heat, warm 2 tablespoons of the olive oil. Add the vegetables and fry gently, stirring frequently, until tender, about 5 minutes. Season to taste with salt and pepper. Remove from the heat and let cool to room temperature.

♣ Preheat an oven to 350°F (180°C). Divide the vegetables into 6 equal portions and roll each portion into a firm ball. With a fingertip, make a hollow in the center of each ball to form a nestlike indentation.

♣ Brush an 8-by-12-in (20-by-30-cm) baking dish with the remaining 2 tablespoons olive oil and arrange the balls in it, hollow side up. Break 1 egg and drop the white of the egg into one of the hollows; set the yolk aside. Repeat with the remaining eggs, dropping a white into each "nest" and setting the yolks aside so that they can also be added individually.

♣ Bake the nests until the egg white solidifies, about 10 minutes. Remove the dish from the oven and drop a yolk over the white in each hollow. Return the dish to the oven and bake for 2 minutes. Transfer to a platter and serve immediately.

SERVES 6

Cheese Mold

Green Nests

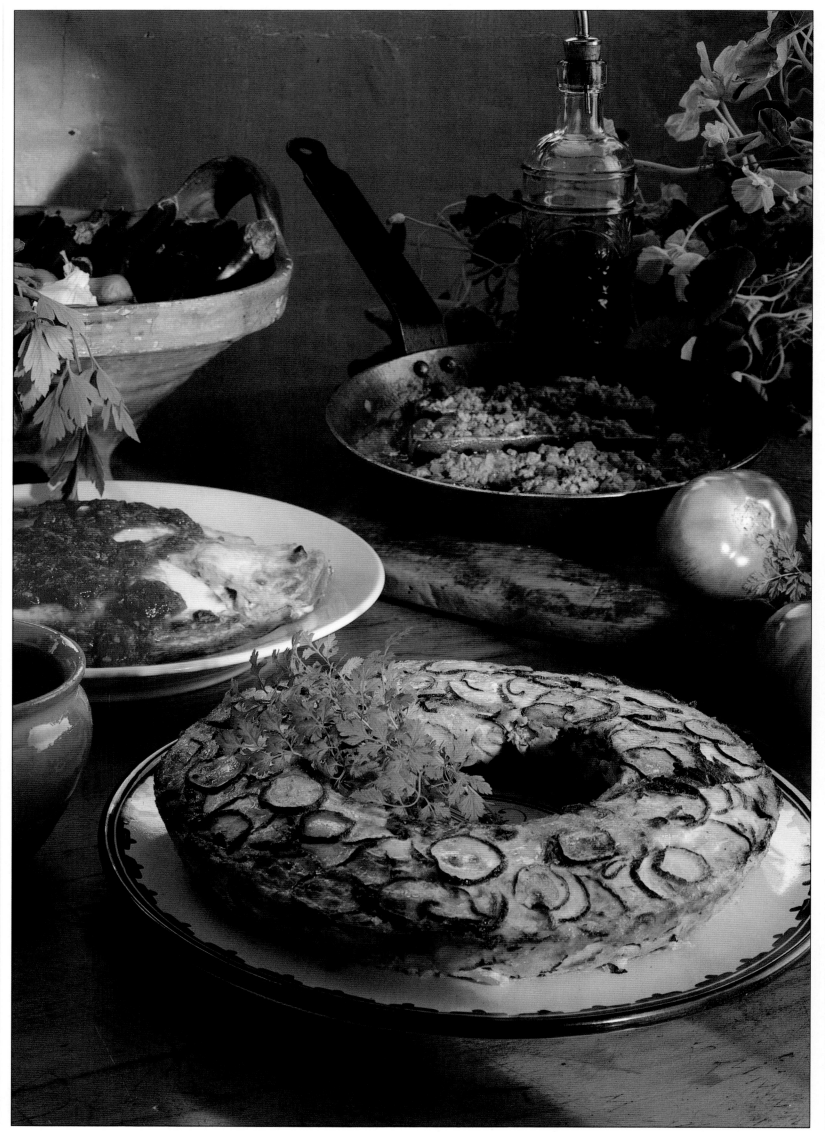

Front to rear: Zucchini Omelet, Omelet Cake and Stuffed Zucchini

TORTINO DI ZUCCHINE
Zucchini Omelet

This omelet may also be served with meat sauce, sautéed sweet-breads or a simple tomato sauce.

3 tablespoons extra virgin olive oil
2 lb (900 g) small zucchini (courgettes), trimmed and thinly
    sliced
4 eggs
3 tablespoons milk
pinch of freshly grated nutmeg
salt and freshly ground pepper
¼ cup (1 oz/30 g) all-purpose (plain) flour
½ cup (2 oz/60 g) freshly grated Parmesan cheese
12 fresh basil leaves, torn into pieces
⅔ cup (3 oz/90 g) fine dry bread crumbs

❧ Preheat an oven to 350°F (180°C).
❧ In a skillet over moderate heat, warm 2 tablespoons of the olive oil. Add the zucchini and fry, stirring frequently, until all the liquid released by the zucchini evaporates and the zucchini are just golden, about 10 minutes.
❧ In a bowl, whisk together the eggs and milk until well blended. Add the nutmeg and season to taste with salt and pepper. Whisking constantly, gradually add the flour through a sieve to prevent lumps from forming. Add the zucchini and Parmesan and mix well. Stir in the basil.
❧ Oil an 8-in (20-cm) ring mold with the remaining 1 tablespoon olive oil. Coat the mold with the bread crumbs. Pour in the egg mixture.
❧ Bake until slightly golden, about 1 hour. Remove the mold from the oven. Run a thin, sharp knife blade around the edge of the mold to loosen it, then invert onto a warm serving dish. Serve hot.
SERVES 6

TORTINO DI FRITTATE
Omelet Cake

This very popular dish makes an excellent lunch when served with sautéed vegetables or a salad. The omelet may be flavored with ham, cheese or mushrooms instead of pancetta.

5 oz (150 g) *pancetta,* finely chopped
3 eggs
¾ cup (3 oz/90 g) all-purpose (plain) flour
2 cups (16 fl oz/480 ml) milk
4 tablespoons (2 fl oz/60 ml) extra virgin olive oil
2 garlic cloves, chopped
1¼ lb (600 g) plum (egg) tomatoes, peeled and chopped
2 tablespoons unsalted butter
½ cup (2 oz/60 g) freshly grated Parmesan cheese
salt and freshly ground black pepper

❧ In a nonstick skillet over low heat, gently fry the *pancetta* until crisp. With a slotted spoon, remove to absorbent paper towels to drain and cool completely.
❧ In a bowl, whisk the eggs until well blended. Whisking constantly, gradually add ½ cup (2 oz/60 g) of the flour and ⅔ cup (5 fl oz/150 ml) of the milk. Stir in 2 tablespoons of the olive oil and the *pancetta.* Let the batter stand for about 30 minutes.
❧ In a medium saucepan over moderate heat, warm 1 tablespoon of the olive oil. Add the garlic and fry gently, stirring

frequently until just golden, about 3 minutes. Add the tomatoes and simmer over low heat until most of the liquid evaporates and the sauce is thick, about 50 minutes. Keep the sauce warm.
❧ Meanwhile, in a heavy-bottomed saucepan over low heat, melt the butter. Add the remaining ¼ cup (1 oz/30 g) flour and cook, stirring constantly, for 2 minutes. Stirring constantly, gradually add the remaining 1⅓ cups (11 oz/330 ml) milk. Cook, continuing to stir, until the sauce thickens, about 5 minutes. When the sauce is ready, remove it from the heat and stir in the Parmesan. Season to taste with salt and pepper.
❧ Lightly oil a 7-in (18-cm) nonstick skillet with a little of the remaining 1 tablespoon olive oil and warm over low heat. Add just enough batter to the skillet to make a very thin omelet, tilting the pan to spread it evenly. Cook until the batter sets, about 2 minutes. Turn the omelet over and cook the other side, about 30 seconds. Slide the omelet from the pan and set aside on a flat surface.
❧ Continue making omelets until you have used all the batter, adding oil to the pan as needed. You should have about 12 omelets in all.
❧ Preheat an oven to 325°F (160°C).
❧ In the center of an ovenproof serving dish, place an omelet. Cover it with a little of the white sauce. Place an omelet on top and spoon a little more white sauce on it. Repeat until all of the omelets and white sauce have been used, ending with some sauce.
❧ Bake until heated through and bubbly, about 20 minutes.
❧ Remove from the oven and spoon the hot tomato sauce over the top. Serve immediately.
SERVES 6

ZUCCHINE RIPIENE
Stuffed Zucchini

Stuffed zucchini are often served as a main course for family suppers. Leftover cooked meats, ham or various cheeses may be used for the stuffing.

4 tablespoons (2 fl oz/60 ml) extra virgin olive oil
1 tablespoon chopped yellow onion
1¼ lb (600 g) plum (egg) tomatoes, peeled and chopped
salt and freshly ground black pepper
6 zucchini (courgettes)
5 oz (150 g) ground (minced) veal
1 tablespoon chopped fresh flat-leaf (Italian) parsley

❧ In a large skillet over low heat, warm 2 tablespoons of the olive oil. Add the onion and fry gently until translucent, about 5 minutes. Add the tomatoes, season to taste with salt and pepper and cook until the sauce has just begun to thicken but is still runny, about 30 minutes.
❧ Trim both ends off the zucchini. Using an apple corer, scoop out the centers, leaving a shell about ¼ in (6 mm) thick. Finely chop the zucchini centers and place in a bowl. Add the meat and mix well. Season to taste with salt and pepper.
❧ In a skillet over moderate heat, warm the remaining 2 tablespoons olive oil. Add the meat-zucchini mixture and cook, stirring, for about 5 minutes. Remove from the heat.
❧ Stuff the hollowed zucchini with the meat mixture. Arrange the stuffed zucchini in the skillet with the tomato sauce. Cook until the sauce is thick and the zucchini is tender, about 20 minutes.
❧ Arrange the zucchini and sauce on a warm platter. Sprinkle with the parsley and serve.
SERVES 6

SFORMATINI DI ZUCCHINE
Zucchini Timbales

At the Mugolone Ristorante in Siena, the chef sometimes makes these timbales with peas or chopped green beans. This recipe is also excellent cooked in a ring mold.

4 tablespoons (2 fl oz/60 ml) extra virgin olive oil
1¼ lb (600 g) zucchini (courgettes), trimmed and thinly
   sliced
¼ cup (1 oz/30 g) all-purpose (plain) flour
1¼ cups (10 fl oz/300 ml) milk, at room temperature
½ cup (2 oz/60 g) freshly grated Parmesan cheese
3 eggs
salt and freshly ground black pepper
2 tablespoons unsalted butter
¾ cup (3 oz/90 g) fine dry bread crumbs

♣ Preheat an oven to 350°F (180°C).
♣ In a skillet over moderate heat, warm 2 tablespoons of the olive oil. Add the zucchini and fry gently, stirring frequently, until the zucchini are just golden, about 10 minutes. Remove from the heat and let cool.
♣ In a medium saucepan over moderate heat, warm the remaining 2 tablespoons olive oil. Add the flour and cook, stirring continuously, until the flour has absorbed all of the oil, about 2 minutes. Continuing to stir, gradually add the milk and cook until a smooth, thick sauce forms, about 5 minutes. Remove from the heat and let cool to room temperature.
♣ Add the zucchini and Parmesan to the sauce. Then add the eggs, one at a time, mixing well after each addition. Season to taste with salt and pepper.
♣ Butter 6 ramekins each about 4 in (10 cm) in diameter and then coat them evenly with the bread crumbs. Divide the egg mixture evenly among the prepared ramekins.
♣ Place the ramekins in a baking dish and pour water into the dish to a depth of 1 in (2.5 cm). Bake in the center of the oven until the custard sets and the tops are golden, about 30 minutes.
♣ Remove the ramekins from the oven. Run a thin, sharp knife blade around the edge of each ramekin and then invert the timbales onto individual serving plates. Serve immediately.

SERVES 6

CANESTRINI DI PATATE
Deep-Fried Potato Baskets

Although usually served on their own, these potato baskets are a perfect accompaniment to roast pork or chicken at a dinner party.

1 oz (30 g) dried *porcini* mushrooms
1 tablespoon extra virgin olive oil
4 oz (120 g) chicken livers
salt and freshly ground black pepper
4 oz (120 g) cooked ham
2½ lb (1.2 kg) boiling potatoes
2 eggs, separated
2 tablespoons all-purpose (plain) flour
1 cup (4 oz/120 g) fine dry bread crumbs
5 cups (40 fl oz/1.2 l) extra virgin olive oil for frying

♣ In a small bowl, soak the mushrooms in warm water to cover for 30 minutes. Drain and squeeze out any excess moisture.

♣ In a medium skillet over moderate heat, warm the olive oil. Add the mushrooms and chicken livers and sauté, stirring occasionally, for 5 minutes. Season to taste with salt and pepper. Remove from the heat and transfer the mushrooms and livers to a cutting surface.
♣ Add the ham to the mushrooms and livers and chop the ingredients together. Return the mixture to the skillet and keep warm without cooking.
♣ Meanwhile, in a saucepan, boil the potatoes in salted water to cover until tender, about 30 minutes. Drain the potatoes

Deep-Fried Potato Baskets (left) and ingredients for Zucchini Timbales (right)

and peel them. Place in a bowl and mash while still hot. Set aside to cool completely.

🍃 When the potatoes are at room temperature, add the egg yolks and mix well. Sprinkle your hands with the flour and roll the potato mixture into 2-in (5-cm) balls. You should have 18 balls in all. Flatten the balls slightly and, with a fingertip, form a hollow in the middle. In a small bowl, beat the egg whites until slightly thick but not stiff. Put the bread crumbs in a small, shallow bowl. Coat the balls with the egg whites and then roll them in the bread crumbs to coat evenly.

Set aside on a plate.

🍃 In a deep skillet, heat the olive oil to 350°F (180°C). Slip the potato baskets, a few at a time, into the hot oil and fry until just golden, about 5 minutes. With a slotted spoon, remove to absorbent paper towels to drain. Continue frying all the baskets in the same manner.

🍃 Fill the hollows of the hot potato baskets with the ham-liver mixture. Serve immediately.

SERVES 6

119

Top to bottom: Potato Croquettes, Stuffed Celery and Frittata with Pancetta

CROCCHETTE DI PATATE

Potato Croquettes

Deep-fried vegetables, a Tuscan specialty, are particularly good in Lucchesia, where excellent extra virgin olive oil is produced. Frying oil should be used only once, because when the oil is reheated it releases toxins.

2¼ lb (1.2 kg) boiling potatoes
½ cup (2 oz/60 g) freshly grated Parmesan cheese
3 eggs, separated
pinch of freshly grated nutmeg
2 tablespoons chopped fresh flat-leaf (Italian) parsley
salt and fresh ground black pepper
1 cup (4 oz/120 g) all-purpose (plain) flour
1¾ cups (7 oz/210 g) fine dry bread crumbs
4 cups (32 fl oz/1 l) extra virgin olive oil for frying

🍃 In a saucepan, boil the potatoes in their skins in salted water to cover until tender, about 30 minutes. Drain the potatoes and peel them. Place in a bowl and mash while still hot. Let cool completely.

🍃 When the potatoes are at room temperature, add the Parmesan, egg yolks, nutmeg and parsley. Season to taste with salt and pepper and mix thoroughly.

🍃 Sprinkle your hands with a little of the flour and form the potato mixture into ovals about 2 in (5 cm) long. You should have about 30 ovals in all.

🍃 Put the remaining flour in a small, shallow bowl. Put the bread crumbs in a separate bowl. In another small bowl, lightly beat the egg whites until blended. Roll the ovals in the flour, dip them in the egg white and then roll them in the bread crumbs.

🍃 In a deep skillet, heat the olive oil to 350°F (180°C). Slip the ovals, a few at a time, into the hot oil and fry until golden, about 5 minutes. With a slotted spoon, remove to absorbent paper towels to drain. Continue frying the remaining ovals in the same manner.

🍃 Serve piping hot.

SERVES 6

SEDANI RIPIENI

Stuffed Celery

Every Tuscan cook seems to have his or her own version of this old favorite. Served with meat sauce, this is a good supper dish. The celery is sometimes fried before going into the sauce. Green celery can be used in place of the white, but it is slightly bitter.

¼ cup (2 fl oz/60 ml) extra virgin olive oil
1 small yellow onion, chopped
1 garlic clove, chopped

1¼ lb (600 g) plum (egg) tomatoes, peeled and chopped
salt and freshly ground black pepper
1 oz (30 g) dried *porcini* mushrooms
4 oz (120 g) crustless coarse country bread
1 cup (8 fl oz/240 ml) milk
2 large heads white celery
4 oz (120 g) sweet Italian sausages
½ cup (2 oz/60 g) freshly grated Parmesan cheese
1 egg

🍂 In a medium saucepan, warm the olive oil over low heat. Add the onion and garlic and fry gently for 2 minutes. Add the tomatoes and season to taste with salt and pepper. Cook over low heat until the liquid evaporates, about 50 minutes.

🍂 Meanwhile, in a small bowl, soak the mushrooms in warm water to cover for 30 minutes. In a separate bowl, soak the bread in the milk for about 10 minutes.

🍂 Break off the celery stalks. With a small knife, remove the strings and cut off and discard the leaves.

🍂 In a large saucepan, blanch the celery in boiling salted water to cover for 1 minute. Drain the celery and cut into pieces about 2 in (5 cm) long. Press the hollow side of each piece lightly to open it up.

🍂 Drain the mushrooms and squeeze out any excess liquid. Chop them finely and place in a mixing bowl. Drain the bread and squeeze out the milk.

🍂 Add the bread to the bowl. Skin the sausages and crumble the meat into the bowl as well.

🍂 Add the Parmesan and egg to the bowl and mix well. Fill half of the pieces of celery with this mixture. Cover with the remaining halves, hollow side down, and press firmly together.

🍂 Add the stuffed celery to the tomato sauce. Cook over low heat until the filling is cooked and the celery is tender and has absorbed the flavor of the sauce, about 10 minutes. Serve immediately.

SERVES 6

CARDI TRIPPATI

Fried Cardoon in Tomato Sauce

Tuscans describe these cardoons as being trippati, *or "triped," because they are served in the same sauce used for tripe in Florence.*

juice of 1 lemon
1 large cardoon, about 3 lb (1.3 kg)
2 eggs
salt
1 tablespoon extra virgin olive oil, plus 5 cups (40 fl oz/1.2 l) for frying
2 oz (60 g) *pancetta*
1 tablespoon chopped yellow onion
2 garlic cloves, chopped
1¼ lb (600 g) plum (egg) tomatoes, peeled and chopped
⅔ cup (3 oz/90 g) all-purpose (plain) flour
¾ cup (3 oz/90 g) freshly grated Parmesan cheese

🍂 Fill a large bowl with water and add the lemon juice. Remove and discard the base from the cardoon and discard any tough stalks. Trim and discard the leaves and spurs from the tender stalks and then scrape the stalks with a small knife to remove all strings and fibers. Cut each stalk crosswise into pieces 2 in (5 cm) long and immediately drop them into the water so that they do not discolor. Drain and pat dry with absorbent paper towels.

🍂 In a deep bowl, whisk the eggs with a little salt. Add the cardoon to the bowl and set aside.

🍂 In a medium saucepan over moderate heat, warm the 1 tablespoon olive oil and the *pancetta*. Add the onion and garlic

and fry gently until the onion is translucent, about 5 minutes. Add the tomatoes and simmer until the liquid evaporates and the sauce thickens, about 50 minutes.

🍂 Meanwhile, in a deep, heavy skillet, heat the olive oil for frying to 350°F (180°C). Put the flour in a small shallow bowl. Remove the cardoon pieces from the egg and roll them in the flour. Slip the pieces a few at a time into the hot oil and fry until golden, about 5 minutes. Remove with a slotted spoon to absorbent paper towels to drain. Continue cooking the remaining cardoon pieces in the same manner.

🍂 When all of the cardoon pieces have been fried, transfer them to the tomato sauce. Cook gently over low heat to allow the cardoon pieces to absorb the flavor of the sauce, about 10 minutes.

🍂 Arrange the cardoon pieces and sauce on a warm serving dish, sprinkle with the Parmesan and serve.

SERVES 6

FRITTATA CON GLI ZOCCOLI

Frittata with Pancetta

In Tuscany bits of crisp pancetta *are called* zoccoli, *or "clogs." Here* pancetta *is saltier and sharper than that of other regions, and it is often eaten raw on bread.*

8 eggs
salt and freshly ground black pepper
2 tablespoons extra virgin olive oil
4 oz (120 g) thick *pancetta* slices, diced

🍂 In a medium bowl, whisk the eggs until well blended. Season to taste with salt and pepper.

🍂 In a skillet over moderate heat, warm the olive oil. Add the *pancetta* and fry until crisp and golden, about 5 minutes. With a slotted spoon, remove to absorbent paper towels to drain and cool. Reserve the drippings in the skillet.

🍂 Stir the cooled *pancetta* bits into the beaten egg.

🍂 Pour 1 tablespoon of the *pancetta* drippings into an 8-in (20-cm) nonstick skillet and warm over moderate heat. Pour in the egg mixture and cook, occasionally moving the egg with a wooden spoon, until the egg sets and only the surface is runny, about 5 minutes. Turn the frittata out onto a plate, browned side up. Slide the frittata back into the skillet and cook the other side for 1 minute. Turn the frittata out onto a serving plate. Serve hot.

SERVES 6

Fried Cardoon in Tomato Sauce

Livorno

UOVA STRASCICATE AL POMODORO E CIPOLLE

Scrambled Eggs with Onion and Tomato

A very simple family dish that can be made with fresh tomatoes or the excellent canned tomatoes from Donoratico, a coastal village famous for the quality of its plum tomatoes. The flavor of the olive oil gives scrambled eggs a real lift.

3 tablespoons extra virgin olive oil
2 large yellow onions, chopped

1¼ lb (600 g) plum (egg) tomatoes, peeled and chopped
6 eggs
salt and freshly ground black pepper

❧ In a nonstick skillet over moderate heat, warm the olive oil. Add the onion and fry gently until it starts to turn golden, about 6 minutes. Add the tomatoes and cook over low heat until the liquid evaporates, about 40 minutes.

❧ Meanwhile, in a bowl, whisk the eggs until well blended. Season with a little salt and pepper. Add the eggs to the tomato and cook over moderate heat, stirring constantly and scraping the bottom of the skillet with a wooden fork. Remove from the heat as soon as the eggs begin to set but are still very moist, about 3 minutes.

❧ Turn the eggs out onto a serving plate. Serve immediately.

SERVES 6

Scrambled Eggs with Onion and Tomato

Game Terrine

PASTICCIO DI CACCIA

Game Terrine

This terrine is prepared with whatever the hunter has bagged, from pheasant to hare. Guinea fowl or quail, which have a lot of flavor and are now raised commercially, may be substituted for the game.

1 pheasant, about 3 lb (1.3 kg), including the liver
¼ cup (2 fl oz/60 ml) extra virgin olive oil
6 oz (180 g) mild Italian sausages, skinned and crumbled
1 yellow onion, chopped
2 garlic cloves, chopped
3 fresh bay leaves
1 tablespoon juniper berries
½ cup (4 fl oz/120 ml) Vin Santo or white dessert wine
salt and freshly ground black pepper
2 egg yolks
6 tablespoons (3 oz/90 g) unsalted butter, at room temperature, cut into small pieces, plus extra for buttering pan

❧ Cut the pheasant into large pieces.

❧ In a heavy pot over moderate heat, warm the olive oil. Add the pheasant, liver, sausage, onion, garlic, bay leaves and juniper berries and cook over moderate heat, stirring occasionally, until the pheasant is golden, about 10 minutes.

❧ Add the wine and stir well, scraping the pot bottom to dislodge any browned bits. Season to taste with salt and pepper. Cover and cook over low heat for about 1 hour. Add a little water if necessary to keep the contents moist.

❧ Remove the pot from the heat and let cool. Bone the pheasant and put the meat in a food processor fitted with a metal blade. Remove and discard the bay leaves. Add the remaining contents of the pot to the food processor. Add the egg yolks and butter and process just long enough to form a well-blended mixture that is not too loose.

❧ Line a 3-by-8-in (8-by-20-cm) bread pan with parchment (greaseproof) paper, then butter the paper well. Pour the pheasant mixture into the pan and smooth the top. Cover and refrigerate for about 2 hours before serving.

❧ Invert onto a serving dish, lift off the pan and peel off the paper. Serve at room temperature.

SERVES 6

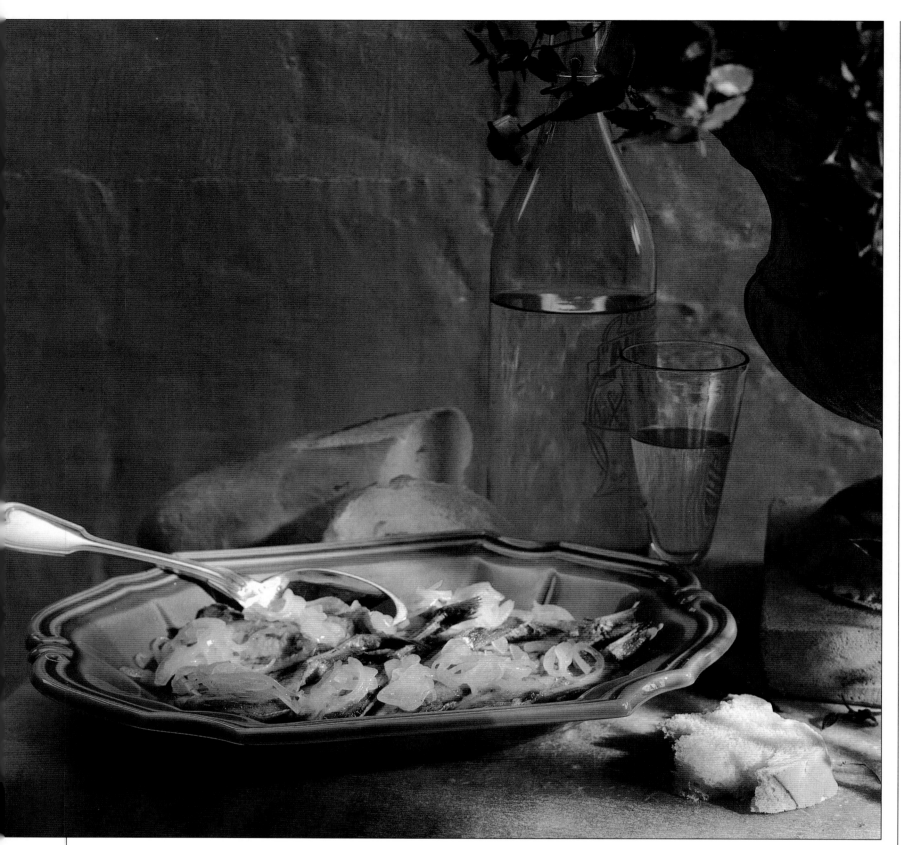

Anchovies in Vinegar

Livorno

ALICI IN CARPIONE

Anchovies in Vinegar

Fresh anchovies are always available in the fish markets near Livorno. Every morning fishing boats set out and return in the evening with their catch.

1¼ lb (600 g) fresh anchovies
1 cup (4 oz/120 g) all-purpose (plain) flour
5 cups (40 fl oz/1.2 l) extra virgin olive oil for frying
salt
2 large yellow onions, sliced
⅞ cup (7 fl oz/210 ml) white wine vinegar
pinch of ground dried chili

🔸 Remove and discard the heads from the anchovies. Slit the bodies lengthwise along the belly and remove and discard the bones. Rinse the anchovies and pat dry on absorbent paper towels. Dredge the anchovies in the flour.

🔸 Reserve 3 tablespoons of the olive oil and pour the remainder into a deep, heavy skillet. Heat the oil in the skillet to 350°F (180°C). A few at a time, add the anchovies and fry until they begin to turn golden, about 3 minutes. With a slotted spoon, remove to absorbent paper towels to drain. Season with salt. Continue frying the remaining anchovies in the same manner.

🔸 In a large skillet over low heat, warm the 3 tablespoons olive oil. Add the onions, season to taste with salt and fry gently until translucent, about 5 minutes. Add the vinegar and continue cooking until it evaporates, about 5 minutes. Remove from the heat.

🦋 Arrange the anchovies on a serving plate. Sprinkle them with the chili and then cover them with the onion.

🦋 Let stand at room temperature for about 2 hours before serving.

SERVES 6

FOGLIE DI CAVOLO RIPIENE DI SALSICCIA

Stuffed Cabbage Leaves

In Arezzo, cooks often use wild boar sausages, which are more strongly flavored than pork sausages. This recipe is very successful when leftover roast or stewed meat is used for the stuffing.

4 oz (120 g) crustless coarse country bread
1 cup (8 fl oz/240 ml) milk
10 oz (300 g) plum (egg) tomatoes, peeled
18 large Savoy cabbage leaves
10 oz (300 g) sweet Italian sausages, skinned and crumbled
½ cup (2 oz/60 g) freshly grated Parmesan cheese
1 egg
3 tablespoons extra virgin olive oil
salt

🦋 In a bowl, soak the bread in the milk for 10 minutes. Drain the bread and squeeze out any excess moisture; set aside.

🦋 Put the tomatoes through a food mill; set aside.

🦋 Bring a large saucepan filled with salted water to a boil. Add the cabbage leaves, a few at a time, and blanch for 30 seconds. Remove the leaves with a slotted spoon, drain well and place them side by side on a board. Continue blanching the remaining leaves in the same manner.

🦋 In a mixing bowl, combine the sausage, Parmesan, egg and bread. Blend well.

🦋 Divide the sausage mixture evenly among the cabbage leaves, placing a mound of it about one third of the way in from the stalk end of the leaf. First fold in the sides of each leaf, then roll them up to enclose the mixture completely.

🦋 Secure the rolls loosely with kitchen string and place them side by side in a heavy pot. Sprinkle the olive oil over the rolls and cook over moderate heat for 5 minutes, carefully turning the rolls occasionally.

🦋 Pour the sieved tomatoes over the rolls and cook for 15 minutes. Season to taste with salt.

🦋 Arrange the rolls with the tomato sauce on a warm platter and serve hot.

SERVES 6

FRITTELLE DI PESCE

Fish Rissoles

These rissoles may be made with any boiled or baked fish. If you have a mix of leftovers, the rissoles will be even more interesting. The fish should be chopped very finely by hand; a food processor makes it too smooth.

1 large boiling potato
1 lb (450 g) any variety of white fish, cooked and boned
2 tablespoons chopped fresh flat-leaf (Italian) parsley
1 garlic clove, chopped
2 egg yolks, plus 2 whole eggs
salt
1 cup (4 oz/120 g) all-purpose (plain) flour
5 cups (40 fl oz/1.2 l) extra virgin olive oil for frying
lemon wedges

🦋 In a small saucepan, boil the potato in its skin in salted water to cover until tender, about 30 minutes. Drain and peel. Place in a mixing bowl and mash while still hot. Set aside to cool completely.

🦋 Chop the fish finely and add to the bowl with the potato. Add the parsley, garlic and egg yolks. Season to taste with salt and mix well.

🦋 In a small bowl, beat the whole eggs until well blended. Pour the flour into a separate small bowl. Roll the fish mixture into balls about the size of an egg. Flatten the balls slightly. Dredge the balls in the flour and then dip them in the beaten egg.

🦋 In a deep skillet, heat the oil to 350°F (180°C). A few at a time, slip the rissoles into the hot oil and fry until golden, about 5 minutes. With a slotted spoon, remove to absorbent paper towels to drain. Continue frying the remaining rissoles in the same manner.

🦋 Arrange on a warm platter. Serve hot with lemon wedges.

SERVES 6

Stuffed Cabbage Leaves (top) and Fish Rissoles (bottom)

AREZZO

AREZZO

"V*a, mia canzone, ad Arezzo in Toscana,*" Guittone d'Arezzo sang in the thirteenth century. "Go, my song, to Arezzo in Tuscany." One of the greatest lyric poets of his time, he was the first sonneteer and he described his birthplace as "sweet Aretine land . . . of every delight."

Arezzo, known as Aretium to the Etruscans when it was their economic capital, is still a pleasant land. Its charms, however, are revealed little by little. This is upland Tuscany, the severest and the coldest area of the region. Consequently, its cuisine is often said to be less refined and inventive than in the rest of Tuscany, but that is a mistake! Aretine cooking, with its ancient flavors and mountain simplicity, is well worth discovering.

Others say that Arezzo is more like a northern city than a Tuscan one, that it is hard and never lets itself go. But this is quite fallacious too. Arezzo could be described as reserved, but when it does relax it produces the very best that Tuscany has to offer.

Over the centuries many great men of letters have come from here: Maecenas, the friend and patron of Horace and Virgil; Petrarch, who rivals Dante as the greatest Italian poet; Guido d'Arezzo, the father of the modern system of musical notation; Titian's friend, Pietro Aretino, whose satirical pen was highly feared during the Renaissance; and Giorgio Vasari, whose *Lives* has for centuries been indispensable to the study of the history of Italian art. Some of Italy's foremost painters were also

Left: The medieval hill town of Cortona is known for its steep, narrow streets. Built atop ancient Etruscan foundations, the town is one of Italy's oldest. Previous pages: An evening vignette in the village of Poppi, stronghold of the powerful Guidi family, who ruled this region until defeated by Florence in 1440.

Piazza San Francesco lies at the heart of Arezzo, a bustling city in the midst of a rich agricultural region defined by the Val di Chiana and Valdarno.

born here: Piero della Francesca, Luca Signorelli, Masaccio, Paolo Uccello and, above all, Michelangelo, who was born in Michelangelo Caprese, just a few miles from Arezzo. Michelangelo told Vasari that if there was anything good in his talent, it was most certainly due to the fine air in Arezzo.

It is also a land of mysticism. Many great Italian monasteries stand majestic on the Casentino mountains: the Abbey of Vallombrosa, the Hermitage of Camaldoli, and La Verna, where St. Francis received the stigmata in the autumn of 1224.

Arezzo and its surroundings can arouse deep emotions. This may even happen when one takes up a knife and fork in an extraordinary restaurant like Il Vicolo del Convento in Castelfranco di Sopra. The tastes and aromas can somehow remind one that this land belonged to Etruscans and Romans, to poets and writers, to painters and great noble families.

One such family were the Tarlati, whose name was given to a very famous Aretine recipe, *zuppa del Vescovo Tarlati,* or Bishop Tarlati's soup. It is said that the bishop, who was also Signore d'Arezzo in 1312, took this chicken-and-egg soup from Arezzo to Avignon when he had an audience with Pope John XXII, and that it was appropriated by the French, who named it *soupe à la reine.* But there is the usual dispute about the provenance of this recipe, some claiming that in fact the bishop brought it back with him from France.

Chicken soup is very popular in this area because the indigenous black hens from the Valdarno make an excellent stock. Furthermore, local legend maintains that chicken stock gives strength and increases virility, which is probably why a soup called *ginestrata,* "yellow broom," is still to be found. Actually there is no broom in the soup,

but the color is the same as the flower. A glance at the ingredients lends support to the popular belief. It is made with strong chicken stock, an egg per person, Vin Santo, cinnamon, saffron, nutmeg, lemon and a little sugar, all beaten together. It is perhaps not surprising that this soup was traditionally served to couples when they returned from their honeymoon.

In addition to such benefits, good chicken stock in Arezzo is also the perfect foil for the delicious local *cappelletti.* These stuffed pasta "hats" originated in Emilia, but the ones made in Arezzo provide serious competition.

Brodo del parto, "childbirth soup," probably originated in these parts, too. The Madonna del Parto, one of Piero della Francesca's most famous frescoes, is on the wall of a little chapel in the cemetery at Monterchi. Pregnant women visit this chapel, light a candle before the magnificent Madonna and pray for an easy delivery. *Brodo del parto* is a meat stock seasoned with herbs to which a little strong wine is added as a tonic.

There are many other first courses in Arezzo beyond soups, the most famous being *gnocchi del Casentino.* The Guidi family, who were the lords of Poppi, are said to have eaten large quantities of them in their castle above the Arno. Gnocchi are little dumplings that are one of the earliest forms of pasta. When Boccaccio described "maccheroni rolled down a mountain of grated cheese" in the *Decameron,* he was probably referring to gnocchi, which in the Casentino are made of ricotta and spinach.

Another very early recipe that is said to be Etruscan is *bringoli,* thick spaghetti from Anghiari, a place not far from Arezzo noted for a great battle fought there between the armies of Florence and the Duke of Milan in 1440. Drawings made by Leonardo da Vinci for a fresco in Florence's Palazzo Vecchio depicting this famous battle can still be seen here. *Acquacotta,* a soup made all over Tuscany, is also considered Etruscan. It is particularly well liked in the Casentino, where, at one time, it was a favorite with the many coopers living there.

In this district, gravy from Aretine ducks is used to dress *pappardelle,* wide egg pasta. Ducks had a significant role in Etruscan culture, and frescoes portraying them were found in tombs in Tarquinia. They served as a symbol of marital fidelity, and a special duck was raised to celebrate a wedding.

Pork liver is treated in a unique way in Arezzo. In the rest of Tuscany it is seasoned with bay leaves and sage, but here only fennel seed is used. Traditionally, cooked pork liver is preserved in lard and stored in either glass jars or earthenware pots.

Many other Aretine recipes include fennel seed as well. After being crushed in a mortar with a pestle, it is sprinkled abundantly over duck and chicken, a custom dating from the thirteenth century. Fennel was also used for medicinal purposes. The leaves cooked with chickpeas were considered an efficient diuretic and effective in the treatment of snake and scorpion bites.

The most celebrated main course in Arezzo is undoubtedly *scottiglia,* which is very much like the Sienese *buglione.* Both dishes are composed of mixed meats, but while *buglione* has tomato in it and the meat is cooked to a mush, the various meats in *scottiglia* are still distinguishable. A good *scottiglia* should include pieces of beef, pork, chicken, guineafowl, duck, rabbit and lamb.

As usual, there are two tales describing the origin of this very ancient stew. Some say that it goes back to the Middle Ages, when the landowners left the remains of their banquets—chicken wings and necks, pork trotters and lamb offal—for the peasants. Others maintain that it comes from the age-old Tuscan custom of gathering to

A farmhouse enjoys views of the fertile Casentino valley. These fields of the upper Arno were first cultivated by the Etruscans, who exported crops and wine to Greece.

The piazzas of Arezzo come alive during the evening passegiata. *Among the famous Aretines who once walked these streets are the poet Petrarch and the artist-historian Giorgio Vasari.*

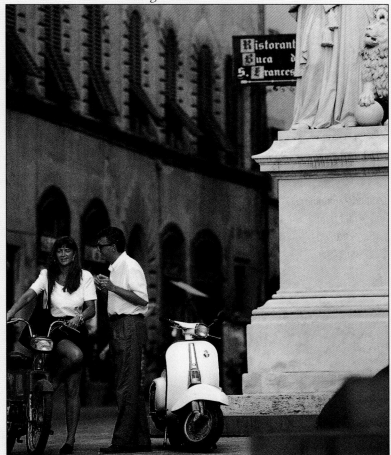

chat in front of the farmhouse fire during the long winter evenings. Everyone apparently arrived bearing his own piece of meat.

Pietro Aretino, the Renaissance writer, praised this Tuscan country custom: "Sitting at table requires bird song, the murmur of running water, a breath of breeze and the sweet smell of fresh grass; but four dry logs are all you need to sit and chat for four or five hours with chestnuts on the fire and a bottle of wine between your knees. We love winter, the springtime for lively minds." A man who certainly did not mince his words, Aretino was also convinced that the best oil and olives came from his part of the world. In writing to Madonna Bartolina he said, "Spanish olives are so huge they are conceited . . . the olives from Puglia are so small they should be called bread crumbs. So it is your side [Tuscany] that may boast the best." Perhaps because Arezzo has fewer olives than other parts of Tuscany, the appreciation of olive oil has always been a cult. But there have been olive trees in the area for centuries. In Roman times, Minerva, the goddess of wisdom, was worshipped in Arezzo, and olive oil has always been associated with her rites.

The "sweet Aretine land" also offers several local desserts. *Berlingozzo* is a fifteenth-century Easter cake; *baldino* is a chestnut cake; and *gatò aretino* is served at country weddings. Then there is *panina gialla*, also known as *pan co' l'uve*—bread dough to which olive oil, raisins, saffron, cinnamon, cloves and coriander are added with pleasing results.

I SECONDI

Ewes and their lambs graze in the Maremma.

I SECONDI

Main dishes—*i secondi*—were the glory of Tuscan cuisine during the Renaissance. Although many of today's main courses were served at the Florentine court, at that time they were divided into three distinct groups. *Il primo servizio di cucina,* the first service from the kitchen, included roast turkey, chicken and duck, often stuffed and flavored with truffles. *Il secondo servizio di cucina,* the second service, offered boiled meats: choice cuts of beef, capon stuffed with chestnuts, and lamb flavored with spices, served with a variety of sauces. *Il terzo servizio di cucina,* the third service, consisted of braised meats, meat loaves, soup, and fish and shellfish.

It is, above all, in the main courses that Florentine cooking lost its supremacy over French cuisine. Many famous French dishes originated in Tuscany, the outstanding example being the renowned duck *à l'orange,* the very same Tuscan *papero alla melarancia* described by an anonymous author in a fourteenth-century book on Tuscan cooking.

During the Renaissance, however, the Italians dedicated themselves far more to painting and sculpture and left the art of cooking to the French. It is hard to say who was correct, but one thing is certain: Michelangelo, Leonardo da Vinci and Raphael are well-known all over the world, while it is a little more difficult to remember the names of famous French chefs of the same period. But enough of national pride.

The celebrated *bistecca alla fiorentina* should be mentioned at once, although it is so-called only outside Tuscany. Here it is simply called *costata.* Apparently nothing could be more simple than grilling a steak, but a great deal depends on the quality of the meat and the cook's skill. The word *bistecca,* a corruption of the English

Fresh fish is available in the large towns of Tuscany every day. Delivery trucks bring fish to the small hill towns on Thursdays and Fridays.

Previous pages: Lamb with Artichokes (left, page 172) and Fried Pork Chops with Tarragon (right, page 177).

134

The end of summer signals the start of porcini *season, when the most enthusiastic* porcini *lovers take to the woods and begin their search. The coveted mushroom shows up in many* secondi *recipes.*

"beef steak," came into being with the advent of the first British tourists, who were actually noblemen doing the Grand Tour. For centuries before that, these steaks were called *carbonata,* because they were grilled on *carbone,* or wood charcoal. A real *fiorentina* should be hung for several days and should never be thicker or thinner than 1⅛ inches (3 centimeters).

Another typically Tuscan meat dish is *arista di maiale,* or loin of pork. There has been considerable debate over why this roast is called *arista.* No two experts seem to agree. What is certain is that the name comes from the Greek word *aristos,* meaning "the best," and the dish in its simplicity is undoubtedly exquisite.

On Sundays, roast or fried chicken or rabbit is nearly always found on the Tuscan table. Until the 1950s, the peasants lived off the land as they had for centuries, so it is understandable that farmyard animals still play an important role in the Tuscan kitchen.

There are also excellent Tuscan braised meats and stews. Many visitors to Florence have been converted to tripe after tasting it there. Some of these tripe dishes, like *cibreo fiorentino* and *cioncia* from Pescia, originated in the Middle Ages. It is well worth seeking out such specialties in the few restaurants where they are now served after years of neglect. *Cibreo,* for example, was reintroduced by Annie Feolde of the famous Enoteca Pinchiorri in Florence.

As Tuscany is a land of enthusiastic hunters, many main courses are made with venison and game birds. Wild boar and hare, pheasant and woodcock, quail and mallard are excellent reasons for visiting the numerous restaurants and trattorias where they are served during the hunting season.

Tuscany is also blessed with a long coastline. To tell the truth, however, fish is not one of the highlights of the Tuscan kitchen, except for the famous Livornese fish soup called *cacciucco,* and *cee,* baby eels from Pisa. Although there are not many Tuscan recipes for fresh fish, curiously enough there are several original dishes made with salt cod, dried cod and herring. Cooking fish *in zimino,* or with vegetables—usually spinach or Swiss chard—is another regional tradition.

Grosseto

PICCIONI IN TEGAME

Pot-Roasted Pigeons

Starting the pigeons in cold oil with raw vegetables adds to their flavor. They may also be prepared this way but first stuffed with bread, egg, Parmesan, and their sautéed and chopped giblets.

6 oz (180 g) *pancetta,* chopped
2 garlic cloves, chopped
1 small yellow onion, chopped
1 carrot, peeled and chopped
1 celery stalk, trimmed and chopped
1 tablespoon chopped fresh flat-leaf (Italian) parsley
1 tablespoon chopped fresh rosemary
3 tablespoons extra virgin olive oil
3 pigeons (squab), about 1 lb (450 g) each

lower the heat, cover and cook for 1½ hours, gradually adding the rest of the wine as the pan becomes dry.

🐾 Remove the pigeons from the pan and cut each pigeon in half. Spoon the cooking juices over the pigeons and serve immediately.

SERVES 6

Livorno

POLLO FRITTO

Fried Chicken

The Livornese are fond of fried food, which they are masters at cooking. It is always crisp and golden and free of oil. Fried chicken is usually served with a salad only.

1 chicken, about 4 lb (1.8 kg), cut into serving pieces
⅔ cup (3 oz/90 g) all-purpose (plain) flour
2 eggs
salt and freshly ground black pepper
5 cups (40 fl oz/1.2 l) extra virgin olive oil for frying

🐾 Dredge the chicken pieces in the flour, shaking off any excess. In a bowl, whisk the eggs with a little pepper.

🐾 In a deep, heavy skillet, heat the olive oil to 350°F (180°C). A few pieces at a time, dip the floured chicken pieces into the egg and then slip them into the hot oil without crowding the pan. Fry until crisp and golden on all sides, about 7 minutes. With a slotted utensil, remove to absorbent paper towels to drain. Sprinkle with salt and pepper. Continue frying the remaining chicken in the same manner.

🐾 Arrange the chicken on a platter and serve very hot.

SERVES 6

Siena

POLLO AI FUNGHI

Braised Chicken with Mushrooms

Monte Amiata, near Siena, is famous for its autumn mushrooms. If porcini *mushrooms are not available, button mushrooms or* shiitake *may be used instead.*

6 tablespoons (3 fl oz/90 ml) extra virgin olive oil
3 garlic cloves, chopped
1 chicken, about 4 lb (1.8 kg), cut into serving pieces
1 cup (8 fl oz/240 ml) dry white wine
salt and freshly ground black pepper
1¼ lb (600 g) fresh mushrooms
1 tablespoon fresh calamint or thyme leaves

🐾 In a heavy pot over low heat, warm 3 tablespoons of the olive oil. Add the garlic and fry gently until translucent, about 3 minutes. Add the chicken pieces and fry, turning occasionally, until golden, about 10 minutes. Pour in the wine and season to taste with salt and pepper. Cover and cook over very low heat until tender, about 1½ hours, adding a couple of tablespoons of water from time to time to keep the contents very moist.

🐾 Clean the mushrooms by rubbing them with a dampened cloth; do not wash them. Trim the mushroom stems, then slice the mushrooms. In a skillet over moderate heat, warm the remaining 3 tablespoons olive oil. Add the mushrooms and calamint and cook, stirring occasionally, for 3 minutes. Add the mushrooms to the chicken, stir well and cook for 2 minutes.

🐾 Arrange the chicken on a platter and serve immediately.

SERVES 6

Left to right: Pot-Roasted Pigeons, Braised Chicken with Mushrooms, and Fried Chicken

salt and freshly ground black pepper
1½ cups (12 fl oz/360 ml) dry red wine

🐾 In a shallow pan, combine the *pancetta,* garlic, onion, carrot, celery, parsley and rosemary. Drizzle the olive oil over the vegetable mixture and place the pigeons on top. Season to taste with salt and pepper.

🐾 Place the pan over moderate heat and cook, stirring the vegetables and turning the pigeons once, until the pigeons start to turn golden, about 10 minutes. Add half of the wine,

PICCIONI SUL CROSTONE

Stuffed Pigeons

Although very tasty wild pigeons are shot during the hunting season, most of the pigeons eaten in Tuscany are raised by farmers. In fact, nearly all the farmhouses have small, square towerlike constructions that serve as dovecotes.

3 oz (90 g) crustless coarse country bread
1 cup (8 fl oz/240 ml) milk
6 oz (180 g) sweet Italian sausages, skinned
1 egg
1 tablespoon chopped fresh flat-leaf (Italian) parsley
2 tablespoons chopped celery stalk
2 tablespoons chopped carrot
2 tablespoons chopped yellow onion
salt and freshly ground black pepper
3 pigeons (squab), about 1 lb (450 g) each
2 oz (60 g) *pancetta,* thinly sliced
6 tablespoons (3 fl oz/90 ml) extra virgin olive oil

Goose Stuffed with Sausage

1 cup (8 fl oz/240 ml) dry red wine
6 slices coarse country bread

❧ Soak the 3 oz (90 g) bread in the milk for 10 minutes. Squeeze out any excess milk from the bread and place the bread in a mixing bowl.
❧ Preheat an oven to 350°F (180°C). Skin the sausages and crumble them into the bowl with the bread. Add the egg, parsley and 1 tablespoon each of the chopped celery, carrot and onion. Mix well and season to taste with salt and pepper.
❧ Stuff the pigeons with the sausage mixture and truss them securely with kitchen string. Cover the breasts with the *pancetta.*
❧ In a roasting pan over moderate heat, warm 3 tablespoons of the olive oil. Arrange the pigeons in the pan and brown on all sides for about 10 minutes. Place in the oven and roast for 1 hour, turning frequently.
❧ Add the remaining chopped vegetables and the wine to the pan and roast for 30 minutes longer. At the same time, brush the bread slices with the remaining 3 tablespoons olive oil and toast in the oven until golden, about 10 minutes.
❧ Remove the pigeons from the pan and keep warm. Purée the cooking juices and return them to the pan. Reheat gently over low heat. If the sauce is too thin, reduce it over moderate heat.
❧ Cut the pigeons in half. Arrange the toast slices on a platter and place half a pigeon on each slice. Pour the sauce over the pigeons and serve immediately.

SERVES 6

OCIO RIPIENO ALLA SALSICCIA

Goose Stuffed with Sausage

Stuffed goose with chestnuts is traditional Christmas fare in Lucca. As geese are fairly large, this recipe will serve twelve.

1 goose, about 9 lb (4.2 kg)
10 oz (300 g) sweet Italian sausages
1 teaspoon fresh thyme
1 teaspoon juniper berries
3 tablespoons extra virgin olive oil
1 cup (8 fl oz/240 ml) dry red wine
salt and freshly ground black pepper

❧ Preheat an oven to 325°F (160°C).
❧ If the liver and gizzard have come with the goose, remove them from the cavity and reserve them for another use. Skin the sausages and place the meat in a bowl. Add the thyme and juniper berries and mix well. Stuff the goose with this mixture and truss it closed with kitchen string.
❧ In a roasting pan over moderate heat, warm the olive oil. Add the goose and cook, turning the goose so that it browns on all sides, for about 10 minutes.
❧ Place the pan in the oven and roast the goose, basting occasionally, until tender, about 3 hours.
❧ Remove the goose from the pan and keep it warm. Skim most of the fat off the cooking juices. Add the wine to the pan juices and place over moderate heat. Cook, scraping the browned bits from the bottom of the pan, until the sauce reduces a little. Season to taste with salt and pepper.
❧ Scoop the stuffing from the goose cavity and place it on a large platter. Cut the goose into serving pieces and arrange them alongside the stuffing. Serve the sauce in a bowl on the side.

SERVES 12

Top to bottom: Chicken in Red Wine, Braised Chicken with Mushrooms, and Deviled Chicken on the Bone

POLLO AL VINO ROSSO

Chicken in Red Wine

Chicken cooked in red wine with the addition of baby onions is a popular Sunday lunch in Lucca.

1 chicken, about 4 lb (1.8 kg)
3 tablespoons extra virgin olive oil

3 oz (90 g) *pancetta*, chopped
1½ cups (12 fl oz/400 ml) dry red wine
1¼ lb (600 g) pearl onions
salt and freshly ground black pepper

🌲 Preheat an oven to 400°F (200°C). Truss the chicken with kitchen string.
🌲 Pour the olive oil into a roasting pan. Add the *pancetta* and place the chicken in the pan. Roast for 30 minutes, turning a couple of times so that it is golden all over.

🍂 Add the wine and lower the temperature to 350°F (180°C). Cook for another 40 minutes, basting occasionally.

🍂 Add the onions and season to taste with salt and pepper. Cook until the onions are tender, about 20 minutes.

🍂 Transfer the chicken and onions to a serving dish and keep warm. Skim the fat off the cooking juices and then strain the juices into a small saucepan. Reduce the juices over high heat until you have a fairly thick sauce. Pour the sauce over the chicken and serve immediately.

SERVES 6

Livorno

POLLO IN CACCIUCCO

Braised Chicken with Mushrooms

The chicken should be cut into serving pieces and cooked very slowly for this classic Livornese dish. The name comes from the similarity in preparation to the fish dish called cacciucco.

6 slices dried *porcini* mushrooms
3 tablespoons extra virgin olive oil
2 garlic cloves, chopped
1 yellow onion, chopped
1 carrot, peeled and chopped
1 celery stalk, trimmed and chopped
2 tablespoons chopped fresh flat-leaf (Italian) parsley
1 chicken, about 4 lb (1.8 kg), cut into serving pieces
2 lb (900 g) plum (egg) tomatoes, peeled and chopped
salt and freshly ground black pepper

🍂 In a bowl, soak the mushrooms in warm water to cover for 30 minutes. Drain the mushrooms and set aside.

🍂 In a heavy pot over low heat, warm the olive oil. Add the garlic, onion, carrot, celery and parsley and fry gently until the onion is translucent, about 5 minutes. Add the chicken and cook over moderate heat, turning the pieces, until golden on all sides, about 10 minutes.

🍂 Add the mushrooms and tomatoes and season to taste with salt and pepper. Lower the heat, cover and cook for 1½ hours, adding a little water if the sauce becomes too thick.

🍂 Arrange the chicken and sauce on a platter and serve.

SERVES 6

Firenze

POLLO ALLA DIAVOLA

Deviled Chicken on the Bone

This dish, one of the most famous Florentine specialties, is served in nearly all the city's restaurants. It is particularly good at a very old trattoria called Oreste, in Pian dei Giullari, one of the loveliest parts of Florence. Traditionally it is grilled over an open fire, but it can be cooked under an ordinary broiler.

2 chickens, about 2 lb (900 g) each
⅓ cup (3 fl oz/90 ml) extra virgin olive oil
salt and freshly ground black pepper
1 lemon

🍂 Cut the chickens along the length of the breastbone and open them up. With a meat mallet, gently flatten each chicken, being careful not to shatter the bones. In a shallow plate, stir together the olive oil and salt and pepper to taste. Brush the chicken thoroughly with this mixture and marinate for about 2 hours. Remove the chicken from the dish, reserving the olive oil.

🍂 Prepare a fire in a charcoal grill or preheat a broiler (grill).

🍂 Place the chickens on the grill rack over a hot fire or slip it under the broiler. Cook for about 10 minutes on each side, frequently brushing them with the reserved oil and turning them when necessary to prevent burning. The chickens should be crisp and golden when they are done.

🍂 Cut the chickens into serving pieces and arrange them on a platter. Squeeze the lemon over the top and serve.

SERVES 6

Firenze

FEGATINI DI POLLO ALLA SALVIA

Sautéed Chicken Livers with Sage

Sage is not only used in the preparation of several first courses, but also often serves as a seasoning for white meat as well as chicken and pork liver. The fragrant herb is at its best during the summer but, because of Florence's mild climate, it is in leaf throughout the year.

2 lb (900 g) chicken livers
¼ cup (2 fl oz/60 ml) extra virgin olive oil
1 large handful of fresh sage leaves
salt and freshly ground black pepper

🍂 Remove and discard any fat and connective tissue from the chicken livers. Cut the livers in half.

🍂 In a skillet over high heat, warm the olive oil and sage leaves. Add the chicken livers and cook, stirring, for about 3 minutes. Season to taste with salt and pepper.

🍂 Transfer to a serving dish and serve immediately.

SERVES 6

Sautéed Chicken Livers with Sage

Siena

ANATRA ALL'ARANCIA

Roast Duck with Orange Sauce

Duck with orange sauce is said to have originated in Siena and then taken to France by Caterina de' Medici's chefs. It is usually prepared with wild duck during the hunting season, but is also very good when domestic duck is used.

2 oranges
2 ducks, about 3 lb (1.5 kg) each
3 tablespoons extra virgin olive oil
2 tablespoons granulated sugar
1 tablespoon white wine vinegar
1 cup (8 fl oz/240 ml) dry white wine
salt and freshly ground black pepper

🪶 Preheat an oven to 350°F (180°C). Remove the zest from the oranges in long, thin strips; make sure that none of the pith is attached. Squeeze the juice from the oranges. Set the juice and zest aside.
🪶 Truss the ducks with kitchen string. In a heavy ovenproof pot over moderate heat, warm the olive oil. Add the trussed ducks and cook them, turning, until they start to turn golden on all sides, about 10 minutes.
🪶 Transfer the pot to the oven and roast the ducks until tender, about 1½ hours.
🪶 Meanwhile, combine the sugar and vinegar in a small, heavy saucepan and caramelize the sugar by placing it over moderate heat until the sugar dissolves, then stir while the sugar deepens to a rich brown. Be sure that the sugar does not burn. Remove from the heat, add the orange zest, stir well and pour in the orange juice. Set the pan aside.
🪶 Remove the ducks from the pot and cut them into serving pieces. Place the pieces on a platter and keep them warm.
🪶 Skim the fat off the roasting juices and reheat the juices over moderate heat. Add the wine and scrape the browned bits off the bottom of the pan. Add the caramelized orange mixture and cook the juices until they reduce and thicken to a sauce. Season to taste with salt and pepper. Pour the hot sauce over the duck pieces and serve immediately.
SERVES 6

Arezzo

ANATRA IN PORCHETTA

Duck Stuffed with Pork

This duck is called in porchetta *because the herb-sausage stuffing gives it the flavor of the whole pigs cooked for country fairs. Because ducks have so much fat, they should be cooked slowly at low temperature so that the fat dissolves and the meat is tender.*

6 oz (180 g) sweet Italian sausages
1 tablespoon chopped fresh sage
1 tablespoon chopped fresh rosemary
2 garlic cloves, chopped
salt and freshly ground black pepper
1 duck, about 4 lb (1.8 kg)
2 bay leaves
3 oz (90 g) *pancetta,* thinly sliced
¼ cup (2 fl oz/60 ml) extra virgin olive oil

🪶 Preheat an oven to 325°F (160°C).
🪶 Skin the sausages and crumble them into a bowl. Add the sage, rosemary and garlic and mix well. Season to taste with salt and pepper. Stuff the duck with this mixture and truss it securely with kitchen string. Lay the bay leaves on the breast and cover with the *pancetta* slices. Tie in place with kitchen string.
🪶 Pour the olive oil into a roasting pan and place the duck in the pan, breast side up. Roast in the oven for about 3 hours, basting occasionally. When the duck is ready, the skin should be fairly dark and very crisp.
🪶 Remove the duck from the oven, draining off as much of the fat as possible. Discard the *pancetta* and bay leaves. Cut the duck into serving pieces. Arrange on a platter and serve immediately.
SERVES 6

Duck Stuffed with Pork

Roast Duck with Orange Sauce

Lucca

PETTO DI TACCHINO AI FUNGHI

Turkey Breast with Mushrooms

Tuscans consider turkey breast very much a family dish, as it is easy to prepare and inexpensive. Any leftovers are delicious served cold with mayonnaise and salad.

1 tablespoon chopped fresh sage
1 tablespoon chopped fresh rosemary
3 garlic cloves, chopped
salt and freshly ground black pepper
2 lb (900 g) turkey breast, butterflied
4 oz (120 g) *pancetta,* thinly sliced
1 piece caul fat, about 20 in (50 cm) long
3 tablespoons extra virgin olive oil
6 slices dried *porcini* mushrooms
1 cup (8 fl oz/240 ml) dry white wine

🌿 Preheat an oven to 350°F (180°C).
🌿 In a small bowl, combine the sage, rosemary, garlic and salt and pepper to taste. Spread the turkey breast out flat and pound it with a meat mallet until it is about ¼ in (6 mm) thick. Cover it with the *pancetta* and sprinkle it with the sage mixture. Roll up the turkey breast into a cylinder shape, wrap it in the caul fat, and tie tightly with kitchen string.
🌿 In a roasting pan over moderate heat, warm the olive oil. Add the turkey and cook, turning, until golden on all sides, about 10 minutes. Place the pan in the oven and cook for about 1 hour.
🌿 Meanwhile, in a small bowl, soak the mushrooms in warm water to cover for 30 minutes. Drain and squeeze out any excess water. Finely chop the mushrooms and add them and the wine to the pan. Cook for 10 more minutes.
🌿 Remove the turkey breast from the pan. Reheat the pan juices on the stovetop, scraping up any browned bits on the pan bottom, and reduce slightly to form a sauce. Snip the string off the turkey breast. Slice the breast and arrange on a platter. Pour the sauce over the slices and serve immediately.

SERVES 6

Arezzo

POLLO AFFINOCCHIATO

Roast Chicken with Fennel Seed

Despite the fact that excellent beef is raised in the Val di Chiana, the people of Arezzo are very fond of chicken, rabbit and pork, prepared in a variety of ways.

2 garlic cloves, chopped
3 tablespoons fennel seed
salt and freshly ground black pepper
1 chicken, about 4 lb (1.8 kg)
¼ cup (2 fl oz/60 ml) extra virgin olive oil

🌿 Preheat an oven to 350°F (180°C).
🌿 In a small bowl, combine the garlic, fennel seed and salt and pepper to taste. With a fingertip and starting from the breast, gently loosen the skin from the chicken, being careful not to tear the skin. Still using a fingertip, gently spread the garlic mixture evenly between the meat and skin of the chicken breast, back and legs. Truss the chicken.
🌿 Pour the olive oil into a roasting pan and place the chicken in the pan. Roast for 1½ hours, basting frequently with the pan juices. When the chicken is ready, the skin should be fairly dark and crisp. Remove the chicken from the oven. Cut into serving pieces and arrange on a platter. Serve immediately.

SERVES 6

Grosseto

POLLO CON LE OLIVE

Sautéed Chicken with Olives

In Grosseto the local olives are cured in brine with grated orange zest, fennel seed and a little garlic. Chicken cooked with these olives is quite tasty. If they are not available, the same result can b obtained by cooking the chicken with the ingredients in this recipe.

Left to right: Sautéed Chicken with Olives, Turkey Breast with Mushrooms, and Roast Chicken with Fennel Seed

3 tablespoons extra virgin olive oil
2 garlic cloves
1 chicken, about 4 lb (1.8 kg), cut into serving pieces
1 tablespoon fennel seed
chopped zest of 1 orange
salt and freshly ground black pepper
1 cup (8 fl oz/240 ml) dry white wine
6 oz (180 g) black Gaeta olives, pitted

❧ In a heavy pot over moderate heat, warm the olive oil and garlic. Add the chicken pieces and cook over moderate heat, turning the pieces occasionally, until they start to turn golden, about 10 minutes.

❧ Add the fennel seed, orange zest and salt and pepper to taste. Pour in the wine, cover the pot and lower the heat. Cook for 1 hour, occasionally adding a little water if the pan becomes too dry. Add the olives and cook for another 10 minutes.

❧ Arrange the chicken and olives on a platter and serve immediately.

SERVES 6

Left to right: Roast Rabbit, Braised Rabbit and Rabbit Cooked in Wine and Stock

Siena

CONIGLIO ARROSTO

Roast Rabbit

All around the walls outside Siena there are small private vegetable gardens where chickens and rabbits are also raised.

2 fresh rosemary sprigs
2 bunches of fresh sage
1 rabbit, about 4 lb (1.8 kg)
3 garlic cloves, chopped
salt and freshly ground black pepper
3 tablespoons extra virgin olive oil
1 cup (8 fl oz/240 ml) dry white wine

♣ Preheat an oven to 350°F (180°C).
♣ Chop half of the rosemary and sage. Rub the rabbit with the chopped rosemary, sage, garlic and salt and pepper to taste. Place the rest of the rosemary and sage in the cavity. Fold the rabbit in half by bringing the head and tail end together. Truss the rabbit securely with kitchen string.
♣ Pour the olive oil into a roasting pan and add the rabbit. Place in the oven and roast until tender, about 1½ hours. Baste the rabbit frequently with the pan juices and turn it over frequently so that it browns well on both sides.

♣ Remove the rabbit and discard the herbs. Cut the rabbit into serving pieces and place on a serving platter; keep warm.
♣ Add the wine to the pan juices and place over high heat. Cook, scraping the browned bits from the bottom of the pan, until the wine reduces a little. Pour the sauce over the rabbit and serve very hot.

SERVES 6

Grosseto

CONIGLIO STRASCICATO

Braised Rabbit

Wild rabbits thrive in the Maremma, the coastal area of Grosseto. Their meat is darker than that of domestic rabbits, and they are usually larger and taste more like hare. They also take longer to cook than ordinary rabbit and should be braised in plenty of liquid.

2 tablespoons extra virgin olive oil
2 oz (60 g) *pancetta,* chopped
1 stewing rabbit, about 4 lb (1.8 kg), cut into serving pieces
2 garlic cloves
1 small bunch of fresh sage, tied with kitchen string

146

1 fresh rosemary sprig
1 cup (8 fl oz/240 ml) dry white wine
1 yellow onion, chopped
1 celery stalk, trimmed and chopped
salt and freshly ground black pepper
1¼ lb (600 g) plum (egg) tomatoes, peeled and puréed

🍂 In a heavy pot over moderate heat, warm the olive oil. Add the *pancetta* and fry until transparent, about 5 minutes. Add the rabbit, garlic, sage and rosemary. Cook, turning the rabbit pieces until they are golden on all sides, about 10 minutes. Pour in the wine and add the onion, celery and salt and pepper to taste. Cover, lower the heat and cook until the wine evaporates, about 10 minutes.
🍂 Add the puréed tomatoes, stir well, cover and simmer for about 1½ hours, adding a little water if the pan becomes too dry.
🍂 Remove and discard the sage, rosemary and garlic and arrange the rabbit on a platter. Serve immediately.

SERVES 6

Grosseto

LEPRE IN DOLCEFORTE

Hare in Sweet and Sour Sauce

This recipe may also be used for wild boar, although the cooking time would be slightly longer. As is always the case, the wine should be of high quality, because a sauce is only ever as good as the wine that went into it.

4 lb (1.8 kg) hare, cut into serving pieces
1 bottle (3 cups/24 fl oz/750 ml) good red wine
2 yellow onions, quartered
2 carrots, peeled and halved
2 celery stalks, trimmed and halved
2 bay leaves
1 tablespoon juniper berries
2 whole cloves
3 tablespoons extra virgin olive oil
salt and freshly ground black pepper
¼ cup (2 oz/60 g) granulated sugar
2 garlic cloves
1 cup (8 fl oz/240 ml) red wine vinegar

🍂 Place the hare pieces in a glass or ceramic dish. Add the wine, onions, carrots, celery, bay leaves, juniper berries and cloves. Mix well, cover and marinate in the refrigerator for 24 hours.
🍂 Remove the hare pieces from the marinade, reserving the marinade, and dry them with absorbent paper towels. In a heavy pot over moderate heat, warm the olive oil. Add the hare and cook, turning occasionally, until browned on all sides, about 10 minutes.
🍂 Meanwhile, drain the marinade, reserving both the liquid and the vegetables. Add the vegetables to the browned hare, stir well and season to taste with salt and pepper. Pour in 1 cup of the marinade liquid. Cover and simmer over very low heat for 2 hours, gradually adding the remaining marinade as the pan becomes dry.
🍂 Put the sugar in a small saucepan. Crush the garlic and add it to the sugar. Place over moderate heat until the sugar dissolves, then cook, stirring, until the sugar caramelizes and turns a golden brown. Remove from the heat and stir in the vinegar. Add the sugar mixture to the pan with the hare and stir well. Simmer for another 10 minutes.
🍂 With a slotted utensil, remove the hare pieces from the sauce and arrange them on a serving dish; keep warm. Put the vegetables from the sauce through the fine disc of a food mill. Return the puréed vegetables to the sauce, stir well and reheat to serving temperature.
🍂 Pour the sauce over the hare and serve immediately.

SERVES 6

Lucca

CONIGLIO ARROSTO MORTO

Rabbit Cooked in Wine and Stock

Arrosto morto, literally "dead roast," *is halfway between roasting and braising. In Lucca this method is often used for cooking chicken and veal. The meat is started in oil, with wine and stock added later.*

1 rabbit, about 4 lb (1.8 kg)
3 tablespoons extra virgin olive oil
6 fresh sage leaves
1 fresh rosemary sprig
1 cup (8 fl oz/240 ml) white wine
salt and freshly ground black pepper
1 small carrot, peeled and diced
1 celery stalk, trimmed and diced
1 small yellow onion, diced
1 cup (8 fl oz/240 ml) light meat stock (recipe on page 73)
1 bay leaf

🍂 Preheat an oven to 350°F (180°C).
🍂 Fold the rabbit in half by bringing the head and tail end together. Truss the rabbit securely with kitchen string.
🍂 In a heavy ovenproof pot over moderate heat, warm the olive oil. Add the rabbit, sage and rosemary. Cook, turning the rabbit so that it browns lightly on all sides, for about 10 minutes. Add the wine and season to taste with salt and pepper.
🍂 Cover the pot, place in the oven and cook for 1 hour. Add the carrot, celery, onion, stock and bay leaf. Re-cover and cook for 30 minutes longer, turning occasionally.
🍂 Remove the rabbit from the pot and cut it into serving pieces. Place on a serving dish and keep warm. Remove and discard the bay leaf from the pot. Put the vegetables through the fine disc on a food mill and return them to the pot. Stir the puréed vegetables into the pan juices and reheat on the stovetop. If the sauce is too thin, reduce it over moderate heat.
🍂 Pour the sauce over the rabbit and serve.

SERVES 6

Hare in Sweet and Sour Sauce

Arezzo

POLPETTONE ALL'ARETINA

Meat Loaf from Arezzo

The meat loaf made in Arezzo is particularly delicious because it uses fresh mushrooms when they are in season and dried ones the rest of the year. This meat loaf is excellent served cold.

7 oz (210 g) coarse country bread
1 cup (8 fl oz/240 ml) milk
1 oz (30 g) dried *porcini* mushrooms
1¼ lb (600 g) lean ground (minced) beef
2 eggs
½ cup (2 oz/60 g) freshly grated Parmesan cheese
3 oz (90 g) *prosciutto,* chopped
pinch of freshly grated nutmeg
salt and freshly ground black pepper
3 tablespoons all-purpose (plain) flour
2 tablespoons extra virgin olive oil
⅓ cup (3 fl oz/90 ml) dry white wine

🐟 In a bowl, soak the bread in the milk for 30 minutes. At the same time, in a separate bowl, soak the mushrooms in warm water to cover for 30 minutes.

🐟 Preheat an oven to 350°F (180°C). Squeeze out any excess moisture from the bread and place it in a large bowl. Drain the mushrooms and squeeze out any excess moisture. Chop them and add them to the bowl with the bread.

🐟 Add the beef, eggs, Parmesan, *prosciutto* and nutmeg. Season to taste with salt and pepper. Thoroughly mix the ingredients with your hands and then shape the mixture into an oval about 2½ in (6 cm) in diameter. Dredge the loaf lightly with the flour.

🐟 In a roasting pan over moderate heat, warm the olive oil. Add the meat loaf and brown it on all sides, turning it very gently, about 10 minutes. Pour in half of the wine and place the pan in the oven. Bake for 1 hour, gradually adding the rest of the wine as the pan becomes dry.

🐟 Remove the meat loaf from the pan and let it cool slightly. Slice and arrange on a serving dish. Serve warm or at room temperature.

SERVES 6

Arezzo

SCOTTIGLIA

Medley of Mixed Meats

Braised mixed meats, a feature of the Arezzo kitchen, sometimes appear on menus as cacciucco di carne. *The name comes from the fact that there are always at least seven different varieties of meat, cooked in the same way as the famous* cacciucco *from Livorno, which is composed of fish varieties.*

4 lb (1.8 kg) mixed meats (rabbit, chicken, veal, pork, guinea hen, pigeon or squab or lamb)
2 garlic cloves
¼ cup (2 fl oz/60 ml) extra virgin olive oil
1 small carrot, peeled and chopped
½ celery stalk, trimmed and chopped
½ yellow onion, chopped
1¼ lb (600 g) plum (egg) tomatoes, peeled and puréed
½ cup (4 fl oz/120 ml) light meat stock (recipe on page 73)
salt and freshly ground black pepper
6 slices coarse country bread
1 tablespoon chopped fresh flat-leaf (Italian) parsley
1 tablespoon chopped fresh basil

🐟 Chop all the meats into medium-sized pieces and set aside.

🐟 Chop 1 of the garlic cloves. In a heavy pot over low heat, warm the olive oil. Add the chopped garlic, carrot, celery and onion and fry gently until translucent, about 5 minutes.

🐟 Raise the heat to moderate and add the meats. Brown well on all sides. Add the tomatoes and lower the heat. Cover and cook for about 10 minutes.

🐟 Pour the stock into the pot, stir to mix and season to taste with salt and pepper. Cook, stirring occasionally, until the sauce is thick, about 1 hour. If necessary, add a little water to keep the meats moist.

🐟 Meanwhile, preheat an oven to 350°F (180°C). Toast the bread slices in the oven until golden. Rub one side of each slice of toast with the remaining garlic clove and place the slices on individual serving plates, garlic side up.

🐟 Divide the meats and sauce among the 6 slices of toast. Sprinkle with the parsley and basil and serve very hot.

SERVES 6

Scottiglia, Pork on a Spit and Meat Loaf from Arezzo (rear)

PORCHETTA ALLO SPIEDO

Pork on a Spit

In Tuscan markets there is always a freshly roasted whole pig, which is carved on the spot and is generally still warm. Pigs weighing as much as 200 lb (100 kg) are highly seasoned with garlic, rosemary and sage and baked in enormous bread ovens. On market days there are always groups of people standing patiently waiting for their pork served on thick slices of country bread. This is the recipe for the homemade version.

1 tablespoon chopped fresh sage
1 tablespoon chopped fresh rosemary
6 garlic cloves, chopped
salt and freshly ground black pepper

2½ lb (1.2 kg) boneless tied pork loin
¼ cup (2 fl oz/60 ml) extra virgin olive oil

🍂 Preheat an oven with or without a spit to 350°F (180°C).
🍂 In a small bowl, combine the sage, rosemary, garlic and salt and pepper to taste. Mix well and rub this mixture onto the entire surface of the prepared roast. In a roasting pan over moderate heat, warm the olive oil. Add the pork and brown it on all sides, about 10 minutes.
🍂 Thread the pork onto the oven spit and cook for 1½ hours, basting frequently with the olive oil. If your oven does not have a spit, pour the olive oil into a roasting pan. Add the pork and roast in the oven, turning frequently, for 1½ hours.
🍂 Remove the pork from the spit or pan and snip off the string. Cut the pork into slices and arrange them on a platter to serve.

SERVES 6

Pan-Fried Sausage and Mushrooms (front) and Beef Croquettes (rear)

Grosseto

TEGAMATA DI SALSICCIA E FUNGHI

Pan-Fried Sausage and Mushrooms

Around Grosseto this dish is usually prepared with sharp-tasting wild boar sausages, but sweet Italian sausages are a satisfactory substitute. If porcini *mushrooms are unavailable, you may use* shiitake *or button mushrooms. If the latter are used, add a few dried* porcini *to give the dish more flavor.*

1¼ lb (600 g) fresh *porcini* mushrooms
2 lb (900 g) wild boar sausages or sweet Italian sausages
3 tablespoons extra virgin olive oil
⅓ cup (3 fl oz/90 ml) red wine vinegar
3 garlic cloves, chopped
salt
1 tablespoon chopped fresh mint or thyme

❧ Clean the mushrooms by rubbing them with a dampened cloth; do not wash them. Trim the mushroom stems, then slice the mushrooms; set aside.
❧ Prick the sausages with a fork. In a skillet over moderate heat, warm the olive oil. Add the sausages and fry until they start to turn brown, about 5 minutes. Remove some of the cooking fat and pour in the vinegar. Continue cooking until the vinegar evaporates, about 5 minutes.
❧ Add the mushrooms and garlic and cook for another 5 minutes. Season to taste with salt, sprinkle with the mint and stir well.
❧ Arrange the sausages on a platter and serve very hot.

SERVES 6

Grosseto

POLPETTE RIFATTE

Beef Croquettes

Tuscan pancetta *is cured with salt and a lot of pepper, is flat and not round, and is called* rigatino, *meaning "little line," because it is fatty with thin layers of pink meat.*

3 oz (90 g) crustless coarse country bread
1¼ lb (600 g) beef bottom round or top round, very thinly sliced
4 oz (120 g) ground (minced) beef
1 garlic clove, chopped
3 oz (90 g) *pancetta,* chopped
1 tablespoon chopped fresh flat-leaf (Italian) parsley
3 tablespoons extra virgin olive oil
1 cup (8 fl oz/240 ml) dry red wine
1¼ lb (600 g) plum (egg) tomatoes, peeled and puréed
salt and freshly ground black pepper

❧ Soak the bread in water to cover for 30 minutes. Drain, squeeze out any excess moisture and place in a bowl.
❧ With a meat mallet, gently flatten the beef slices until they are about ⅛ in (3 mm) thick.
❧ Add the ground beef, garlic, *pancetta* and parsley to the bowl with the bread and mix well. Spread a little of this mixture evenly on each slice of beef, fold in the sides, roll up and secure with a wooden toothpick.
❧ In a roasting pan over moderate heat, warm the olive oil. Add the beef rolls and brown them on all sides, about 10 minutes. Pour in the wine and cook until it evaporates, about 10 minutes.
❧ Add the tomatoes and season to taste with salt and pepper. Lower the heat, cover and cook until the sauce thickens, about 40 minutes.
❧ Arrange the rolls and sauce on a platter. Serve immediately.

SERVES 6

Firenze

ANIMELLE CON PISELLI
Sweetbreads with Peas

In Italy sweetbreads are very popular, as are all the other variety meats (offal)—brains, liver, kidney and tripe.

2 lb (900 g) calf's sweetbreads
juice of 1 lemon
3 tablespoons all-purpose (plain) flour
¼ cup (2 fl oz/60 ml) extra virgin olive oil
3 oz (90 g) *prosciutto,* diced
⅓ cup (3 fl oz/90 ml) Marsala wine
3½ cups (14 oz/420 g) shelled green peas
½ cup (4 fl oz/120 ml) water, boiling
salt and freshly ground black pepper

❧ Soak the sweetbreads in cold water to cover for 1 hour; drain.

❧ Bring a large saucepan of water to a boil and add the lemon juice. Add the sweetbreads and boil for about 6 minutes. Drain the sweetbreads and plunge in cold water to cool. Carefully remove the membrane covering the lobes and any tough connective tissue. Place the sweetbreads between 2 plates and top with a weight. Chill for 2 hours in the refrigerator.

❧ Cut the sweetbreads into fairly large pieces. Dredge the pieces in the flour.

❧ In a deep skillet over moderate heat, warm the olive oil. Add the sweetbreads and cook until they are golden on both sides, about 10 minutes total cooking time. Add the *prosciutto* and cook, stirring, for another 2 minutes. Pour in the Marsala and cook until it evaporates, about 5 minutes.

❧ Add the peas and boiling water, lower the heat, cover and cook until the peas are tender, about 10 minutes. Season to taste with salt and pepper.

❧ Transfer the sweetbreads to a serving dish and serve immediately.

SERVES 6

Firenze

COSTATA ALLA FIORENTINA
Florentine Steaks

Florentine steaks, which are 1¼ in (3 cm) thick and weigh a minimum of 2½ lb (1.2 kg), come from the cattle raised in the Val di Chiana and are very similar to T-bone steaks. They are the classic Sunday lunch and are generally grilled on an open wood-burning fire; they may, however, be cooked under an ordinary broiler. One costata is the usual portion for just two people!

2 T-bone steaks, about 2½ lb (1.2 kg) each
2 tablespoons extra virgin olive oil
salt and freshly ground black pepper

❧ Brush the steaks with the olive oil and sprinkle with pepper to taste. Marinate at room temperature for about 30 minutes.

❧ Meanwhile, prepare a fire in a charcoal grill or preheat a broiler (grill). Place the steaks on the grill rack over a hot fire or slip them under the broiler. Cook, turning occasionally, until done to your liking, about 15 minutes for medium-rare.

❧ Remove the steaks to a serving dish, sprinkle them with salt and serve.

SERVES 6

Sweetbreads with Peas

Florentine Steak

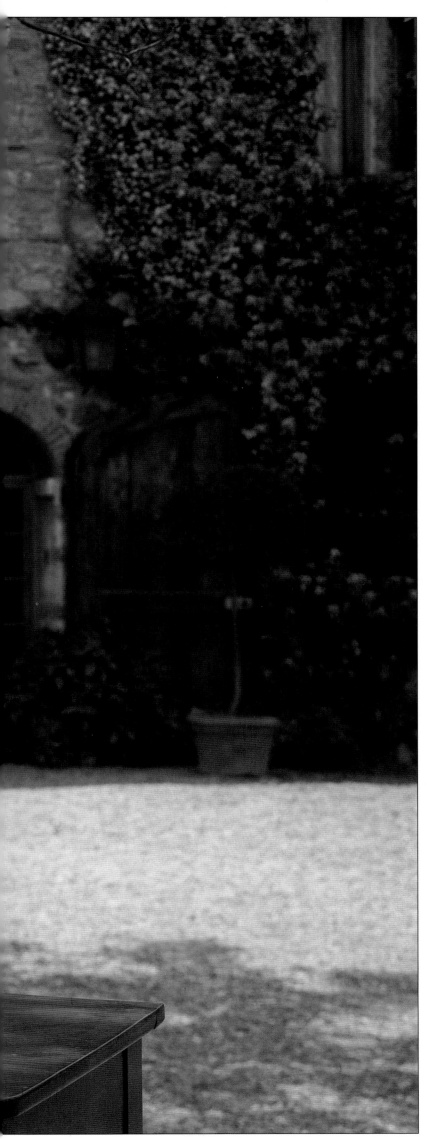

OSSIBUCHI AL POMODORO
Ossobuco with Tomato

The best ossibuchi *(veal shanks) are those cut from about halfway down the shank part of the leg, because that is where the proportion of meat and marrow is just right. Although this dish is a specialty of Lombardy, the people of Lucca have developed their own distinctive recipe that uses onions and tomato.*

6 slices dried *porcini* mushrooms
6 veal shanks, about 8 oz (240 g) each
3 tablespoons extra virgin olive oil
2 yellow onions, chopped
1 tablespoon finely chopped celery stalk
1 tablespoon finely chopped carrot
10 oz (300 g) plum (egg) tomatoes, peeled and puréed
salt and freshly ground black pepper
⅓ cup (3 fl oz/90 ml) dry white wine
1 tablespoon chopped fresh flat-leaf (Italian) parsley

♣ In a small bowl, soak the mushrooms in warm water to cover for 30 minutes. Drain and squeeze out any excess water. Chop the mushrooms and set aside.
♣ Tie each *ossobuco* around the edges with a piece of kitchen string. In a roasting pan over moderate heat, warm the olive oil. Add the *ossibuchi* and brown them on both sides for a few minutes. Add the onions, celery and carrot. Lower the heat, cover and cook until the vegetables are translucent, about 5 minutes.
♣ Add the mushrooms and tomatoes and season to taste with salt and pepper. Cover the pan and cook over low heat for 1½ hours, gradually adding the wine to keep the contents moist.
♣ Snip the string off the *ossibuchi* and arrange them on a platter. Cover them with the hot pan juices, sprinkle with the parsley and serve.

SERVES 6

AGNELLO AL FORNO
Roast Lamb

Spring lamb is considered the choicest because it is tender and has a mild flavor. Around Arezzo, farmers' wives cook lamb in their bread ovens after they have finished baking because the wood-burning ovens are at just the right temperature. Diced potatoes are often added for the last half hour.

3 garlic cloves, chopped
2 tablespoons fresh rosemary leaves
salt and freshly ground black pepper
5 lb (2.5 kg) leg of lamb
¼ cup (2 fl oz/60 ml) extra virgin olive oil
20 bay leaves

♣ Preheat an oven to 350°F (180°C).
♣ In a small bowl, mix together the garlic, rosemary and salt and pepper to taste. Rub the lamb with this mixture. Place the lamb in a large roasting pan. Sprinkle the olive oil over the lamb and add the bay leaves. Place the pan in the oven and roast for about 1½ hours, turning the lamb occasionally so that it browns on all sides.
♣ Remove the lamb from the roasting pan and carve into servings. Arrange on a platter and serve very hot.

SERVES 6

Roast Lamb (left) and Ossobuco with Tomato (right)

Grosseto

BISTECCHE ALLA CACCIATORA

Steak with Mushrooms and Marjoram

These steaks are cooked in a tomato sauce flavored with the marjoram that grows wild all along the Grosseto coast. They owe their name to the fact that they are suited to the robust appetites of the cacciatori, or huntsmen.

1 oz (30 g) dried *porcini* mushrooms
6 thin flank (rump) steaks, about 6 oz (180 g) each

Steak with Mushrooms and Marjoram

2 tablespoons extra virgin olive oil
2 garlic cloves, chopped
1 cup (8 fl oz/240 ml) dry red wine
1 tablespoon tomato paste
1 tablespoon fresh marjoram leaves or 1 teaspoon dried
  marjoram
1 tablespoon juniper berries
salt and freshly ground black pepper

❧ In a bowl, soak the mushrooms in warm water to cover for 30 minutes. Drain the mushrooms and reserve the soaking liquid. Strain the liquid and set aside. Squeeze out any excess moisture from the mushrooms and chop the mushrooms.

❧ In a skillet large enough to hold the steaks in a single layer, warm the olive oil over moderate heat. Add the garlic and steaks and cook on each side for 2 minutes, when they will start to brown.

❧ Lower the heat and add the wine, tomato paste, marjoram, juniper berries and mushrooms. Season to taste with salt and pepper and cover the skillet. Cook for 10 minutes, adding a little of the mushroom liquid if the pan becomes too dry. The sauce should not be too thick.

❧ Arrange the steaks and sauce on a platter. Serve at once.

SERVES 6

Firenze

POLPETTE DI LESSO

Fried Meatballs

Tuscans are very parsimonious and never waste food. Any leftovers are transformed into something quite different. These meatballs are an interesting way of using leftover boiled meat.

2 boiling potatoes
2 lb (900 g) boiled or roasted beef, chicken or veal
2 eggs
1 tablespoon chopped fresh flat-leaf (Italian) parsley
1 tablespoon chopped fresh sage
1 garlic clove, chopped
1 teaspoon freshly grated lemon zest
pinch of freshly grated nutmeg
3 tablespoons freshly grated Parmesan
salt and freshly ground black pepper
⅔ cup (3 oz/90 g) fine dry bread crumbs
5 cups (40 fl oz/1.2 l) extra virgin olive oil for frying

❧ In a saucepan, boil the potatoes in salted water to cover until tender, about 30 minutes. Drain the potatoes and peel and mash them while still hot.

❧ Chop the meat very finely using a knife or *mezzaluna* and place in a bowl. Add the mashed potato, eggs, parsley, sage, garlic, lemon zest, nutmeg and Parmesan. Mix thoroughly and season to taste with salt and pepper. Using your hands, form the mixture into ovals about 2½ in (6 cm) long and 1 in (2.5 cm) in diameter. Coat them evenly with the bread crumbs.

❧ In a deep, heavy skillet, heat the olive oil to 350°F (180°C). A few at a time, slip the meatballs into the hot oil without crowding the pan. Fry until golden, about 5 minutes. With a slotted spoon, remove the meatballs to absorbent paper towels to drain briefly. Continue frying the remaining meatballs in the same manner.

❧ Arrange the meatballs on a platter and serve piping hot.

SERVES 6

Siena

BRASATO AL CHIANTI

Beef Braised in Chianti

Several different cuts of beef may be used to prepare good braised meat, but one of the best is chuck or rump roast. The meat is usually simmered for at least 4 hours in order for it to become very tender.

2½ lb (1.2 kg) beef chuck or rump roast (boned and rolled beef topside)
1 bottle (24 fl oz/750 ml) Chianti Riserva
1 carrot, peeled and sliced
1 yellow onion, sliced
1 celery stalk, trimmed and sliced
2 bay leaves

½ tablespoon whole black peppercorns
1 tablespoon juniper berries
6 slices dried *porcini* mushrooms
3 tablespoons extra virgin olive oil
2 plum (egg) tomatoes, peeled and chopped
salt

🦐 Place the meat in a large bowl and pour the bottle of wine over it. Add the carrot, onion, celery, bay leaves, peppercorns and juniper berries. Marinate in the refrigerator for at least 24 hours, turning the meat occasionally so that it is always moist.
🦐 In a small bowl, soak the mushrooms in warm water to cover for 30 minutes. Meanwhile, remove the meat from the marinade and dry it with absorbent paper towels. Strain the marinade and set the vegetables aside. Reserve the marinade liquid.
🦐 In a heavy oval pot just large enough to accommodate the meat, warm the olive oil over moderate heat. Add the meat

Twice-Cooked Boiled Beef (left), Beef Braised in Chianti (right) and
Meat Loaf with Mushroom-Tomato Sauce (rear)

and brown well on all sides, about 10 minutes.

❧ While the meat is browning, drain the mushrooms and reserve the liquid. Strain the liquid and set the mushrooms and liquid aside. Lower the heat under the beef and add the reserved vegetables, tomatoes, mushrooms and salt to taste. Add a little of the marinade liquid; cover and simmer very gently. As the beef cooks, gradually add the marinade liquid, alternating it with the mushroom liquid, so that the meat always remains very moist.

❧ After about 4 hours, remove the meat and place on a serving platter. Slice the meat and keep it warm.

❧ Pass the vegetables through a fine sieve and return them to the pot. Stir the puréed vegetables into the cooking juices and cook over moderate heat until thickened to a sauce.

❧ Pour the sauce over the sliced meat and serve immediately.

SERVES 6

Siena

POLPETTONE IN UMIDO
Meat Loaf with Mushroom-Tomato Sauce

In Tuscany there are various ways of making meat loaf. It is sometimes boiled, resulting in the added bonus of an excellent stock, but in Siena it is usually served with a mushroom-tomato sauce.

6 slices dried *porcini* mushrooms
6 oz (180 g) crustless coarse country bread
1 cup (8 fl oz/240 ml) milk
1¼ lb (600 g) lean ground (minced) beef
2 eggs
1 tablespoon fresh thyme leaves
3 oz (90 g) *prosciutto,* chopped
salt and freshly ground black pepper
⅓ cup (3 fl oz/90 ml) extra virgin olive oil
1 cup (8 fl oz/240 ml) dry red wine
1 lb (450 g) plum (egg) tomatoes, peeled and puréed
1 tablespoon chopped fresh flat-leaf (Italian) parsley

❧ In a small bowl, soak the mushrooms in warm water to cover for 30 minutes. In a separate bowl, soak the bread in the milk for 10 minutes.

❧ Preheat an oven to 350°F (180°C).

❧ Squeeze out any excess milk from the bread and place it in a large bowl. Add the beef, eggs, thyme, *prosciutto* and salt and pepper to taste. Thoroughly mix the ingredients with your hands, and then shape the mixture into an oval about 2½ in (6 cm) in diameter.

❧ In a heavy ovenproof pot over moderate heat, warm the olive oil. Add the meat loaf and cook, turning, until browned on all sides, about 10 minutes.

❧ Meanwhile, drain the mushrooms and reserve the liquid. Squeeze the mushrooms dry and then chop them finely. Strain the liquid and set aside.

❧ Add the wine, puréed tomatoes and mushrooms to the pot and bring slowly to a boil. As soon as the tomato mixture starts to boil, transfer the pot to the oven and cook, turning the meat a few times, until tender, about 1 hour. Should the sauce become too dry, add a little of the reserved mushroom liquid.

❧ Remove the pot from the oven and place the meat loaf on a serving platter. Slice the meat. Season the sauce to taste with salt and pepper; pour it over the meat. Sprinkle with parsley and serve.

SERVES 6

Siena

LESSO RIFATTO
Twice-Cooked Boiled Beef

Being very thrifty, the Tuscans have many different ways of disguising leftovers. This excellent dish is traditionally made with boiled meat, but roast meat can also be used.

3 tablespoons extra virgin olive oil
1 lb (450 g) yellow onions, thinly sliced
1¼ lb (600 g) plum (egg) tomatoes, peeled and chopped
pinch of freshly grated nutmeg
salt and freshly ground black pepper
2 lb (900 g) boiled beef or veal, sliced

❧ In a skillet over low heat, warm the olive oil. Add the onions and fry gently until they are translucent, about 5 minutes. Add the tomatoes and nutmeg and continue cooking until the sauce thickens slightly and the onion disintegrates, about 30 minutes. Season to taste with salt and pepper. Add the meat and cook for 10 minutes to allow the flavors to blend.

❧ Arrange the meat and sauce on a platter. Serve immediately.

SERVES 6

TRIPPA ALLA FIORENTINA

Florentine Tripe

Tripe is very popular all over Tuscany, but particularly so in Florence. When buying tripe, always choose the honeycomb type, which has the best texture. Because tripe is tough it should be well cooked, but care should be taken not to overcook it or it loses its flavor.

2 carrots
2 yellow onions
2 celery stalks
1 bay leaf
1 teaspoon green peppercorns
2 lb (900 g) veal or beef tripe
¼ cup (2 fl oz/60 ml) extra virgin olive oil
1 lb (450 g) plum (egg) tomatoes, peeled and chopped
salt and freshly ground black pepper
½ cup (2 oz/60 g) freshly grated Parmesan cheese

❧ Bring a large saucepan of salted water to a boil. Add 1 each of the carrots, onions and celery stalks, the bay leaf and the peppercorns. When the water returns to a boil, add the tripe, cover and simmer for 30 minutes.

❧ Drain the tripe and discard the vegetables. Cut the tripe into narrow strips. Peel the remaining carrot and trim the remaining celery stalk. Chop the carrot, celery and onion.

❧ In a fairly large saucepan over low heat, warm the olive oil. Add the chopped carrot, celery and onion and cook until the onion is translucent, about 5 minutes. Add the tripe and stir for a few minutes. Add the tomatoes and cook until the liquid evaporates, about 30 minutes.

❧ Season to taste with salt and pepper. Ladle the tripe onto a platter, sprinkle with the Parmesan and serve.

SERVES 6

Braised Veal Cubes (left) and Beef Stew from Impruneta (right)

PEPOSO DEL FORNACIARI DELL'IMPRUNETA

Beef Stew from Impruneta

Impruneta is a village outside Florence where the most beautiful handmade tiles and terra-cotta pots are produced. The wives of the furnace workmen make this robust stew for their husbands to take to their jobs.

¼ cup (2 fl oz/60 ml) extra virgin olive oil
1 white onion, chopped
1 garlic clove, chopped
2 lb (900 g) boneless beef shank (shin), cut into 1¼-in (3-cm) cubes
2 bay leaves
1 teaspoon whole black peppercorns
⅓ cup (3 fl oz/90 ml) dry red wine
1 lb (450 g) plum (egg) tomatoes, peeled and chopped
salt

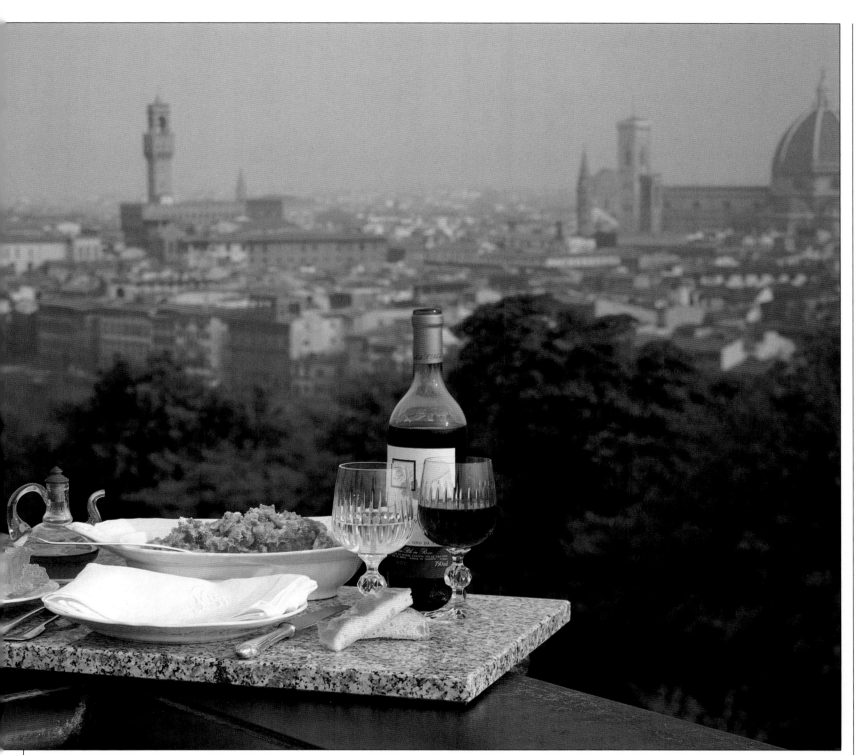

Florentine Tripe

In a heavy pot over moderate heat, warm the olive oil and onion. Add the garlic, meat, bay leaves and peppercorns.

Cook, stirring occasionally, until the meat is browned on all sides, about 10 minutes. Pour in the red wine and cook until it evaporates, about 5 minutes.

Add the tomatoes, cover and lower the heat. Simmer until the meat is tender, about 1½ hours. Should the stew become too dry, add water, a little at a time. Season to taste with salt.

Ladle the stew into a serving dish and serve immediately.

SERVES 6

Firenze

SPEZZATINO IN UMIDO

Braised Veal Cubes

This stew is usually served either with a vegetable mold, potatoes stewed in a tomato sauce, or fresh green peas sautéed in oil.

¼ cup (2 fl oz/60 ml) extra virgin olive oil
1½ lb (900 g) veal rump roast (boneless veal topside),
cut into 1¼-in (3-cm) cubes
1 tablespoon all-purpose (plain) flour
⅓ cup (3 fl oz/90 ml) dry white wine
½ white onion, chopped
1 carrot, peeled and chopped
1 celery stalk, trimmed and chopped
⅓ cup (3 fl oz/90 ml) light meat stock (recipe on page 73)
salt and freshly ground black pepper
juice and grated zest of 1 lemon
2 tablespoons chopped fresh flat-leaf (Italian) parsley

In a heavy pot over moderate heat, warm the olive oil. Add the veal cubes and cook, stirring occasionally, until the meat is browned on all sides, about 10 minutes. Sprinkle the meat with the flour and pour in the wine. Lower the heat, cover and cook for 10 minutes over low heat.

Add the onion, carrot, celery and stock and stir well. Re-cover and continue cooking for 1½ hours. Should the stew become too dry, add water, a little at a time.

Season to taste with salt and pepper. Add the lemon juice and zest, stir well and sprinkle with the parsley. Place the veal on a platter and serve.

SERVES 6

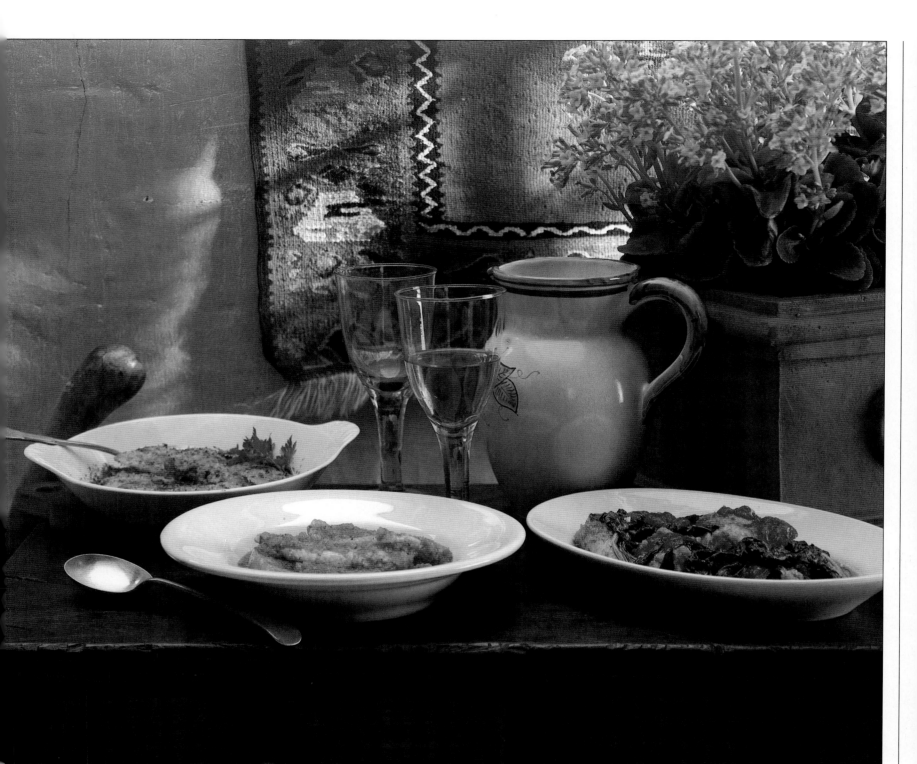

Left to right: Baked Anchovies, Sole and Red Mullet Soup, and Salt Cod with Spinach

ZUPPA DI SOGLIOLE E TRIGLIE

Sole and Red Mullet Soup

Livorno is famous for both its sole and its red mullet. In this recipe local cooks manage to combine them in a delicious and filling soup that is usually served as a main course.

2 sole, about 1⅓ lb (690 g) total weight
3 red mullet, about 1⅓ lb (690 g) total weight
¼ cup (2 fl oz/60 ml) extra virgin olive oil
2 garlic cloves, chopped, plus 1 whole garlic clove
1 small yellow onion, chopped
1 carrot, peeled and chopped
1 celery stalk, trimmed and chopped
2 tablespoons chopped fresh flat-leaf (Italian) parsley
1 cup (8 fl oz/240 ml) dry white wine
1¼ lb (600 g) plum (egg) tomatoes, peeled and chopped

salt and freshly ground black pepper
6 slices coarse country bread

🐟 Cut the heads off the fish and save them. Fillet the bodies and discard the bones. Set the fillets and heads aside.
🐟 In a heavy pot over low heat, warm the olive oil. Add the chopped garlic, onion, carrot, celery and parsley and cook until the onion is translucent, about 5 minutes. Add the fish heads and wine and cook until the wine evaporates, about 10 minutes. Add the tomatoes and cook until the sauce begins to thicken, about 40 minutes.
🐟 Preheat an oven to 350°F (180°C).
🐟 Remove and discard the fish heads from the pot and then put the sauce through a food mill. Return the puréed sauce to the pot and add the fish fillets. Season to taste with salt and pepper. Cook over low heat for no more than 10 minutes, gradually adding a little water to keep the sauce fairly thin.
🐟 Meanwhile, toast the bread slices in the oven until golden. Rub one side of each slice with the remaining whole garlic clove. Place the slices in individual soup bowls, garlic side up.
🐟 Ladle the soup and fish over the toast. Serve immediately.
SERVES 6

SEPPIE COI FAGIOLI
Squid and Beans

Although the Florentines are not great fish-eaters, they are very fond of salt cod, eel and squid. This is a particularly delicious recipe for squid.

1½ cups (10 oz/300 g) dried *cannellini* beans
6 tablespoons (3 fl oz/90 ml) extra virgin olive oil
1 handful of fresh sage leaves
2 lb (900 g) squid
2 garlic cloves
1¼ lb (600 g) plum (egg) tomatoes, peeled and chopped
salt and freshly ground black pepper

🦐 In a bowl, soak the beans in water to cover for 12 hours.
🦐 Drain the beans and transfer them to a heavy saucepan. Add 2 tablespoons of the olive oil, the sage and water just to cover. Bring slowly to a boil over low heat. Simmer gently for 1½ hours, by which time the water should be absorbed and the beans will be almost the consistency of porridge.
🦐 Meanwhile, clean the squid. Pull the tentacles from each body. Discard the entrails, ink sac and the cartilage from the body. Cut the tentacles off at the point just above the eyes and discard the head. Rinse the body and tentacles under cold running water. When all of the squid are cleaned, slice the squid bodies and chop the tentacles.
🦐 In a large skillet over moderate heat, warm the remaining 4 tablespoons (2 fl oz/60 ml) olive oil with the garlic. Add the squid and cook, stirring occasionally, for 5 minutes. Add the tomatoes, lower the heat and cook until the liquid almost completely evaporates, about 30 minutes.
🦐 Add the beans to the squid. Stir and heat together for about 5 minutes. Season to taste with salt and pepper.
🦐 Transfer to a serving dish and serve immediately.

SERVES 6

TORTA DI ACCIUGHE
Baked Anchovies

In this classic Livornese recipe, filleted anchovies or sardines are opened flat and arranged in concentric circles in a baking dish.

¾ cup (3 oz/90 g) fine dry bread crumbs
1 tablespoon dried marjoram or oregano
3 garlic cloves, chopped
salt
2½ lb (1.2 kg) fresh anchovies or sardines
¼ cup (2 fl oz/60 ml) extra virgin olive oil

🦐 Preheat an oven to 350°F (180°C).
🦐 In a small bowl, combine half of the bread crumbs, the marjoram, garlic and salt to taste. Mix well and set aside.
🦐 Remove the heads from the fish. Slit the bodies lengthwise along the belly and open them flat. Remove and discard the bones. Rinse the fish and pat dry on absorbent paper towels.
🦐 Pour half of the olive oil into a round ovenproof dish. Sprinkle with the bread crumb mixture. Arrange the fish in the dish in concentric circles, slightly overlapping them if necessary. Sprinkle the fish with the remaining crumbs and then drizzle with the remaining olive oil. Bake for 20 minutes. Serve hot.

SERVES 6

BACCALÀ ALL'INZIMINO
Salt Cod with Spinach

All'inzimino means "cooked with leaf vegetables," and all over Tuscany cuttlefish, tuna and salt cod are cooked in this way.

2 lb (900 g) salt cod
2½ lb (1.2 kg) Swiss chard (silverbeet) or spinach, trimmed
⅓ cup (3 fl oz/90 ml) extra virgin olive oil
2 garlic cloves, chopped
pinch of ground dried chili
10 oz (300 g) plum (egg) tomatoes, peeled and chopped

🦐 Soak the salt cod in water to cover in the refrigerator for 24 hours, changing the water 3 or 4 times.
🦐 Bring a large saucepan of water to a boil. Add the Swiss chard (or spinach) and boil for 1 minute. Drain well and chop; set aside.
🦐 Drain the salt cod. Remove and discard the bones and skin. Dry with absorbent paper towels. Cut the cod into large pieces.
🦐 In a heavy saucepan over moderate heat, warm the olive oil. Add the garlic and salt cod. Sprinkle the chili over the top and cook, turning the cod, until it is just golden on all sides, about 5 minutes.
🦐 Add the Swiss chard and tomatoes. Lower the heat, cover the pan and continue cooking over low heat until the liquid evaporates and a fairly thick sauce forms, about 20 minutes.
🦐 Arrange the cod pieces and sauce on a platter and serve.

SERVES 6

Squid and Beans

Top to bottom: Baked Marinated Prawns, Stuffed Cuttlefish and Grilled Trout

164

SEPPIE RIPIENE
Stuffed Cuttlefish

The long coastline near Grosseto accounts for the numerous fish recipes in the area.

6 cuttlefish or squid, about 6 oz (180 g) each
7 oz (210 g) crustless coarse country bread
1 egg
1 tablespoon chopped fresh flat-leaf (Italian) parsley
1 tablespoon chopped fresh basil
½ cup (2 oz/60 g) freshly grated Parmesan cheese
2 garlic cloves, chopped
pinch of ground dried chili
salt and freshly ground black pepper
3 tablespoons extra virgin olive oil
1 cup (8 fl oz/240 ml) dry white wine

♣ Pull the tentacles from each cuttlefish (or squid) body. Discard the entrails, ink sac and cartilage from each body, being careful not to tear it. Cut the tentacles off at the point just above the eyes and discard each head.
♣ Rinse the bodies and tentacles under cold running water. Chop the tentacles and place in a mixing bowl. Set the bodies aside.
♣ In a bowl, soak the bread in water to cover for 10 minutes. Drain and squeeze out any excess moisture. To the bowl with the tentacles, add the bread, egg, parsley, basil, Parmesan, garlic, chili and salt and pepper. Mix thoroughly. Stuff the cuttlefish with this mixture and secure them closed with wooden toothpicks.
♣ In a large skillet over moderate heat, warm the olive oil. Add the cuttlefish and cook, turning once, until pink, about 6 minutes.
♣ Pour in the wine and season to taste with salt and pepper. Lower the heat, cover and cook for 30 minutes, adding a little water if the pan becomes too dry.
♣ Arrange the cuttlefish on a platter and serve.

SERVES 6

TROTE AL FRANTOIO
Grilled Trout

Fishing in the small lakes around Arezzo is a favorite Sunday pastime. The fishermen build fires beside the lake to grill their catch. They are called al frantoio *(olive oil press) because they are cooked with olive oil that has just been pressed.*

6 bay leaves
6 whole trout, about 8 oz (240 g) each
6 tablespoons (3 fl oz/90 ml) extra virgin olive oil
salt and freshly ground black pepper
½ lemon

♣ Prepare a fire in a charcoal grill or preheat a broiler (grill).
♣ Place a bay leaf in the cavity of each trout.
♣ Brush a grill rack with 3 tablespoons of the olive oil. Arrange the trout on the rack over the charcoal or slip into a broiler and cook for a few minutes on each side. Sprinkle the trout with salt and pepper to taste while they are cooking.
♣ Place the fish on a serving dish, squeeze the lemon over them, sprinkle with the remaining 3 tablespoons olive oil and serve.

SERVES 6

TRIGLIE ALLA LIVORNESE
Fried Red Mullet in Tomato Sauce

This is one of the tastiest ways of cooking red mullet, which are particularly excellent in Livorno because they are fished near rocks. Red mullet are quite fragile, so they should be handled with great care.

6 red mullet, about ½ lb (240 g) each
⅔ cup (3 oz/90 g) all-purpose (plain) flour
5 cups (40 fl oz/1.2 l) extra virgin olive oil for frying
3 garlic cloves, chopped
1¼ lb (600 g) plum (egg) tomatoes, peeled and puréed
salt and freshly ground black pepper
2 tablespoons chopped fresh flat-leaf (Italian) parsley

♣ Gently pat the fish dry with absorbent paper towels. Dredge the fish in the flour.
♣ Reserve 3 tablespoons of the olive oil and pour the remaining olive oil into a deep, heavy skillet. Heat the oil in the skillet to 350°F (180°C). One at a time, slip the mullet into the hot oil and fry until golden, about 5 minutes. With a slotted utensil, remove to absorbent paper towels to drain. Continue frying the remaining mullet in the same manner.
♣ In a heavy saucepan over low heat, warm the 3 tablespoons olive oil. Add the garlic and fry gently until translucent, about 3 minutes. Add the tomatoes and continue cooking over low heat until the sauce is fairly thick, about 40 minutes.
♣ Gently place the mullet in the sauce and heat them for a few minutes. Season to taste with salt and pepper and sprinkle with the parsley.
♣ Arrange the mullet and sauce on a platter and serve.

SERVES 6   *Photograph page 10*

SPANNOCCHIE ALLO SCOGLIO
Baked Marinated Shrimp

On the long coast of Lucchesia there are several holiday resorts, the most famous of which are Forte dei Marmi and Viareggio. Their celebrated fish restaurants are as much of an attraction as the sandy beaches. Spannocchie are large clawed crustaceans caught on the rocks off the coast. As they are impossible to find elsewhere, you can use large headless shrimp in their place.

juice of 1 lemon
5 tablespoons (2½ fl oz/80 ml) extra virgin olive oil
salt and freshly ground black pepper
2 lb (900 g) peeled headless shrimp (prawns)
2 garlic cloves
1 tablespoon chopped fresh flat-leaf (Italian) parsley

♣ Stir the lemon juice into the olive oil and season to taste with salt and pepper. Brush the shrimp with this mixture and marinate at room temperature for 30 minutes.
♣ Pour off the marinade into a roasting pan and warm over moderate heat with the garlic. Add the prawns to the pan and sauté them until opaque and curled, not more than 5 minutes. Season to taste with salt and pepper and discard the garlic.
♣ Arrange the shellfish on a platter and sprinkle with the parsley. Serve hot.

SERVES 6

Livorno

TONNO CON PISELLI

Fresh Tuna with Peas

In Tuscany fish is often prepared with vegetables. The flavors marry well as long as the vegetables have a mild taste.

6 tuna steaks, about 8 oz (240 g) each
3 tablespoons extra virgin olive oil
5 cups (1¼ lb/600 g) shelled green peas
1 tablespoon chopped fresh flat-leaf (Italian) parsley
½ cup (4 fl oz/120 ml) dry white wine
salt and freshly ground black pepper

❧ In a skillet large enough to contain the tuna steaks in a single layer, warm the olive oil over moderate heat. Add the fish and cook on both sides for 5 minutes. Add the peas, parsley and wine; cook for another 5 minutes. Season to taste with salt and pepper.
❧ Arrange the tuna and peas on a platter and serve immediately.

SERVES 6

Pork Escalopes with Mushrooms

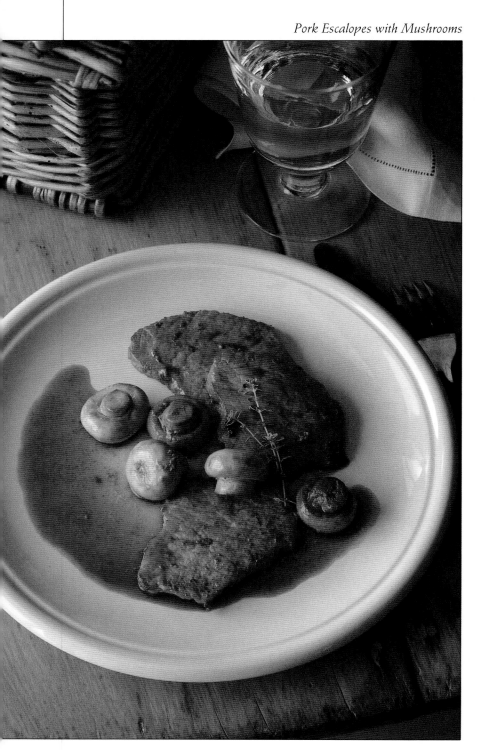

Lucca

SCALOPPINE ALLA BOSCAIOLA

Pork Escalopes with Mushrooms

The people of Lucchesia prefer white meat to beef. These escalopes are traditionally cut from uncured ham and then cooked in a mushroom sauce. They are called alla boscaiola, *or "woodcutter style," because of the great quantity of mushrooms in the woods.*

10 oz (300 g) fresh *porcini, shiitake* or button mushrooms
⅓ cup (3 fl oz/90 ml) extra virgin olive oil
2 lb (900 g) lean pork, thinly sliced
3 garlic cloves
⅓ cup (3 fl oz/90 ml) dry white wine
1 tablespoon fresh thyme leaves
salt and freshly ground black pepper

❧ Clean the mushrooms by rubbing them with a dampened cloth; do not wash them. Trim the mushroom stems, then slice the mushrooms fairly thinly; set aside.
❧ In a heavy ovenproof pot over moderate heat, warm the olive oil. Add the pork slices and cook, turning once, until golden on both sides, about 2 minutes per side. Add the mushrooms and garlic and sauté for 2 more minutes. Pour in the wine and sprinkle with the thyme. Cook, scraping the browned bits from the bottom of the pan, until the wine evaporates, about 2 minutes. Season to taste with salt and pepper and remove and discard the garlic.
❧ Arrange the pork and mushrooms on a platter and serve.

SERVES 6

Livorno

ZUPPA DI MUSCOLI

Mussel Soup

This hearty mussel soup makes an excellent luncheon dish served with a green salad, and is just as interesting made with clams.

6 lb (3 kg) large mussels in the shell
⅓ cup (3 fl oz/90 ml) extra virgin olive oil
2 garlic cloves, chopped
1 lb (450 g) plum (egg) tomatoes, peeled and puréed
1 cup (8 fl oz/240 ml) dry white wine
2 cups (16 fl oz/480 ml) water
salt and freshly ground black pepper
6 slices coarse country bread
2 tablespoons chopped fresh flat-leaf (Italian) parsley

❧ Scrub and debeard the mussels. Put the mussels in a shallow saucepan, cover and place over moderate heat until the shells open, about 5 minutes. Remove from the heat and discard any mussels that did not open; set the mussels aside in their shells. Strain the liquid that the mussels released into the saucepan and set aside.
❧ Preheat an oven to 350°F (180°C).
❧ In a heavy ovenproof pot over low heat, warm the olive oil. Add the garlic and fry gently until translucent, about 5 minutes. Add the tomatoes, wine, liquid from the mussels and the water. Cook over low heat for 30 minutes. Add the mussels and allow the flavors to blend for another 2 minutes. Season to taste with salt and pepper.
❧ Meanwhile, toast the bread slices in the oven until golden, about 10 minutes. Place the slices in individual soup dishes. Ladle the soup over the toast, sprinkle with the parsley and serve immediately.

SERVES 6

Fresh Tuna with Peas (left) and Mussel Soup (right)

Baked Swordfish with Potatoes (left) and Stockfish and Potatoes (right)

STOCCAFISSO CON PATATE
Stockfish and Potatoes

Stockfish is unsalted dried cod. Because drying fish without salt is a more difficult process, stockfish is harder to find and more expensive than salt cod.

2½ lb (1.2 kg) stockfish
⅓ cup (3 fl oz/90 ml) extra virgin olive oil
1 small yellow onion, chopped
2 garlic cloves, chopped
¾ cup (6 fl oz/180 ml) dry white wine
2½ lb (1.2 kg) potatoes, peeled and diced
1 tablespoon chopped fresh rosemary
salt and freshly ground black pepper

🐟 In a large bowl, soak the stockfish in cold water to cover in the refrigerator for 24 hours, changing the water 3 or 4 times. Drain the fish and remove and discard the bones and skin. Dry with absorbent paper towels. Cut the fish into fairly large pieces.

🐟 In a heavy saucepan over moderate heat, warm the olive oil. Add the onion and garlic and fry gently until translucent, about 5 minutes. Add the stockfish and cook, turning the fish, until golden on all sides, about 5 minutes. Pour in the wine, cover and lower the heat. Cook for 10 minutes.

🐟 Add the potatoes and rosemary and season to taste with salt and pepper. Cover and cook, stirring occasionally, until the potatoes are tender, about 20 minutes. Add a little water if the pan becomes too dry, and turn the fish and potatoes very gently so that they do not break.

🐟 Arrange the stockfish and potatoes on a warm platter and serve hot.

SERVES 6

PESCE SPADA CON PATATE
Baked Swordfish with Potatoes

Although swordfish is generally fished in southern Italy, it is also popular on the coast near Grosseto. There the locals prepare it in the same way as the eels that are bred at Orbetello, a village situated on a beautiful lagoon. Orbetello is also the capital of Monte Argentario, a famous resort area.

1¼ lb (600 g) boiling potatoes
6 tablespoons (3 fl oz/90 ml) extra virgin olive oil
6 pieces filleted swordfish, about 6 oz (180 g) each
2 tablespoons chopped fresh rosemary
3 tablespoons fine dry bread crumbs
3 ripe tomatoes, peeled and sliced
salt and freshly ground black pepper
1 cup (8 fl oz/240 ml) dry white wine

🐟 In a saucepan, boil the potatoes in salted water to cover until tender, about 30 minutes. Drain the potatoes, then peel and slice them.

🐟 Preheat an oven to 350°F (180°C). Pour 3 tablespoons of the olive oil into an ovenproof earthenware dish. Arrange the potato slices in overlapping concentric circles in the bottom of the dish. Lay the fish on top of the potatoes and sprinkle with the rosemary and bread crumbs. Place the tomato slices on the fish and season to taste with salt and pepper. Drizzle the remaining 3 tablespoons olive oil over the top and pour in the wine. Bake for 20 minutes.

🐟 Serve hot directly from the dish.

SERVES 6

Arezzo

ARISTA AL RAMERINO

Roast Pork Loin with Rosemary

Roast pork loin is a traditional Sunday lunch in Arezzo. In spring it is served with peas and artichokes; in the winter, cubed, peeled potatoes are added to the roasting pan with the pork during the last half hour of cooking.

4 lb (1.8 kg) pork loin on the bone
2 tablespoons chopped fresh rosemary, plus 4 fresh rosemary sprigs
3 garlic cloves, chopped
salt and freshly ground black pepper
¼ cup (2 fl oz/60 ml) extra virgin olive oil

🦃 Preheat an oven to 350°F (180°C).
🦃 Using a sharp knife, cut the meat from the bone in a single piece, working very carefully, or ask your butcher to do it. Reserve the rack of bones.
🦃 In a small bowl, mix together the chopped rosemary, garlic and salt and pepper to taste. Using a larding needle or something similar, make a hole in the center of the meat through its entire length. Fill this cavity with the rosemary mixture.
🦃 Lay the meat back on the bone, place the rosemary sprigs along the top and tie the meat and sprigs to the bone with kitchen string.
🦃 Pour the olive oil into a roasting pan and place the meat in it, fat side up. Place in the oven and roast for about 1½ hours, turning occasionally to brown on all sides.
🦃 Remove the roast from the oven and snip off the string. Lift the meat from the bone and carve it. Arrange the pork on a platter and serve.

SERVES 6

Arezzo

BRACIOLE COL CAVOLO

Braised Pork with Cabbage

This particularly hearty dish is prepared after the first frosts, when the black cabbage is at its tastiest. Savoy cabbage may be used as a substitute.

6 slices lean pork, about 6 oz (180 g) each
2 lb (900 g) black cabbage or Savoy cabbage
2 tablespoons extra virgin olive oil
2 garlic cloves
¼ cup (2 fl oz/60 ml) dry white wine
salt and freshly ground black pepper

🦃 With a meat mallet, gently flatten the pork slices to about ⅛ in (3 mm) thick.
🦃 Remove and discard the hard stalks from the cabbage and slice the leaves thinly.
🦃 In a large skillet over moderate heat, warm the olive oil. Add the pork and garlic and cook until the pork is lightly browned on both sides, about 5 minutes' total cooking time. Pour the wine over the meat and add the cabbage. Lower the heat, cover the skillet and cook for another 30 minutes, adding a little water if necessary to keep the meat moist.
🦃 Season to taste with salt and pepper. Transfer to a platter and serve immediately.

SERVES 6

Roast Pork Loin with Rosemary (top) and Braised Pork with Cabbage (bottom)

Siena

SPIEDINI ALLA CHIANTIGIANA

Skewered Pork with Sausage

Every butcher in Chianti has his own version of mixed skewered meats, to which some add tomatoes and slices of sweet pepper (capsicum). The classic version, however, sandwiches pieces of bread between the fattier meats. The bread turns crisp and tasty during the cooking.

6 oz (180 g) sweet Italian sausages
6 oz (180 g) *pancetta*
6 oz (180 g) pork tenderloin (fillet)
6 oz (180 g) pork liver
10 oz (300 g) coarse country bread
salt and freshly ground black pepper
¼ cup (2 fl oz/60 ml) extra virgin olive oil

🍃 Preheat an oven to 350°F (180°C).
🍃 Cut the sausages, *pancetta,* pork tenderloin, pork liver and bread into pieces about 1½ in (4 cm) long and ¼ in (6 mm) thick. Thread the meats onto 6 metal skewers, alternating the various types and always putting a piece of bread between pieces of bacon and sausage. Sprinkle with salt and pepper.
🍃 Select a shallow baking dish slightly narrower than the length of the skewers. Balance the skewers on the rim, with the points resting securely on either side so that the cooking juices will fall into the dish. Brush the meats with the olive oil. Place in the oven and cook for about 30 minutes, turning the skewers and brushing them frequently with the juices.
🍃 Arrange the skewers on a platter and serve hot.
SERVES 6

Siena

COSTOLECCIO ALLA GRIGLIA

Grilled Spareribs

In Sienese farmhouses, spareribs are often cooked over an open fire. They absorb the flavor of the wood and are juicy and tender. They may also be grilled under a broiler.

4 lb (1.8 kg) pork spareribs
salt and freshly ground black pepper
3 tablespoons extra virgin olive oil

🍃 Divide the spareribs into 6 equal pieces and place in a shallow plate. Season to taste with salt and pepper and brush with the oil. Marinate at room temperature for 30 minutes.
🍃 Meanwhile, prepare a fire in a charcoal grill. Remove the ribs from the plate, reserving the olive oil. Place the ribs on the grill rack over a hot fire and cook, turning a few times and brushing with the reserved oil until done, about 15 minutes.
🍃 Arrange the ribs on a serving platter and serve very hot.
SERVES 6

Lucca

AGNELLO COI CARCIOFI

Lamb with Artichokes

The best cut for this recipe is a leg with a few chops. In Italy we slaughter lamb when it is still quite young and weighs no more than 20 to 25 lb (10 to 12 kg). If you cannot find such young lamb, you can use just the leg. For the artichokes, choose small ones that have been trimmed but left whole.

6 tablespoons (3 fl oz/90 ml) extra virgin olive oil
1 garlic clove
5 lb (2.5 kg) leg of lamb, boned and cut into serving pieces
juice of 1 lemon
6 globe artichokes
1 cup (8 fl oz/240 ml) dry white wine
salt and freshly ground black pepper
1 tablespoon chopped fresh flat-leaf (Italian) parsley

Skewered Pork with Sausage (left) and Grilled Spareribs (right)

In a heavy pan over moderate heat, warm the olive oil and garlic. Add the lamb and cook, turning the lamb so that it browns on all sides, about 10 minutes.

Meanwhile, fill a large bowl with water and add the lemon juice. Cut the stalks off the artichokes. Remove the tough outer leaves and cut away any sharp leaf points. Cut the artichokes into quarters and remove and discard the furry chokes. Immediately drop them into the bowl of water to prevent discoloration. When all of the artichokes have been cut, drain them and dry with absorbent paper towels.

Add the artichoke to the lamb and cook for 10 minutes. Add the wine to the pan and cook for another 10 minutes, adding a little water if the juices become too dry. Season to taste with salt and pepper.

Arrange the lamb and artichokes on a platter, sprinkle with the parsley and serve.

SERVES 6   *Photograph pages 132–133*

ROGNONI COL BATTUTO

Kidneys with Chopped Vegetables and Pancetta

Unless kidneys are cooked very quickly they become tough. In Lucca they are sautéed with chopped vegetables and pancetta. *Liver is excellent cooked in the same way.*

2 lb (900 g) veal kidneys
3 oz (90 g) *pancetta,* chopped
1 tablespoon finely chopped carrot
1 tablespoon finely chopped fresh flat-leaf (Italian) parsley
1 tablespoon finely chopped yellow onion
3 tablespoons extra virgin olive oil
⅓ cup (3 fl oz/90 ml) dry white wine
salt and freshly ground black pepper

🦐 Cut the kidneys in half lengthwise; remove the fat and hard white core and the thin membrane covering the lobes. Cut into slices about ¼ in (6 mm) thick; set aside.
🦐 In a small skillet over moderate heat, warm the *pancetta.* Add the carrot, parsley and onion and fry gently until the *pancetta* and vegetables are slightly golden, about 3 minutes. Keep warm.
🦐 In a large skillet over moderate heat, warm the olive oil. Add the kidney slices and sauté until golden on one side, about 2 minutes. Turn over gently and sauté the other side until golden. Add the wine, scrape the browned bits from the bottom of the skillet and cook over high heat until the wine evaporates, about 1 minute. Season to taste with salt and pepper. Add the vegetables and *pancetta* and stir to blend the flavors.
🦐 Transfer to a platter and serve immediately.

SERVES 6

SCOTTIGLIA DI CINGHIALE

Mixed Wild Boar Stew

The hunting season for wild boar is from November to the end of January, and as there is an abundance of wild boar in the Maremma, there are many different ways of cooking it. In this recipe the less choice cuts are traditionally used, so they must be cooked for a fairly long time.

4 lb (1.8 kg) mixed wild boar cuts, such as leg or loin chops, including bone
¼ cup (2 fl oz/60 ml) extra virgin olive oil
2 garlic cloves, chopped
salt and freshly ground black pepper
1 carrot, peeled and chopped
1 celery stalk, trimmed and chopped
1 tablespoon chopped fresh flat-leaf (Italian) parsley
1 tablespoon chopped fresh thyme
small piece of dried chili
1 cup (8 fl oz/240 ml) dry red wine
1¼ lb (600 g) plum (egg) tomatoes, peeled and chopped
1 cup (8 fl oz/240 ml) light meat stock (recipe on page 73)

🦐 Cut the meat into bite-sized pieces. In a roasting pan over moderate heat, warm the olive oil. Add the garlic and fry gently for a few minutes. Add the wild boar and brown on all sides, about 10 minutes. Season to taste with salt and pepper.
🦐 Add the carrot, celery, parsley, thyme and chili. Stir well and pour in the wine. Lower the heat and cook until the wine evaporates, about 10 minutes. Add the tomatoes and cook for 2 hours, gradually adding the stock when the pan becomes too dry.
🦐 Ladle the meat and sauce onto a platter and serve.

SERVES 6

Kidneys with Chopped Vegetables and Pancetta (left) and Pork Liver with Fennel (right)

Mixed Wild Boar Stew

FEGATELLI DI MAIALE AL FINOCCHIO

Pork Liver with Fennel

Pork liver is cooked in a variety of ways around Siena, sometimes with pieces of bread and occasionally with sausage or other types of meat.

2 tablespoons fennel seed
salt and freshly ground black pepper
2 lb (900 g) pork liver
1 piece caul fat, about 20 in (50 cm) long
3 tablespoons extra virgin olive oil

🐾 In a small dish, mix together the fennel seed with salt and pepper to taste. Cut the pork liver into 18 pieces and sprinkle it with the fennel mixture.

🐾 Cut the caul fat into 18 pieces and wrap a piece of the fat around each piece of pork liver, fastening it in place with a wooden toothpick.

🐾 In a large skillet over moderate heat, warm the olive oil. Add the pork liver and cook, gently turning the meat from time to time so that it browns all over, until tender but still pink, about 10 minutes.

🐾 Transfer the liver pieces to a platter and serve very hot.

SERVES 6

Drowned Veal Escalopes

BRACIOLINE AFFOGATE

Drowned Veal Escalopes

This dish is cooked very slowly over low heat so that the sauce is thick and the full flavor of the mushrooms comes through.

6 slices dried *porcini* mushrooms
6 boneless veal escalopes, about 6 oz (180 g) each
2 tablespoons extra virgin olive oil
2 garlic cloves, chopped
1 tablespoon fresh thyme
1 lb (450 g) plum (egg) tomatoes, peeled and chopped
salt and freshly ground black pepper

In a small bowl, soak the mushrooms in warm water to cover for 30 minutes. Drain the mushrooms, reserving the liquid, and squeeze out any excess moisture. Chop the mushrooms and set aside. Strain and reserve the liquid.

With a meat mallet, gently flatten the escalopes until they are about ¼ in (3 mm) thick. In a large skillet over high heat, warm the olive oil and garlic. Add the escalopes and cook, turning, until they begin to brown, about 5 minutes. Add the mushrooms, thyme and tomatoes. Cover the skillet, lower the heat and simmer very gently until the sauce is thick, about 1 hour, adding a few tablespoons of the mushroom liquid if the pan becomes too dry.

Season to taste with salt and pepper. Arrange on a platter and serve.

SERVES 6

MAIALE UBRIACO

Drunken Pork

In Livorno in summertime, pork chops are generally grilled over an open fire and sprinkled with a little garlic and rosemary. On winter days, when the weather is cool and rosemary is more difficult to find, these chops are popular served with mashed potatoes.

6 pork chops, about 8 oz (240 g) each
1 tablespoon extra virgin olive oil
½ teaspoon fennel seed
2 bay leaves
½ cup (4 fl oz/120 ml) dry red wine
salt and freshly ground black pepper

❧ In a skillet large enough to hold all 6 chops in a single layer, warm the olive oil over moderate heat. Add the pork chops; sprinkle them with the fennel seed and top with the bay leaves. Cook for 3 minutes, turn the chops and cook for another 3 minutes on the second side.
❧ Pour in the wine and continue cooking until it evaporates, about 2 minutes. Season to taste with salt and pepper.
❧ Arrange the chops on a platter and serve.

SERVES 6

COSTOLETTE DI MAIALE AL DRAGONCELLO

Fried Pork Chops with Tarragon

Here pork chops are fried quickly and seasoned with fresh tarragon, the most commonly used herb in Siena. This popularity is probably due to the fact that tarragon grows well in the area and has a strong aroma, which may be the result of the quality of the soil.

6 pork chops, about 8 oz (240 g) each
3 tablespoons extra virgin olive oil
½ cup (4 fl oz/120 ml) dry white wine
salt and freshly ground black pepper
3 tablespoons fresh tarragon leaves

❧ In a skillet large enough to hold all the chops in one layer, warm the olive oil over moderate heat. Cook the chops until they begin to turn golden, about 5 minutes on each side.
❧ Add the wine, season to taste with salt and pepper, and sprinkle with the tarragon. Cook a few minutes, turning once, to allow the chops to absorb the flavors and the wine to evaporate a little.
❧ Transfer the chops to a platter and serve hot.

SERVES 6

Photograph pages 132–133

Drunken Pork

LIVORNO

LIVORNO

A few years ago the Italian and foreign press devoted a great deal of space to a story that divided the most authoritative art experts. Two stone heads had been fished out of a canal in Livorno and the vast majority of experts pronounced them to be the work of Modigliani, the great Livornese artist. Only after this attribution had been officially accepted did three young men appear on the scene to declare that they had created the heads with the help of an electric drill. To prove their point, they sculpted two more heads live on television. With the exception of several highly embarrassed art experts, the whole of Italy laughed. And those who did not already know the people of Livorno discovered that this is the most ironical and anarchic city in Italy.

This spirit is reproduced in Livorno's most famous recipe, *cacciucco alla livornese,* a soup of mixed fish of the cheaper kinds that deservedly has made Livorno known to cooks the world over. But before going into details about *cacciucco,* it should be explained why the Livornese are like their soup—a great mixture of people who have lived together in harmony for centuries.

In the fourteenth century, when Livorno was just a small village in the middle of the marshes, the Pisans decided to build a port there because their own was silting up. Later Pisa was conquered by Genoa and, in 1451, the Genoese sold the port of Livorno to the Florentines. Cosimo I, a Medici, fortified it, and a village almost abandoned because of malaria was quickly

Left: Weekend sunworshippers and water-lovers flock to the Piazzale Mascagni, the seaside terrace of Livorno. Previous pages: The finish line of Livorno's annual Palio Marinaro boat race. Held every summer, the race takes place between local teams of rowers in traditional boats.

transformed into the second most important city in Tuscany. Later Ferdinand I decided to build a new city close to the original one. He also constructed a new port, which to this day is called the Medici Port and is one of the most important in the Mediterranean.

In order to attract immigrants to the town, the Medicis granted freedom of residence, and Livorno became an open zone for both people and merchandise. It attracted Jews escaping from Spanish persecution, Greeks, Armenians, Englishmen and Dutchmen, as well as outlaws who were safe from arrest there. In other words, Livorno was a haven for all those seeking refuge or an open market. The population rose rapidly, and by the end of 1600 there were twenty thousand inhabitants, of whom five thousand were Jews. There were also many Turks. It was out of this great melting pot that the Livornese, a very particular type of Tuscan, emerged.

It is perhaps not surprising that the Italian Communist Party was established here in 1921. Nor that the most bawdy and irreverent satirical magazine in Italy, *Il Vernacoliere,* is published in Livorno and that only Tuscans can understand what it means.

Sadly, the old town was almost completely destroyed by bombs during the last war. The Livornese spirit survived, however, as did the beauty of its women, who seem to have been blessed with the best of this racial mélange. The most frequently heard interjection is still "deh," said to be a mispronunciation of the English "the."

And now back to *cacciucco,* the culinary equivalent of this great mixture. As with all historic recipes, several different theories about its origin have been handed down. The name seems to come from the Turkish word *kucuk,* which means "small." Legend has it that Homer's heroes dined on *cacciucco* and that the Phoenicians took it from Asia Minor to Greece, and from there to Provence in France, where it became bouillabaisse. Even Cicero

Livorno is an important fishing center, on any scale. The day's catch may be used to make cacciucco, *the renowned fish soup from Livorno that is said to have inspired similar creations in other countries.*

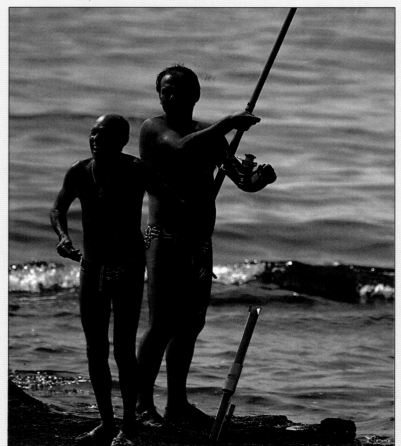

and Caesar are said to have been addicted to it. In Livorno it was undoubtedly improved by the guardians of the watchtowers, whose only pastime was fishing. When their catch was small, bread was added. With the discovery of the Americas came tomatoes and chilies, and so we arrive at the modern *cacciucco.* It was born unpretentious and so it has remained.

There are, of course, many other excellent recipes from Livorno, both those based on fish and those that draw upon the produce of the rich hinterland. But the sea certainly dominates, especially as some of the most beautiful islands in all of Italy lie off the Livorno coast. Napoleon was held prisoner on the isle of Elba, where there is still very limited production of the ancient Aleatico and Moscato wines. Then there is Giglio, greenest of islands, with its rare Ansonica vines, and Capraia, heady with the scent of myrtle and mastic. The well-protected island of Montecristo was made famous by Dumas, while Gorgona and Pianosa are private paradises.

The fish recipes range from *gianchetti* (baby sardines and anchovies) and *cee* (baby eels) to *triglie alla livornese* (red rock mullet in tomato sauce) and from *favolli* (a soup made with large crabs) to the classic *spaghetti alle vongole* (spaghetti tossed with clam sauce). Delicious cooked octopus continue to be hawked by fishermen in the streets of Piombino and on Elba in Portoferraio. And on Elba, it is still maintained that cuttlefish with artichokes was one of Napoleon's favorite dishes.

Bordatino, a Livornese soup, was invented on the old sailing ships but contains no fish. Nowadays it is enriched with fresh vegetables, but originally it was simply a cornmeal mush diluted with red bean soup—ingredients that could easily be stored on ships. There are two explanations for the name. The first is that it was so-called because it was made on board. The other comes from a rough, red-striped cotton cloth of the same name that is used for making aprons. When the bean soup is stirred into the cornmeal, it forms a pattern of red streaks that recalls the cloth. Another Livornese soup, *minestra con la palla,* is made with cauliflower, which is much used here, both raw and cooked as well as pickled in vinegar.

The famous artichokes from Antignano are so big they are called *mazzeferrate,* or "cudgels." They are sometimes cut open nearly to the bottom, stuffed with chopped meat, bread crumbs and egg, dipped in flour and egg, and then fried.

Interestingly enough, couscous was once very common in Livorno, where it is called *cuscussa.* It was originally brought back by sailors who visited North African ports, although today there are no official recipes for it. It is seldom made now and is served with anything the cook chooses, including fish, but semolina from the best durum wheat is always used.

The queen of poultry is the famous leghorn hen. In the nineteenth century these native fowl were taken from Livorno to England for crossbreeding and they came back greatly improved. Although their name is foreign, leghorns are the most celebrated chickens in Tuscany. Black or white with yellow feet, they are prized for their tender meat and are usually cooked either *alla diavola* (flattened and grilled) or with cheese, a recipe from Elba said to have been left by Napoleon's court.

It is above all in the realm of cakes and other desserts that the strong Jewish culinary influence is evident in the Livornese kitchen. *Bollo,* a sweet dough enriched with sugar and egg and flavored with aniseed liqueur, is one example. Another is *orecchie di Amman,* which are much

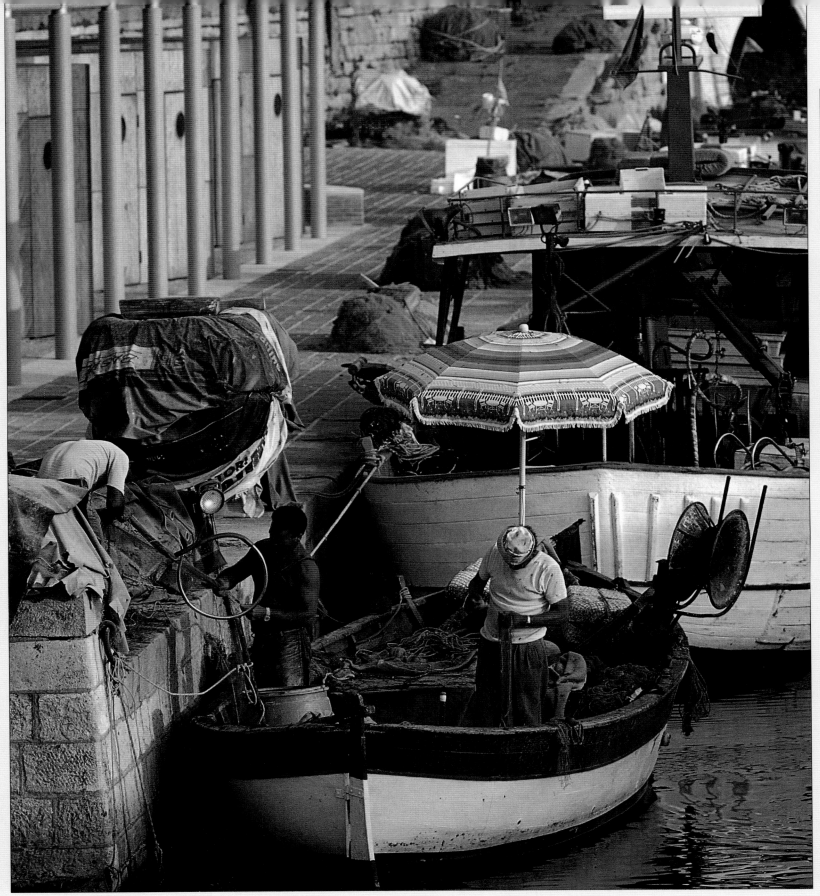

Livorno, often called Leghorn in English, is a major Mediterranean seaport. The town was developed by the Medici family in the late sixteeth century as a free port, bringing goods from around the world to the Grand Duchy of Tuscany.

like the *cenci* (fried biscuits) found in the rest of Tuscany. They take their name from Haman, a favorite of King Ahasuerus of Persia in the biblical book of Esther. Haman advised the king to destroy the Jews, but he failed in his terrible intent and was himself killed. The vendetta continues and "Haman's ears" are still regularly eaten. Then there is Mount Sinai, a typical flourless Passover cake made of almonds. Preserved rosehips, another typical sweet, are, however, of Greek origin.

No visit to Livorno is complete without tasting the famous *ponce alla livornese,* a mispronunciation of punch. The Bar Civili in Livorno is frequented by everyone from bejeweled ladies to stevedores because, although it is far from elegant, the traditional punch is served there. It is prepared in a thick, wide glass that is first half-filled with excellent coffee. Then a spoonful of sugar dissolved under the steam from the coffee machine is added, followed by rum and a slice of lemon peel. Fine Caribbean rum is not used, but rather the dark rum specially made for punch.

The Livornese have two nicknames for their punch—a torpedo and a bomb. Sailors have long found it a very useful drink in winter, when they come ashore shivering from the cold of the sea. At one time anyone with a hoarse voice was described as having a rum-punch voice. That was when the drink was laced with *caramellato,* a mixture of sugar and pure alcohol. Using it was against the law, but all the barkeeps kept it hidden and secretly poured it into the rum. After all, was this pleasant coastal town a haven for outlaws or wasn't it?

Le Verdure

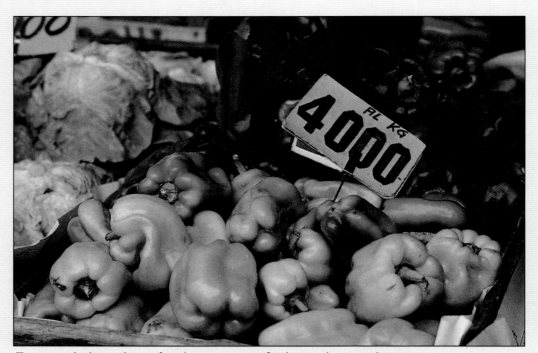

Tuscan cooks have always found inventive uses for the simplest ingredients.

LE VERDURE

Although nutritionists insist that vegetables are vital to our health, fewer and fewer vegetables seem to appear on Italy's restaurant tables these days. It is often hard to find anything more than the ubiquitous—and harmful—fried potato, a few leaves of salad, and vegetables that have been boiled without much enthusiasm.

In Tuscany, however, vegetables have always been important. They are a principal ingredient of molds,

Beans play an important role in the peasant-influenced cucina *of Tuscany. The most popular are white* cannellini *beans.*

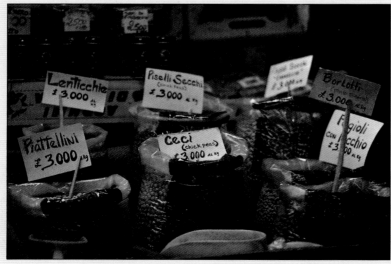

omelets and loaves (see Piatti di Mezzo chapter), soups and sauces, as well as some meat and fish recipes.

The region's traditional vegetable dishes are not available everywhere, of course, but in small trattorias it is not unusual to rediscover familiar flavors and fragrances. A good example of this in Lucchesia is *frissoglia,* a subtle combination of zucchini and their flowers, tomatoes and green beans. One of the specialties of Elba is *gurguglione,* a mixture of bell peppers, eggplants and zucchini reminiscent of *ratatouille.* Lunigiana boasts a very special vegetable loaf made of potatoes, onions and eggs.

Admittedly these are distinctly local dishes, but the average Tuscan restaurant offers a far greater variety of vegetables than its equivalent in northern Italy. There are usually zucchini, green beans, asparagus and artichokes prepared in various ways, as well as Swiss chard, spinach and cabbage in many guises.

Above all, the Tuscan bean is never missing from a menu. It may be cooked with sausage or with pork fat, in a flask with just a little garlic and sage, or *all'uccelletto,* with tomatoes. When beans taste truly excellent, they most likely were cooked in a terra-cotta pot over very low heat. Sometimes they are done in the traditional *fagioliera,* an earthenware jar with a narrow mouth and a wide base. The more esoteric *fagioli al fiasco* is prepared in an old wine flask *(fiasco)* buried in the ashes and embers of a dying fire. If you want to experiment with this method, make quite sure you have an old-fashioned

Previous pages: Potatoes Braised in White Wine (page 196), Braised Onions (page 188), Beans and Tomato (rear, page 192).

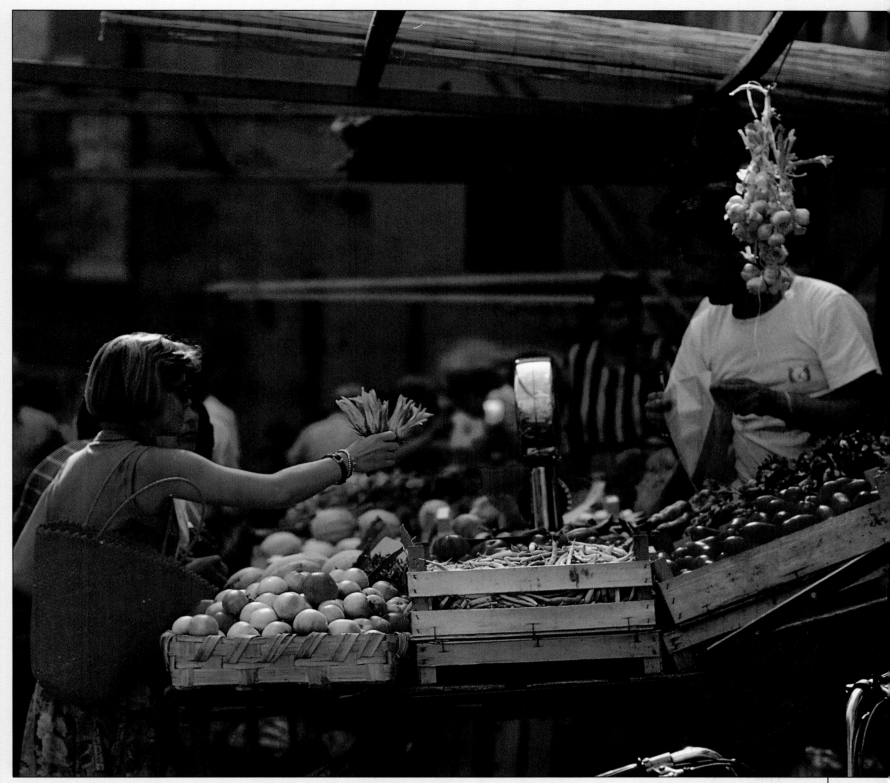

Shoppers in Tuscany visit the market frequently and choose only the freshest ingredients,
planning their meals around what looks best that day.

hand-blown *fiasco,* because the industrially produced flasks sometimes explode in the heat and you might find yourself with a real fiasco. It is probably safer to stick with a *fagioliera* or any other deep earthenware pot.

Broad (fava) beans, or *baccelli* as they are called in Tuscany, are a part of the venerable bean tradition. Dried broad beans are reported to have been found in Egyptian tombs, as well as in prehistoric archaeological sites. Until recently they were considered rather plebeian and left to the farmers, but now they are enjoyed by everyone. When they have just come into season in May, the young, tender beans are presented raw with sheep's milk cheese as an antipasto. The larger ones are stewed with tomatoes and onion and served as a side dish.

Although not botanically a vegetable, mushrooms are treated like one and have always been very popular in Tuscany, where, in some parts, they are found in abundance. The most sought-after mushrooms are *porcini,* meaning "little pigs," so-called because of their shape. They are eaten either fresh or are dried for the winter. Mushrooms, like chestnuts, were once part of the local economy, but recently imports from eastern European countries, particularly Yugoslavia, have come onto the market.

Mushrooms are grilled or fried, served on polenta and pasta, baked with potatoes and parsley, or fried with a little tomato. Although *porcini* are the most highly prized, many other field mushrooms are gathered on the Tuscan hills. Mushroom addicts from every walk of life are prepared to rise at dawn to hunt for them in hidden places that they would not divulge to their closest friends. There is an old saying that only on his deathbed does a Tuscan farmer reveal to his favorite son the exact location of his mushroom ground.

Arezzo

CAROTE IN STUFATO
Braised Carrots

These carrots are so nutritious that woodchoppers often carry them into the forests and have them for lunch on toasted bread. They are more commonly served, however, with lamb or rabbit.

⅓ cup (3 fl oz/90 ml) extra virgin olive oil
4 oz (120 g) *pancetta,* cut into small pieces
1 yellow onion, chopped
1 garlic clove, chopped
2 lb (900 g) carrots, peeled and sliced ⅛ in (2 mm) thick
1 tablespoon chopped fresh flat-leaf (Italian) parsley
⅓ cup (3 fl oz/90 ml) light meat stock (recipe on page 73)
salt and freshly ground black pepper

🍃 In a skillet over low heat, warm the olive oil. Add the *pancetta,* onion and garlic and fry gently, stirring frequently, until the onions are translucent, about 5 minutes. Add the carrots and parsley and stir well.
🍃 Cook gently for 20 minutes, adding just enough of the stock to keep the carrots moist.
🍃 Season to taste with salt and pepper. Spoon the carrots into a serving dish and serve hot.

SERVES 6

Siena

CIPOLLATA
Braised Onions

Generally this dish is prepared with sweet purple or red onions, which can be stored all winter without sprouting. If unavailable, ordinary yellow onions may be used.

2 lb (900 g) purple onions
⅓ cup (3 fl oz/90 ml) extra virgin olive oil
1 cup (8 fl oz/240 ml) dry white wine
½ tablespoon granulated sugar
1 tablespoon fennel seed
salt and freshly ground black pepper

🍃 Slice the onions. If you are using very strong-flavored onions, soak the slices in cold water to cover for about 1 hour. Drain and dry with absorbent paper towels.
🍃 In a heavy pot over moderate heat, warm the olive oil. Add the onions and cook, stirring carefully, until they begin to change color, about 5 minutes. Add the wine and sprinkle with the sugar and fennel seed. Season to taste with salt and pepper, cover and cook over very low heat until all the liquid evaporates, about 10 minutes.
🍃 Spoon the onions onto a serving dish and serve hot.

SERVES 6   *Photograph pages 184–185*

Braised Carrots

Puréed Chick-peas

PASSATO DI CECI

Puréed Chick-peas

Around Grosseto, unlike the rest of Tuscany, chick-peas are just as popular as cannellini *beans, and, when dressed with abundant olive oil, are equally delicious.*

2⅛ cups (14 oz/420 g) dried chick-peas (garbanzos)
1 garlic clove
6 tablespoons (3 fl oz/90 ml) extra virgin olive oil
3 plum (egg) tomatoes, peeled and puréed
salt and freshly ground black pepper

❧ Soak the chick-peas in water to cover for 12 hours.
❧ Drain the chick-peas and place them in a heavy pot. Add the garlic and water to cover and bring slowly to a boil over low heat. Simmer gently until the chick-peas are tender, about 1½ hours.
❧ Drain the chick-peas and put them through the fine disc of a food mill; set aside.
❧ In a heavy pot over low heat, warm 3 tablespoons of the olive oil. Add the puréed chick-peas and the tomato and season to taste with salt and pepper. Cook over low heat, stirring constantly, until the purée is rid of excess moisture.
❧ Arrange the purée in little mounds on a serving platter and make a small hollow in the center of each mound. Pour a little of the remaining 3 tablespoons olive oil into each hollow and sprinkle to taste with salt and pepper. Serve immediately.

SERVES 6

CIPOLLE ALLA GROSSETANA

Baked Stuffed Onions, Grosseto Style

*Spices rather than herbs are used for seasoning these baked
onions, which identifies this as a fairly old recipe. The spices
give the onions a deep, complex taste that goes well with the
local wild boar.*

6 large purple or yellow onions in their skins
3 oz (90 g) beef, finely chopped
3 oz (90 g) sweet Italian sausage, skinned and crumbled
1 egg
pinch of freshly grated nutmeg
1 whole clove, crushed
pinch of ground cinnamon
salt and freshly ground black pepper
1 tablespoon extra virgin olive oil

hollowed-out halves aside. Finely chop the onion centers you have removed.

❧ In a bowl, combine the chopped onion, beef, sausage, egg, nutmeg, clove and cinnamon. Season to taste with salt and pepper. Fill the cavities in the onion halves with this mixture.

❧ In a baking dish in which the stuffed onions will fit without crowding, pour in the olive oil, wine and water. Arrange the onions in the dish. Bake until the onions are tender when pierced with a fork, about 20 minutes.

❧ Arrange the onions on a platter and serve hot.

SERVES 6

Grosseto

CAVOLO STRASCICATO

Cabbage Braised in White Wine

The assertive flavor of cabbage goes well with the red meat eaten in this area. Wild fennel is used for seasoning, but if it is not available, fennel seed may be substituted.

2½ lb (1.2 kg) Savoy cabbage
3 tablespoons extra virgin olive oil
2 oz (60 g) *pancetta*, chopped
salt and freshly ground black pepper
3 sprigs wild fennel or 1 teaspoon fennel seed
½ cup (4 fl oz/120 ml) dry white wine

❧ Remove and discard the hard stalks from the cabbage and slice the leaves into narrow strips.

❧ In a heavy pot over moderate heat, warm the olive oil. Add the *pancetta* and fry gently until transparent, about 5 minutes. Add the cabbage, stir well and cook gently for a few minutes to blend the flavors.

❧ Season to taste with salt and pepper. Sprinkle with the fennel and pour in the wine. Cover and cook over low heat until the cabbage is very tender, about 20 minutes. Check from time to time and add a couple of tablespoons of water if the pan becomes too dry.

❧ Arrange the cabbage on a platter and serve hot.

SERVES 6

Arezzo

FAGIOLINI DI SANT'ANNA

St. Anna Beans

Although in Italy these beans are grown only in Tuscany, they are quite popular in California, which goes to show that Tuscany and California share more than wine. St. Anna beans, which are sometimes called Chinese long beans or snake beans, are very narrow green beans that measure about 16 in (40 cm) in length.

3 tablespoons extra virgin olive oil
3 garlic cloves, chopped
2 lb (900 g) St. Anna beans or runner beans, trimmed
10 oz (300 g) plum (egg) tomatoes, peeled and chopped
salt and freshly ground black pepper

❧ In a large skillet over low heat, warm the olive oil. Add the garlic and fry gently until translucent, about 3 minutes. Add the beans and tomatoes and season to taste with salt and pepper. Lower the heat and cook until the beans are tender, about 15 minutes.

❧ Transfer the beans to a serving dish and serve hot.

SERVES 6

Left to right: Cabbage Braised in White Wine, St. Anna Beans and Baked Stuffed Onions

¼ cup (2 fl oz/60 ml) dry white wine
½ cup (4 fl oz/120 ml) water

❧ Preheat an oven to 350°F (180°C).

❧ Bring a large saucepan of water to a boil. Add the unpeeled onions and boil for about 10 minutes. Drain and, when cool enough to handle, peel the onions and cut them in half horizontally.

❧ Dig out about half of the center of each onion half; set the

FAGIOLI ALL'UCCELLETTO

Beans and Tomato

Fagioli all'uccelletto is undoubtedly the most popular vegetable dish in Siena and is enjoyed all over Tuscany. In Siena this dish is always served with pork liver (recipe on page 175).

2⅛ cups (14 oz/420 g) dried *cannellini* beans
6 tablespoons (3 fl oz/80 ml) extra virgin olive oil
3 garlic cloves
1 large handful of fresh sage leaves
1 lb (480 g) plum (egg) tomatoes, peeled and chopped
salt and freshly ground black pepper

❧ In a bowl, soak the beans in water to cover for 12 hours.
❧ Drain the beans and transfer them to a heavy saucepan. Add 2 tablespoons of the olive oil and water just to cover. Bring slowly to a boil over low heat. Simmer gently for 1½ hours, by which time the water should be absorbed and the beans will be almost the consistency of porridge.
❧ Meanwhile, in a saucepan over low heat, warm the remaining 4 tablespoons (2 fl oz/60 ml) olive oil. Add the garlic and sage and fry gently until they start to change color, about 3 minutes. Add the tomatoes and cook over gentle heat until some of the liquid evaporates, about 10 minutes.
❧ Transfer the beans to the saucepan containing the tomatoes and season to taste with salt and pepper. Stir and then cook over low heat for about 10 minutes to allow the flavors to blend. The final result should be rather thin. Pour into a bowl and serve very hot.

SERVES 6 *Photograph pages 184–185*

Cardoons in Sausage Sauce

GOBBI TRIPPATI

Cardoons in Sausage Sauce

This rich, intensely flavored dish is relished by the local people because wild boar sausages are used for the sauce. The identity of cardoons is strong enough not to be smothered by the sauce.

juice of 1 lemon
4 lb (1.8 kg) cardoons
3 tablespoons extra virgin olive oil
1 carrot, peeled and chopped
1 small yellow onion, chopped
1 celery stalk, trimmed and chopped
1 tablespoon chopped fresh flat-leaf (Italian) parsley
10 oz (300 g) wild boar sausages or sweet Italian sausages, skinned and crumbled
10 oz (300 g) plum (egg) tomatoes, peeled and chopped
¼ cup (2 fl oz/60 ml) light meat stock (recipe on page 73)
salt and freshly ground black pepper

❧ Fill a large bowl with water and add the lemon juice. Remove and discard the base from each cardoon and discard any tough stalks. Trim and discard the leaves and spurs from the tender stalks and then scrape the stalks with a small knife to remove all strings and fibers. Cut each stalk crosswise into pieces 2 in (5 cm) long and immediately drop them into the water to prevent discoloration.
❧ In a heavy pot over low heat, warm the olive oil. Add the carrot, onion, celery, parsley and sausage and fry gently until the carrot is cooked, about 10 minutes.
❧ Drain the cardoon pieces and add to the pot along with the tomatoes. Stir well and add the stock. Cook until the cardoons are very tender and the sauce has thickened, about 20 minutes.
❧ Season to taste with salt and pepper. Transfer to a serving dish and serve hot.

SERVES 6

GURGUGLIONE

Sautéed Mixed Vegetables

This savory vegetable medley resembles certain southern European dishes, probably due to Livorno's sea trade with the Middle East and with Spain.

3 tablespoons extra virgin olive oil
3 garlic cloves, chopped
1 small yellow onion, chopped
2 Asian (slender) eggplants (aubergines), trimmed and cut into ¾-in (2-cm) cubes
3 zucchini (courgettes), trimmed and sliced ¼ in (6 mm) thick
3 yellow or red bell peppers (capsicums), seeded, deveined and cut into long, narrow strips
10 oz (300 g) ripe plum (egg) tomatoes, peeled and chopped
salt and freshly ground black pepper

❧ In a heavy pot over low heat, warm the olive oil. Add the garlic and onion and fry gently until translucent, about 5 minutes.
❧ Add the eggplants, zucchini and peppers and cook, stirring frequently, for 3 minutes.
❧ Add the tomatoes and season to taste with salt and pepper. Cover and cook over gentle heat until the flavors are well blended, about 40 minutes. If necessary, add a little water to keep the vegetables moist.
❧ Spoon into a serving dish and serve hot.

SERVES 6

Sautéed Mixed Vegetables

Roast Diced Potatoes (left) and Artichoke Fritters (right)

Arezzo

FRITTURA DI CARCIOFI

Artichoke Fritters

Traditionally these fried artichokes are served with baby lamb at Easter. They also go well with roast chicken, or they make a satisfying supper when served with a simple omelet.

juice of 1 lemon
2½ lb (1.2 kg) globe artichokes
2 eggs
salt and freshly ground black pepper
⅔ cup (3 oz/90 g) all-purpose (plain) flour
5 cups (40 fl oz/1.2 l) extra virgin olive oil

🐾 Fill a large bowl with water and add the lemon juice. Cut the stalks off the artichokes. Remove the tough outer leaves and cut away any sharp leaf points from the tops. Cut the artichokes lengthwise into eighths and remove and discard the fuzzy chokes. As each artichoke is ready, drop it into the water to prevent discoloration. When all of the artichokes have been trimmed, drain them and pat dry with absorbent paper towels.

🐾 In a bowl, beat the eggs with a little salt and pepper. Dredge the artichokes in the flour and shake off any excess, then dip them in the beaten egg.

🐾 Meanwhile, in a deep, heavy skillet, heat the olive oil to 350°F (180°C).

🐾 A few at a time, slip the artichoke slices into the hot oil without crowding the pan. Fry until golden, about 3 minutes. With a slotted spoon, remove to absorbent paper towels to drain. Continue frying the remaining artichokes in the same manner. Serve piping hot.

SERVES 6

Siena

RAPINI IN PADELLA
Pan-Tossed Broccoli Raab

Broccoli raab is usually picked after the first frosts, when it is tender. It is dressed in various ways and often served with roast pork. At room temperature, splashed with olive oil and lemon, it is excellent.

2 lb (900 g) broccoli raab, trimmed
⅓ cup (3 fl oz/90 ml) extra virgin olive oil
3 garlic cloves
salt and freshly ground black pepper

🦐 Bring a large saucepan of slightly salted water to a boil. Add the broccoli raab to the boiling water and cook for just a few minutes. Drain and immediately transfer to a bowl of iced water so that the leaves remain green. Drain and squeeze out any excess water.

🦐 In a skillet over low heat, warm the olive oil. Add the garlic and fry until just golden, about 5 minutes. Add the drained greens and season to taste with salt and pepper. Fry gently over low heat, stirring occasionally, until tender, about 5 minutes. Remove and discard the garlic.

🦐 Arrange the greens on a serving dish and serve hot.

SERVES 6

Arezzo

PATATE ARROSTO
Roast Diced Potatoes

Arezzo cooks believe that it is practically obligatory to present roast potatoes alongside their celebrated roast pork. The potatoes are seasoned with rosemary and garlic and are generally cooked in the pork drippings. They can, however, also be cooked in olive oil.

1 cup (8 fl oz/240 ml) extra virgin olive oil
2 lb (900 g) baking potatoes, peeled and cut into ¾-in (2-cm) dice
3 garlic cloves
2 tablespoons fresh rosemary leaves

🦐 Preheat the oven to 350°F (180°C). Meanwhile, in a roasting pan, on the stovetop, warm the olive oil over moderate heat. Add the potatoes, garlic and rosemary and stir to coat all the ingredients with the oil. Transfer the pan to the oven and roast the potatoes, stirring frequently, until golden, about 40 minutes.

🦐 Remove the potatoes from the oven. With a slotted spoon, transfer them to absorbent paper towels to drain. Arrange on a warm serving dish and serve immediately.

SERVES 6

Siena

FAGIOLI CON LE COTENNE
Pork and Beans

Cotenne is scalded pork rind with a lot of fat on it and is customarily cooked with dried beans. This dish is usually prepared during the grape harvest when the beans are fresh and everyone is very hungry.

2⅛ cups (14 oz/420 g) dried *cannellini* beans
1 handful of fresh sage leaves
10 oz (300 g) pork rind or *pancetta,* in one piece
3 garlic cloves
salt and freshly ground black pepper

🦐 In a bowl, soak the beans in cold water to cover for 12 hours.

🦐 Drain the beans and transfer them to a heavy saucepan. Add the sage and water just to cover. Bring slowly to a boil over low heat.

🦐 Simmer gently for 1½ hours, by which time the water should be absorbed and the beans will be almost the consistency of porridge.

🦐 Meanwhile, in a saucepan, combine the pork rind (or *pancetta*) with water to cover. Bring to a boil and boil until the pork rind is tender, about 50 minutes. Drain and cut into short, narrow strips.

🦐 In a large skillet over low heat, cook the pork strips and garlic until just golden, about 5 minutes. Add the cooked beans and season to taste with salt and pepper. Stir and then cook over low heat for a few minutes to allow the flavors to blend.

🦐 Pour into a serving bowl and serve hot.

SERVES 6

Pan-Tossed Broccoli Raab (left) and Pork and Beans (right)

Grosseto

TEGAMATA DI PEPERONI
Red and Yellow Peppers with Tomato and Basil

The Grosseto plains are now covered with acres of tomato and pepper plants. The peppers ripen well here and are sweet and tangy.

6 large yellow and red bell peppers (capsicums), in any
    combination
3 tablespoons extra virgin olive oil
2 oz (60 g) *pancetta,* chopped
3 garlic cloves, chopped
10 oz (300 g) ripe plum (egg) tomatoes, peeled and
    chopped
salt and freshly ground black pepper
10 fresh basil leaves

❧ Preheat an oven to 350°F (180°C). Arrange the peppers in a shallow pan and bake for 10 minutes.

❧ Remove the peppers and wrap them in aluminum foil. Let stand for 10 minutes. (This step will make them easy to peel.) Peel the peppers, remove the seeds and veins and cut into narrow strips.

❧ In a skillet over moderate heat, warm the olive oil. Add the *pancetta* and fry gently until transparent, about 5 minutes. Lower the heat, add the garlic and pepper strips and cook, stirring, for 2 minutes.

❧ Add the tomatoes, stir well and season to taste with salt and pepper. Cook over low heat until the peppers have practically disintegrated and the liquid has evaporated, about 20 minutes.

❧ Uncover and sprinkle with the basil. Transfer to a serving platter and serve hot.

SERVES 6

Lucca

BIETOLE CON PINOLI
Swiss Chard and Pine Nuts

All along the coast from Viareggio to Pisa stand great woods of umbrella pines. These trees produce so many pine nuts that the nuts are exported all over Europe.

2 lb (900 g) Swiss chard (silverbeet)
3 tablespoons extra virgin olive oil
salt
1 handful of pine nuts

❧ Bring a large saucepan of lightly salted water to a boil. Meanwhile, trim off the white stalks from the green Swiss chard leaves.

❧ Add the stalks to the boiling water and boil for about 5 minutes. Add the leaves and boil for 2 minutes longer. Drain and immediately transfer to a bowl of iced water so that the leaves remain green. Drain and squeeze out any excess water.

❧ In a skillet over moderate heat, warm the olive oil. Add the chard and fry gently, stirring occasionally, for 2 or 3 minutes to allow the flavors to blend. Season to taste with salt and pepper.

❧ Arrange the chard on a platter and sprinkle with the pine nuts. Serve hot.

SERVES 6

Siena

PATATE ALL'UMIDO
Potatoes Braised in White Wine

These potatoes are braised in white wine and seasoned with rosemary. In some kitchens, a little tomato paste is added. They are an excellent accompaniment to meat loaf or stew.

1 tablespoon tomato paste
¼ cup (2 fl oz/60 ml) light meat stock (recipe on page 73)
3 tablespoons extra virgin olive oil
3 garlic cloves
1 fresh rosemary sprig
2 lb (900 g) boiling potatoes, peeled and sliced about ⅛ in
    (3 mm) thick
1 cup (8 fl oz/240 ml) dry white wine
salt and freshly ground black pepper

❧ Dissolve the tomato paste in the stock and set aside.

❧ In a heavy saucepan over moderate heat, warm the olive oil. Add the garlic, rosemary and potatoes and cook until the garlic is just golden, about 5 minutes.

❧ Pour in the wine, lower the heat and continue cooking gently. As the liquid evaporates, gradually add the stock to keep the contents moist.

❧ After about 20 minutes, the potatoes should be tender. Season to taste with salt and pepper.

❧ Remove and discard the garlic and rosemary. Serve very hot.

SERVES 6   *Photograph pages 184–185*

Lucca

FRISSOGLIA
Green Beans and Zucchini with Flowers

In Lucchesia zucchini are picked when very young. Their flowers are considered a great delicacy. Here the zucchini are cooked with green beans and tomato and flavored with fresh basil.

10 oz (300 g) unopened zucchini (courgette) flowers
⅓ cup (3 fl oz/90 ml) extra virgin olive oil
1 garlic clove, chopped
10 oz (300 g) small zucchini (courgettes), trimmed and sliced
    ⅛ in (3 mm) thick
10 oz (300 g) plum (egg) tomatoes, peeled and chopped
10 oz (300 g) green beans, trimmed
1 tablespoon fresh basil leaves
salt and freshly ground black pepper

❧ With a small, sharp knife, make a small incision in the side of each flower and remove the pistil. Cut off the stalk and set aside.

❧ In a skillet over moderate heat, warm the olive oil. Add the garlic and zucchini and fry gently, turning the zucchini occasionally, until lightly golden, about 10 minutes. Remove the zucchini from the skillet and set aside.

❧ Add the tomatoes, green beans and zucchini flowers to the skillet and stir well. Lower the heat and cook until nearly all the liquid evaporates, about 10 minutes.

❧ Return the zucchini to the skillet and add the basil. Stir and then cook over low heat for 2 minutes to allow the flavors to blend. Season to taste with salt and pepper.

❧ Transfer to a serving bowl and serve hot.

SERVES 6

Red and Yellow Peppers with Tomato and Basil, Swiss Chard and Pine Nuts, and Green Beans and Zucchini with Flowers (rear)

FIORI DI ZUCCA

Stuffed Zucchini Flowers

Throughout spring and summer small bunches of zucchini flowers are available in all the markets of Tuscany. They are fried or stuffed. Anchovy makes a good contrast to the bloom's delicate flavor. Be sure to buy flowers that are still closed.

3 tablespoons extra virgin olive oil
36 unopened zucchini (courgette) flowers
5 oz (150 g) canned flat anchovy fillets in olive oil, drained
½ cup (2 oz/60 g) fine dry bread crumbs
freshly ground black pepper

🔥 Preheat an oven to 350°F (180°C). Brush a 20-by-12-in (50-by-30-cm) baking dish with half of the olive oil.

🔥 With a small, sharp knife, make a small incision in the side of each flower and remove the pistil. Cut off the stalk.

🔥 In a small bowl, combine the anchovies, bread crumbs and a touch of pepper and mash together to blend well. Carefully open the incision in each flower and insert a little of the anchovy mixture. Squeeze the opening closed.

🔥 Arrange the zucchini flowers in one layer in the prepared baking dish and sprinkle with the remaining olive oil. Cover the dish with aluminum foil and bake until the flowers and their stuffing are sizzling hot, about 15 minutes.

🔥 Arrange the flowers on a warm serving dish. Serve very hot.

SERVES 6

6 tablespoons (3 fl oz/90 ml) water
salt and freshly ground black pepper

🍋 In a saucepan over low heat, cook the *pancetta* until the fat is rendered. Add the peas, olive oil, sugar, onion and the water and stir well. Season to taste with salt and pepper.
🍋 Bring the peas to a gentle boil over low heat and cook until the water evaporates, about 20 minutes.
🍋 Transfer to a serving dish and serve hot.

SERVES 6

Left to right: Bean Purée, Stuffed Zucchini Flowers, Green Peas with Pancetta, and Grilled Mushrooms

Firenze

PISELLI ALL'OLIO

Green Peas with Pancetta

The tiny, tender and sweet peas of Tuscany are cooked with a little sugar for quite a long time in this recipe. This permits the peas to absorb the flavor of the oil and pancetta. *They lose a little color but acquire an intense bouquet.*

2 oz (60 g) *pancetta*, chopped
7 cups (2 lb/900 g) shelled peas
3 tablespoons extra virgin olive oil
1 teaspoon granulated sugar
2 thin slices yellow onion

Siena

FUNGHI IN GRATELLA

Grilled Mushrooms

This is the simplest and tastiest way to prepare truly fresh mushrooms. If the stalks are not perfect, cook only the caps.

2 lb (900 g) fresh *porcini* mushrooms or *shiitake* mushrooms
2 garlic cloves, chopped
3 tablespoons extra virgin olive oil
1 tablespoon fresh calamint or thyme
salt and freshly ground black pepper

🍋 Prepare a fire in a charcoal grill or preheat a broiler (grill).
🍋 Trim off the ends of the mushroom stems. Clean the mushrooms by wiping them with a damp cloth; do not wash them. Cut the mushrooms into slices about ¼ in (6 mm) thick.
🍋 In a cup, combine the garlic, olive oil, calamint and salt and pepper to taste. Stir well. Brush the mushrooms with this mixture.
🍋 Arrange the mushrooms on the grill or on a broiler pan (grill tray) and position them so that they are not too close to the source of heat. Grill for 3 minutes. Turn the mushrooms over and grill for another 3 minutes. Serve very hot.

SERVES 6

Firenze

PASSATO DI FAGIOLI

Bean Purée

In Florence puréed beans are served with a variety of meat dishes, in much the same way mashed potatoes are in other regions of Italy. In less traditional kitchens, the same purée is often used for stuffing ravioli or, diluted with stock and a little melted butter, as an excellent sauce on tagliatelle or vegetables.

2⅛ cups (14 oz/420 g) dried *cannellini* beans
1 handful of fresh sage leaves
6 tablespoons (3 fl oz/90 ml) extra virgin olive oil
salt and freshly ground black pepper

🍋 In a bowl, soak the beans in water to cover for 12 hours.
🍋 Drain the beans and place them in a saucepan. Add the sage and water to cover. Cover the pan and bring to a very gentle boil over low heat. Allow to simmer very slowly, until tender, about 1½ hours.
🍋 Remove the beans from the pan and put them through a food mill fitted with a fine disc. Pour 3 tablespoons of the olive oil into a skillet, add the bean purée and place over low heat. Cook, stirring constantly, for a few minutes to allow the moisture to evaporate. Season to taste with salt and pepper.
🍋 Transfer the purée to a serving dish, sprinkle with the remaining 3 tablespoons olive oil and serve hot.

SERVES 6

Livorno

CAVOLO ALL'ACCIUGATA

Braised Cabbage with Anchovies

Part of the large anchovy catch in this area is preserved in salt and used to season numerous dishes. Raw anchovies soaked in lemon juice are also popular.

2½ lb (1.2 kg) black cabbage or Savoy cabbage
3 tablespoons extra virgin olive oil
3 garlic cloves
1 cup (8 fl oz/240 ml) water
6 anchovies in salt
salt and freshly ground black pepper

❧ Remove and discard the hard stalks from the cabbage leaves and slice the leaves into strips about ¾ in (2 cm) wide.
❧ Bring a large saucepan of water to a boil. Add the cabbage and boil for 2 minutes. Drain and immediately transfer to a bowl of iced water so that the leaves remain green. Drain and set aside.
❧ In a heavy pot over low heat, warm the olive oil. Add the garlic and fry gently until translucent, about 5 minutes. Add the cabbage and the 1 cup of water. Cook over low heat until the water evaporates, about 30 minutes.
❧ Meanwhile, remove the heads from the anchovies. Rinse the salt off the anchovies under cold running water. Slit the bodies lengthwise along the belly and remove and discard the bones. Divide the anchovies into fillets. Add the anchovy fillets to the cabbage during the last 10 minutes of cooking.
❧ Season the cabbage lightly with salt and pepper. Arrange on a platter and serve hot.

SERVES 6

Firenze

PINZIMONIO

Vegetables Dipped in Oil

Pinzimonio is the name given to the custom of eating raw vegetables dipped in oil. A variety of vegetables such as carrots, cauliflower, artichokes and radishes may be served, or simply the fennel and Belgian endive suggested here.

1 fennel bulb
2 carrots
2 Belgian endives (witloof/chicory)
1 cup (8 fl oz/240 ml) extra virgin olive oil
salt and freshly ground black pepper

❧ Trim the base of the fennel bulb and cut the bulb into 6 wedges. Peel the carrots and cut them into slender sticks. Trim the Belgian endive and separate the leaves.
❧ Arrange the vegetables on a serving dish. Divide the oil among 6 little bowls. Season each portion with a touch of salt and pepper.
❧ Place the dish of vegetables in the center of the table and pass around the bowls of oil.

SERVES 6

Braised Cabbage with Anchovies

Vegetables Dipped in Oil

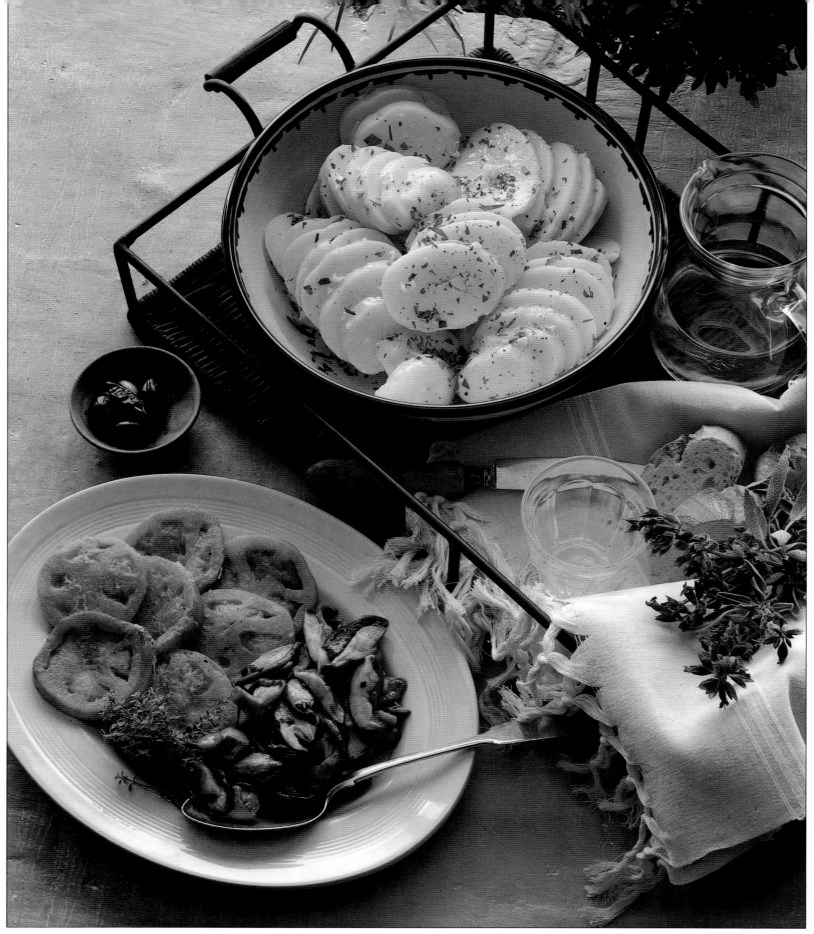

Parslied Potatoes (top), Fried Green Tomatoes and Braised Mushrooms (bottom)

Lucca

POMODORI FRITTI

Fried Green Tomatoes

Slightly sour, hard green tomatoes with very little juice are used in this dish. The golden fried slices are excellent served with boiled meats.

6 large unripe, green tomatoes
salt
⅔ cup (3 oz/90 g) all-purpose (plain) flour
5 cups (40 fl oz/1.2 l) extra virgin olive oil for frying

🍃 Cut the tomatoes into slices about ¾ in (2 cm) thick. Sprinkle the slices with salt and arrange them on a wire rack. Let drain for 2 hours.

🍃 Pat the tomato slices dry with absorbent paper towels. Pour the flour into a shallow bowl.

🍃 In a deep, heavy skillet, heat the olive oil to 350°F (180°C). Dip the tomato slices in the flour, coating well on both sides. A few at a time, slip the slices into the hot oil without crowding the pan. Fry until golden, about 5 minutes. With a slotted spoon, remove the slices to absorbent paper towels to drain briefly. Continue frying the remaining slices in the same manner.

🍃 Transfer the tomato slices to a serving plate and sprinkle with salt. Serve very hot.

SERVES 6

PATATE AL PREZZEMOLO
Parslied Potatoes

This dish offers a good way to enjoy the extraordinary flavor of the olive oil produced near Lucca. The potatoes go well with an omelet or cold meats in the summer.

2 lb (900 g) boiling potatoes
salt and freshly ground black pepper
½ tablespoon white wine vinegar
1 garlic clove, chopped
⅓ cup (3 fl oz/90 ml) extra virgin olive oil
1 tablespoon chopped fresh flat-leaf (Italian) parsley

❦ In a saucepan, boil the unpeeled potatoes in salted water to cover until tender, about 30 minutes. Drain the potatoes and peel them. Let cool to room temperature.
❦ Cut the potatoes crosswise into slices ¼ in (5 mm) thick. Transfer the slices to a salad bowl.
❦ In a small bowl, dissolve salt and pepper to taste in the vinegar and mix in the garlic. Sprinkle the vinegar mixture over the potatoes. Drizzle the olive oil over the potatoes and stir gently to mix well; be careful not to break up the potatoes.
❦ Sprinkle the parsley over the top and serve at room temperature.

SERVES 6

CARCIOFI IN TEGAME
Pan-Roasted Artichokes

For this recipe, the artichokes are always prepared in an earthenware pan, which cooks them gently at a low temperature. If you use an ordinary skillet, they should be transferred to a warm dish for serving. In Lucchesia the artichokes are fairly large but quite tender.

juice of 1 lemon
6 globe artichokes
3 tablespoons extra virgin olive oil
3 oz (90 g) *pancetta,* chopped
6 garlic cloves
1 tablespoon chopped fresh flat-leaf (Italian) parsley
salt and freshly ground black pepper

❦ Fill a large bowl with water and add the lemon juice. Cut the stalks off the artichokes. Remove the tough outer leaves and cut away the sharp leaf points from the tops. Pull the leaves apart gently and, with a spoon, scoop out and discard the prickly choke. Thinly slice the artichokes lengthwise, dropping them as you do into the water to prevent discoloration.
❦ In a flameproof earthenware casserole over moderate heat, warm the olive oil. Add the *pancetta* and garlic and fry gently, stirring occasionally, until just golden, about 5 minutes.
❦ Meanwhile, drain the artichoke slices and pat them dry with absorbent paper towels. Add them to the casserole, sprinkle with the parsley and season to taste with salt and pepper. Cover, lower the heat and cook gently until tender, about 15 minutes, adding a little water to keep the artichokes moist.
❦ Remove and discard the garlic and serve immediately from the casserole.

SERVES 6

FUNGHI IN UMIDO
Braised Mushrooms

At the end of the summer, after the first rains, women carrying baskets of mushrooms walk along the beaches of the Versilia coast and call out, "Bei funghi, funghi morecci"—"beautiful mushrooms, morecci mushrooms." Morecci are the finest porcini, *with dark caps and firm white stalks.*

2 lb (900 g) fresh *porcini* mushrooms or *shiitake* mushrooms
⅓ cup (3 fl oz/90 ml) extra virgin olive oil
2 garlic cloves
1 tablespoon fresh calamint or chopped fresh flat-leaf (Italian) parsley
⅓ cup (3 fl oz/90 ml) dry white wine
salt and freshly ground black pepper
1 tablespoon tomato paste

❦ Trim off and discard the ends of the mushroom stems and then cut off the stems and set aside. Clean the mushrooms by wiping them with a dampened cloth; do not wash them. Cut the mushroom caps vertically into slices about ⅛ in (3 mm) thick; cut the stalks horizontally into slices about ⅛ in (3 mm) thick.
❦ In a skillet over moderate heat, warm the olive oil. Add the garlic and fry gently until translucent, about 3 minutes. Add the mushrooms and the calamint and cook, stirring occasionally, for 5 minutes. Add the wine and season to taste with salt and pepper. Stir in the tomato paste, lower the heat and cook for a few more minutes.
❦ Remove and discard the garlic. Transfer the mushrooms to a serving dish and serve at once.

SERVES 6

Pan-Roasted Artichokes

Livorno

CECI DI MAGRO

Chick-peas with Salt Cod

Traditionally this dish is served on Fridays, which for hundreds of years was a meatless day in Catholic countries. It is substantial enough to be offered as a main course.

10 oz (300 g) salt cod
1½ cups (10 oz/300 g) dried chick-peas (garbanzos)
1 fresh rosemary sprig
⅓ cup (3 fl oz/90 ml) extra virgin olive oil
1 garlic clove
10 oz (300 g) plum (egg) tomatoes, peeled and chopped
freshly ground black pepper

🌶 Soak the salt cod in water to cover in the refrigerator for 24 hours, changing the water 3 or 4 times.
🌶 Meanwhile, soak the chick-peas in water to cover for 12 hours.
🌶 Drain the chick-peas and place them in a heavy pot. Add the rosemary and water to cover and bring slowly to a boil over low heat. Simmer gently until the chick-peas are tender, about 1½ hours. Drain and set aside.
🌶 Drain the salt cod and remove and discard the skin and bones. Slice into fairly large pieces and set aside.
🌶 In a heavy pot over moderate heat, warm the olive oil. Add the garlic and salt cod and fry gently, turning once, until the cod is golden on both sides, about 5 minutes. Add the chick-peas and tomatoes and season to taste with pepper only, as the fish is salty. Lower the heat and cook until the liquid from the tomatoes evaporates, about 20 minutes.
🌶 Arrange on a serving platter and serve hot.

SERVES 6

Chick-peas with Salt Cod

FAGIOLI CON LA BOTTARGA

Beans with Fish Roe

*Bottarga, a great delicacy, is salted fish roe, usually tuna,
pressed and left to mature for at least six months. It is always
sliced very finely and is sometimes dressed with oil and lemon
and served on canapés. Bottarga is also served with pasta. If
unavailable, black lumpfish roe is a good substitute.*

2⅛ cups (14 oz/420 g) dried *cannellini* beans
salt and freshly ground black pepper
¼ cup (2 fl oz/60 ml) extra virgin olive oil
3 oz (90 g) *bottarga,* sliced paper thin, or lumpfish roe
juice of ½ lemon

🍂 In a bowl, soak the beans in water to cover for 12 hours.
🍂 Drain the beans and transfer them to a heavy pot. Add
water to cover by ⅓ in (1 cm) and bring slowly to a boil over
low heat. Simmer gently for 1½ hours, by which time the
water should be absorbed and the beans will be almost the
consistency of porridge.
🍂 Season the beans to taste with salt and pepper. Transfer to
a serving platter and add the olive oil and *bottarga* (or lumpfish
roe). Mix gently. Sprinkle with the lemon juice and serve.

SERVES 6

PATATE AL RAMERINO

Baked Potatoes with Rosemary

*Strongly scented rosemary grows wild all along the Livorno coast
and shows up in many local dishes.*

12 small baking potatoes
12 small fresh rosemary sprigs
salt and freshly ground black pepper
2 tablespoons extra virgin olive oil

🍂 Preheat an oven to 350°F (180°C).
🍂 Cut each unpeeled potato lengthwise, about three quarters of
the way through the center. Insert a sprig of rosemary into each
incision. Sprinkle the potatoes with salt and pepper to taste.
🍂 Pour the olive oil into a baking dish in which the potatoes
will fit without crowding. Add the potatoes and roll them in
the oil to coat all sides. Bake until the potatoes are tender,
about 1 hour. Serve immediately.

SERVES 6

FRITTURA DI ZUCCHINE

Deep-Fried Zucchini

*Deep-fried vegetables are superb in Livorno because they are
always fried in the best available extra virgin olive oil. Fried
zucchini and baby squid are a traditional Livornese combination.*

2 lb (900 g) small zucchini (courgettes)
⅔ cup (3 oz/90 g) all-purpose (plain) flour
5 cups (40 fl oz/1.2 l) extra virgin olive oil
salt

*Baked Potatoes with Rosemary, Deep-Fried Zucchini,
and Beans with Fish Roe*

🍂 Trim the ends off the zucchini and cut in half lengthwise.
Scoop out and discard the seeds if large. Cut the zucchini into
strips 2⅜ in (6 cm) long and ⅓ in (1 cm) thick. Place in a bowl
and add iced water to cover. Let stand for 1 hour in the
refrigerator. Drain and dry on absorbent paper towels. (This
procedure keeps the zucchini strips crisp.)
🍂 Sprinkle the zucchini strips with the flour and shake off any
excess. Meanwhile, in a deep, heavy skillet, heat the olive oil
to 350°F (180°C). A few at a time, slip the zucchini strips into
the hot oil without crowding the pan. Fry until golden, about
3 minutes. With a slotted spoon, remove the strips to absorbent paper towels to drain. Continue frying the remaining
strips in the same manner.
🍂 Arrange the zucchini strips on a serving plate and sprinkle
with salt. Serve hot.

SERVES 6

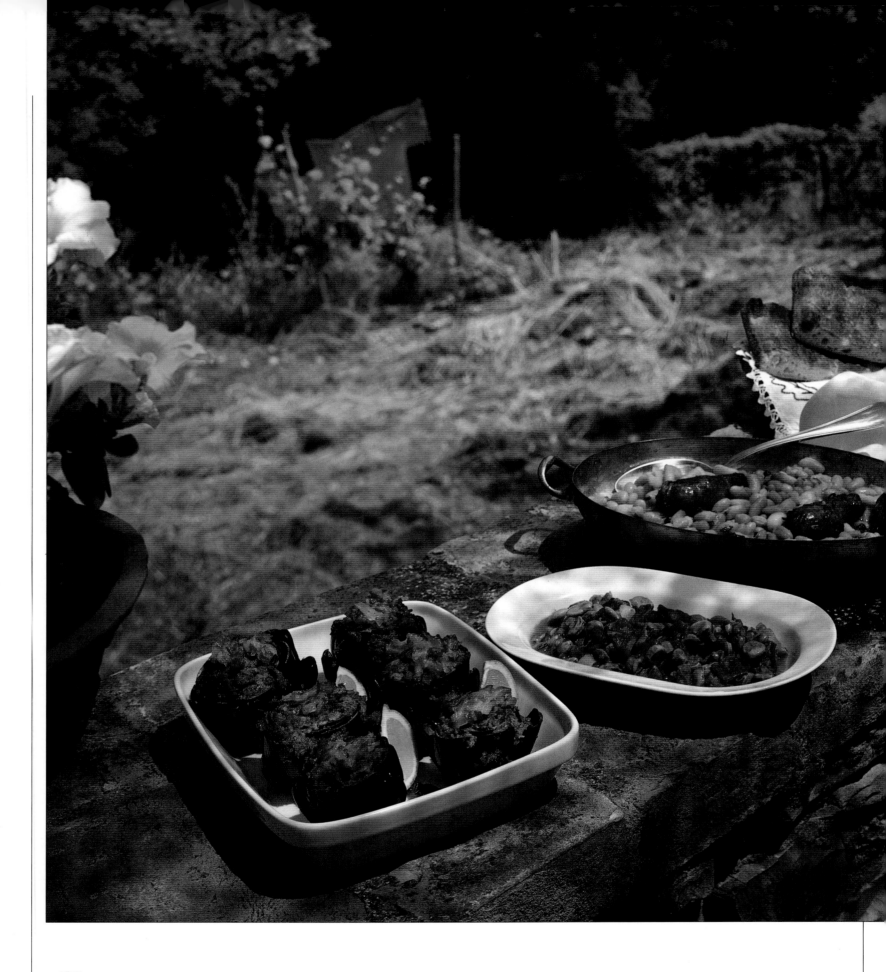

Carciofi Ritti

Upright Artichokes

These artichokes are so-called because they are stuffed and cooked standing up, side by side. The stuffing varies and may be made with sweetbreads, sausage, anchovies, chopped meat or whatever is on hand.

1 slice crustless coarse country bread
1 cup (8 fl oz/240 ml) milk
juice of ½ lemon
6 globe artichokes
2 tablespoons chopped fresh flat-leaf (Italian) parsley

1 tablespoon chopped fresh calamint or mint
1 garlic clove, finely chopped
2 oz (60 g) *pancetta,* chopped
salt and freshly ground black pepper
2 tablespoons extra virgin olive oil
2 tablespoons water

🍃 In a bowl, soak the bread in the milk for 10 minutes. Drain and squeeze out the excess milk.
🍃 Fill a large bowl with water and add the lemon juice. Cut the stalks off the artichokes. Peel the stalks so that only the tender inner part remains, then slice them finely and drop them into the water to prevent discoloration. Remove the tough outer leaves and cut away the sharp leaf points from the tops of the artichokes. Pull the leaves apart gently and, with a spoon, scoop out and discard the prickly choke. Drop

Left to right: Upright Artichokes, Broad Beans with Ham,
and Beans with Sausage

FAGIOLI CON SALSICCE

Beans with Sausage

*The marriage of two of Siena's finest ingredients makes for a
superb dish. Sienese sausages are fairly lean because a little veal is
added to the pork.*

1½ cups (10 oz/300 g) dried *cannellini* beans
1 garlic clove
1 handful of fresh sage leaves
3 tablespoons extra virgin olive oil
1¼ lb (600 g) sweet Italian sausages
1 tablespoon red wine vinegar
salt and freshly ground black pepper

❧ In a bowl, soak the beans in water to cover for 12 hours.
❧ Drain the beans and transfer them to a heavy pot. Add
the garlic, sage, 1 tablespoon of the olive oil and water just
to cover. Bring slowly to a boil over low heat. Simmer
gently for about 1½ hours, by which time the water should
be absorbed and the beans will be almost the consistency of
porridge.
❧ In a heavy pot over moderate heat, warm the remaining 2
tablespoons olive oil. Add the sausages and cook until browned
on all sides, about 10 minutes.
❧ Add the vinegar and cook until it evaporates, about 2
minutes.
❧ Skim the excess fat from the sausages. Add the beans and
lower the heat. Cover and cook for about 5 minutes to allow
the flavors to blend. Season to taste with salt and pepper.
❧ Transfer the beans and sausages to a warm platter and
serve hot.

SERVES 6

BACCELLI AL PROSCIUTTO

Broad Beans with Ham

*Tuscan broad (fava) beans are more tender than most other broad
beans, so they are shelled and cooked without removing the
bean's thin outer skin, which is very sweet. If the outer skins of the
beans are tough they should be removed, in which case you will
need an additional 1 lb (480 g) for this recipe. Broad beans are
often eaten raw with pecorino cheese at the end of a meal or
cooked and served as an accompaniment to white meats like
chicken or turkey.*

3 tablespoons extra virgin olive oil
1 small yellow onion, sliced
3 oz (90 g) *prosciutto,* diced
3½ cups (2 lb/900 g) shelled broad (fava) beans or 4¼ lb
    (2.1 kg) unshelled
3 plum (egg) tomatoes, peeled and chopped
¼ cup (2 fl oz/60 ml) dry white wine
salt and freshly ground black pepper

❧ In a saucepan over low heat, warm the olive oil. Add the
onion and fry gently, stirring, until translucent, about 5 minutes. Add the *prosciutto* and cook, stirring, for 2 minutes. Add
the beans, tomatoes and wine and season to taste with salt and
pepper. Cook over low heat until the beans are tender and
most of the liquid evaporates, about 10 minutes.
❧ Transfer the beans to a platter and serve hot.

SERVES 6

the artichokes into the water.
❧ Finely chop the bread and sliced artichoke stalks. In a small
bowl, combine the bread, artichoke stalks, parsley, calamint,
garlic and *pancetta.* Mix well and season to taste with salt and
pepper.
❧ Push the artichoke leaves slightly apart and stuff the bread
mixture in between the rows of leaves.
❧ Pour the oil into a shallow pan large enough to hold the
artichokes upright in a single layer. Arrange the artichokes
side by side, stem end down. Add the water and cover the pan.
Cook over low heat, occasionally adding a little water to keep
the contents moist, until the artichokes are tender, about 20
minutes.
❧ Arrange them on a serving platter and serve hot.

SERVES 6

FAGIOLI AL FORNO

Baked Beans

Beans taste best when they are cooked very, very slowly. Traditionally they are put into old wine flasks from which the straw covering has been removed and nestled overnight in hot embers. By morning the beans are perfectly cooked. They can, however, also be baked successfully.

2⅛ cups (14 oz/420 g) dried *cannellini* beans
1 handful of fresh sage leaves
1 tablespoon extra virgin olive oil
salt and freshly ground black pepper

� In a bowl, soak the beans in water to cover for 12 hours.
🌱 Preheat an oven to 250°F (120°C).
🌱 Drain the beans and place them in an ovenproof pot, preferably of earthenware. Mix in the sage and sprinkle with the olive oil. Pour in water to cover the beans by about ½ in (12 mm). Cover, place in the oven and slowly bring to a boil.
🌱 When the beans begin to boil, reduce the heat to 225°F (100°C) and simmer very gently until they are tender and have absorbed nearly all the water, about 3 hours.
🌱 The beans should still be slightly soupy when they are done. Season to taste with salt and pepper. Serve hot.

SERVES 6

SEDANI AL SUGO DI CARNE

Celery with Meat Sauce

This is another of those dishes that, during the winter, when celery is at its best, the farmers take to the fields for their lunch and eat with a chunk of hearty salt-free Tuscan bread.

2½ lb (1.2 kg) white celery
3 tablespoons extra virgin olive oil
1 garlic clove, finely chopped
1 tablespoon finely chopped yellow onion
2 oz (60 g) *pancetta,* coarsely chopped
3 oz (90 g) sweet Italian sausages, skinned and crumbled
3 oz (90 g) beef, coarsely chopped
3 oz (90 g) pork, coarsely chopped
1 tablespoon finely chopped fresh flat-leaf (Italian) parsley
1 cup (8 fl oz/240 ml) dry white wine
1 large plum (egg) tomato, peeled and coarsely chopped
salt and freshly ground black pepper

🌱 Break off the celery stalks. With a small knife, remove the strings and cut off and discard the leaves. Cut the stalks into 2-in (5-cm) lengths; set aside.
🌱 In a heavy saucepan over moderate heat, warm the olive oil. Add the garlic, onion, *pancetta,* sausage, beef and pork and fry, stirring frequently, for 5 minutes. Add the parsley and wine and cook until the liquid evaporates, about 10 minutes.
🌱 Add the tomato and celery. Season to taste with salt and pepper, cover and cook over low heat until the celery is tender, about 20 minutes, adding a little water if the pan becomes too dry.
🌱 Arrange on a platter and serve hot.

SERVES 6

Baked Beans (left) and Celery with Meat Sauce (right)

Sautéed Green Beans (top) and Swiss Chard with Lemon Dressing (bottom)

BIETE ALL'AGRO DI LIMONE

Swiss Chard with Lemon Dressing

This is an excellent preparation for other green vegetables as well, especially spinach and young broccoli raab.

2 lb (900 g) Swiss chard (silverbeet)
salt and freshly ground black pepper
2 tablespoons fresh lemon juice
½ cup (4 fl oz/120 ml) extra virgin olive oil

🌢 Bring a large saucepan of lightly salted water to a boil. Meanwhile, trim off the white stalks from the green Swiss chard leaves. Cut the stalks into pieces 2 in (5 cm) long, removing any strings.
🌢 Add the stalks to the boiling water and boil for about 5 minutes. Add the leaves and cook for 2 minutes longer. Drain and immediately transfer to a bowl of iced water so that the leaves remain green. Drain and pat dry with absorbent paper towels.
🌢 Arrange the Swiss chard in a serving dish. In a small bowl, dissolve salt and pepper to taste in the lemon juice. Sprinkle the lemon juice mixture over the Swiss chard. Drizzle the olive oil over the Swiss chard and stir well. Serve warm or at room temperature.

SERVES 6

broiler and grill, turning to cook evenly and brushing them with more of the oil mixture, until tender, about 10 minutes.

🏵 Arrange the cardoons on a serving plate. Serve hot.

SERVES 6

Arezzo

GOBBI IN GRATELLA

Grilled Cardoons

Tuscans call cardoons gobbi, *or "hunchbacks," because they are curved. They flourish here as they need little water. In one of his best-known poems, Tuscan-born Giosue Carducci, who won the Nobel Prize in 1906, describes a gray donkey munching cardoons.*

juice of 1 lemon
4 lb (1.8 kg) cardoons
1 tablespoon all-purpose (plain) flour
3 tablespoons extra virgin olive oil
salt and freshly ground black pepper

🏵 Preheat a broiler (grill).

🏵 Fill a large bowl with water and add the lemon juice. Remove and discard the base from each cardoon and discard any tough stalks. Trim and discard the leaves and spurs from the tender stalks and then scrape the stalks with a small knife to remove all strings and fibers. Cut each stalk crosswise into pieces 2 in (5 cm) long and immediately drop them into the water to prevent discoloration.

🏵 Bring a large saucepan of lightly salted water to a boil. Drain the cardoons and drop them into the boiling water. Sprinkle the surface of the water with the flour to keep the cardoons from darkening. Boil the cardoons for 5 minutes. Drain well and dry with absorbent paper towels.

🏵 In a small bowl, mix together the olive oil and salt and pepper to taste.

🏵 Arrange the cardoons on a broiler pan (grill tray) and brush them with some of the oil mixture. Slip the cardoons under the

Grosseto

FAGIOLINI RIPASSATI IN PADELLA

Sautéed Green Beans

Because green beans take so long to string, cooks often prepare a large quantity at a time for more than one meal. The beans are boiled and then seasoned with fresh olive oil for the first day, and the following day the leftover cooked beans are sautéed with tomatoes.

3 tablespoons extra virgin olive oil
3 garlic cloves, chopped
2 lb (900 g) green beans, blanched 2 minutes and drained
1 lb (480 g) plum (egg) tomatoes, peeled and chopped
1 tablespoon fresh marjoram leaves
salt and freshly ground black pepper

🏵 In a heavy pot over low heat, warm the olive oil. Add the garlic and fry gently until translucent, about 5 minutes. Add the beans, tomatoes, marjoram and salt and pepper to taste. Cook over low heat until the liquid evaporates, about 20 minutes.

🏵 Transfer the green beans to a platter and serve hot.

SERVES 6

Grilled Cardoons

GROSSETO

GROSSETO

Grosseto is the largest city in the region of western Tuscany known as the Maremma. *"Sia maledetta Maremma . . . Maremma amara,"* an old Tuscan folk song goes. "Maremma be damned . . . Maremma the bitter." The coast of the Maremma was, in fact, until the early 1900s, a malarial and bandit-ridden swamp. Throughout the eighteenth and nineteenth centuries, travelers forced to cross it in order to get to Rome hastened through as fast as their horses would carry them. Nevertheless, since Etruscan times this stretch of indescribably beautiful untamed land lying between the sea and the mountains has been rich in towns, villages and culture.

When the Medicis ruled Tuscany, they reclaimed some of the land with highly advanced drainage systems. Then, at the beginning of this century, all the swamps were drained and a dangerous mosquito-infested coast was transformed into a rich and fertile plain. Since then, the Maremma coast has become one of the most exclusive in Italy. Sadly, some of the coastline was spoiled by overdevelopment, but other parts were spared and are still intact.

Now recognized as a wetland of international value, the Maremma is still enchanting. Orbetello, where there is a lagoon protected by two narrow strips of land, is a fascinating place. The early Romans installed a system of nets there for catching eels, which are even now a specialty of the region. And in 1544, a chronicler reported

Left: A familiar dot on the landscape, the olive trees of Tuscany produce the finest oil in Italy. The Romans introduced olives to Italy; before then olive oil was imported from Greece. Previous pages: Some of Italy's most luxurious pleasure craft are moored at Porto Ercole, an exclusive resort on the south of the Argentario peninsula.

that the area was "swarming with very good mullet, eels and a variety of other fish."

The Argentario, some 2100 feet of granite cliffs rising straight out of the sea, is just as intriguing. So, too, is the pristine interior at Roselle, Saturnia, Pitigliano and Sovana—sites of the most complete Etruscan remains found to date. At the beautiful national park of Uccellina, visitors are allowed to enter at dawn if accompanied by a warden, but must leave by dusk. The park is where the *butteri*—Italian cowboys—oversee on horseback the famous herds of cattle and the last wild horses roaming free. Everywhere the Mediterranean brush is heady with the scent of tamarisk, broom and rosemary. Wild boar, stags, fallow deer and porcupines thrive undisturbed in the woods.

The Maremma cuisine, with its perfect blend of foods from the sea and the land, is equally appealing. Its fragrances and flavors are wisely mixed. This is most apparent around Grosseto, where one still senses the splendor of the past and finds its many traces, first of Etruscan and Roman influences and then those of the Middle Ages. Crossbows are no longer used for hunting and the rudimentary fishing techniques have been abandoned, but game and fish are brought to table with exactly the same enthusiasm. Around here even the simplest trattoria is nearly always a pleasant surprise. Local cooking at its very best, however, is to be found in restaurants like Leonardo Cappelli in Follonica, Buca di San Lorenzo in Grosseto, and La Bussala at Punta Ala

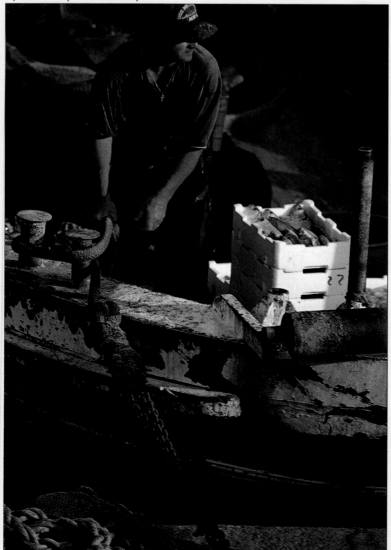

A fisherman at Porto Santo Stefano unloads his catch at the end of the day. The local waters yield an abundance of mullet, sea bass, sardines, squid, cuttlefish and shellfish.

The antipasti range from the classic cured meats to the celebrated *anguille sfumate,* smoked eel from the lagoon at Orbetello. They are called *sfumate* because they are first rubbed with ash, then threaded onto skewers between bay leaves. They are smoked in special rooms filled with smoldering scented herbs and are sprinkled with oil and vinegar. Eels are also found in many other local dishes. *Scaveccio dei bovari,* or "cowboys' halters," are fairly large eels fried with garlic, chili and rosemary and liberally sprinkled with red vinegar.

Nearly all the eels served in Italy come from the breeding grounds in the lagoon at Orbetello, including *capitone,* which is served as the traditional Christmas Eve dinner all over central Italy. A *capitone* is a large female eel just ready to enter the sea. Although eels are generally considered fresh-water fish, they are born, breed and die in the open sea. In this area, an eel soup made with tomatoes and broccoli was once the traditional Christmas lunch.

A variety of crustaceans are found around Orbetello. The most popular are called *femminelle* and are caught in the nets cast to catch eels. *Femminelle* are small crabs that make an excellent soup, and their roe is used to flavor a celebrated risotto.

The local recipe for turtle soup is fortunately no longer used. At one time a great number of turtles were found in the sea, but they are now a protected species. It is interesting to discover that there was once an everyday Tuscan turtle soup, for it is considered very exotic fare by most Italians.

Along the Argentario a typical fish soup called *caldaro* is prepared. It has a unique flavor from the limpets that are prized off the rocks and put straight into the soup with seaweed still attached to their shells, giving the concoction a strong taste of the sea.

The area also offers an excellent bean soup called Lombard soup, although it is completely unknown in Lombardy. Apparently it was first made in the eighteenth century by men from that region who came to work on reclaiming the land.

The best known soup of the Maremma, however, is *acquacotta,* or "cooked water," which, despite its name, is much more than a simple soup. It is the symbol of generations of poverty, when *acquacotta* was just bread, water and herbs. That was when the cowherds, charcoalburners and shepherds had to fill a pot with a little water, bread and whatever the season presented— garlic, an onion, or some tomato. Today there are a hundred different kinds of *acquacotta,* some with mushrooms or asparagus, others with peppers or egg. Every village, indeed every household has its own version, a firmly established family tradition so that no members ever forget the long period when their ancestors lived and died hungry.

Grosseto also enjoys rich and tasty first and second courses, such as *tortelli maremmani al sugo,* stuffed pasta with meat sauce; *pasta alla buttera condita con pancetta,* pasta with bacon sauce; *tagliolini con i fagioli o con i ceci,* fresh pasta with beans or chick-peas; and *zuppa con i funghi,* a soup made with mushrooms gathered on the mountainside. *Ciaffagnoni* is a delicate dish that comes as rather a surprise in these parts. A specialty of Manciano, the dish consists of thin pancakes filled with mushrooms and folded in half. They are as good as their better-known French cousins, crêpes.

Nevertheless, Maremma cooking is at its best with game, and above all wild boar, which have been hunted here for millennia. They grow to an enormous size, some weighing as much as 770 pounds and reaching six and a half feet in length. Wild boar is the ancestor of all domestic pigs and, at least in this area, none of it goes to waste. The cowboys even use the skins for making their saddles. It is a much sought-after hunting trophy and is cooked in many different ways between Grosseto and Rome. It can be roasted with vegetables or herbs, slightly salted, or prepared in the Renaissance manner, *dolceforte*, with a sweet and sharp sauce. In a few country stores it is still possible to find *coppiette di cinghiale*, or "wild boar pairs." They are strips of meat about six inches long that are salted, sprinkled with chili, tied together at both ends, then hung in front of the fire and smoked.

Another Maremma delicacy are *granelli*, testicles of wild boar, sheep, veal or beef. They are deep-fried, sautéed in oil and rosemary, or grilled. On wild boar hunts, the testicles are given to the huntsman who first spotted the prey. According to popular belief the wild boar testicles have a positive effect on the man who is lucky enough to eat them.

But wild boar is not the only game available in the Maremma. At one time there was an unlimited supply of pheasant and woodcock. Nowadays there are far fewer of these birds, but they are still bagged with quail, wild goose, deer and hare. Porcupine is an animal now very seldom eaten because it is protected. For centuries they were hunted because of the excellent flavor of their flesh, usually prepared in a stew, but now they are only cooked if accidentally run over by a car.

Lamb is served in many different ways all over the Maremma, whereas kid is confined to the rockier parts. A typical dish from Capalbio is *buglione d'agnello*, in which wild boar is added to chunks of lamb and stewed in tomato and white wine flavored with garlic and rosemary. At one time, kid was widely available along the rocky Argentario coast, but now fewer goats are raised.

Another Maremma dish that is just as good as its more celebrated French counterpart is *chiocciole alla maremmana*, snails sautéed with celery, onion and carrot and sprinkled with calamint or thyme.

Because there are so many vegetable soups, there is not a great tradition of other vegetable dishes. The Maremma is, however, famous for *cipolle alla grossetana*,

A shepherd with his flock near Pitigliano. Pecorino (sheep's milk cheese) is still made on small farms and vineyards throughout Tuscany.

The town of Sorano clings to its hillside. The Etruscans built their cities atop hills to protect themselves from invaders. Later, Roman and medieval additions grew on the original Etruscan sites.

onions prepared in the style of Grosseto. They are a work of art and not very easy to prepare. Onions are boiled in their skins and half emptied. The pulp is chopped and sautéed with sausage meat and chopped beef seasoned with nutmeg and cinnamon. The mixture is then bound with egg and grated sheep's milk cheese and used to stuff the onions, which are then baked. Needless to say, they are excellent.

This being a land where there never was much to spare, Grosseto and the Maremma do not have many traditional desserts. Those few that can be regarded as typical are extremely simple, such as *sfratti* (round biscuits made with honey and walnuts), *frittelle di San Giuseppe* (St. Joseph's pancakes) or candied figs. These last are usually prepared in a wood-burning oven after bread has been baked. The figs are put into a baking pan, sprinkled with sugar and honey, and moistened with a little lemon juice. Half an hour in the oven, half a glass of Vin Santo allowed to evaporate, and then, when the figs are cold, the discovery that absolute simplicity can give great delight even to the most discriminating palate.

Proof of man's triumph over a hostile countryside is provided by some excellent wines that are now produced in this area. Two names can speak for all: Pitigliano, a white wine that although of ancient origin has only made a name for itself since the 1950s, and Morellino from Scansano.

I Dolci

Panforte, *a spicy cake from Siena traditionally enjoyed at Christmastime.*

I DOLCI

There are not many Tuscan cakes and other desserts, and nearly all of them are linked to some religious celebration, such as the special biscuits served at Carnival and Easter and the traditional cakes for Halloween and Christmas. They are all very simple, their few ingredients occasionally enriched with candied citrus peel and flavored with spices.

Cenci, the traditional Carnival fritters, are direct descendants of *cincius,* which were eaten by the ancient Romans during the Saturnalia, the long orgiastic feast held every year in honor of Saturn. Made with flour and water, *cenci* have changed little in the last two thousand years. Then there are *brigidini* from Lamporecchio, large wafers so celebrated that for centuries almost every Tuscan writer has mentioned them in poetry and prose. *Brigidini* are so much a part of Tuscan life that going to a market or fair inevitably involves buying a bag of them and gobbling them one by one until they are all gone, just like popcorn.

But the real cake and sweet boom comes at Easter, when the forty days of Lent, traditionally spent doing penance and fasting, end in great gastronomic transgressions. Hence the ring cakes, sweet flat breads, rice and semolina puddings, and the sweet rosemary bread from Florence.

Sienese *pan pepato, panforte* and *ricciarelli* were all originally Christmas sweetmeats, and the *sfratti* from Sorano are said to have originated in Etruscan times. On Twelfth Night, when legend says that a witch brings presents to good children and coal to naughty ones, *befanini,* or "little witches" (large biscuits decorated with hundreds and thousands of colored pralines), are seen in abundance in Versilia and Lucchesia.

A match made in heaven: the celebrated almond biscuits from Prato are dipped in Vin Santo before eating.

Previous pages: Candied Figs (left, page 246) and Honey Cake (right, page 230).

Local cakes and biscuits are found in various parts of Tuscany. The famous biscuits of Prato, called *cantucci,* are made with almonds and are so hard that they are always dipped in a glass of Vin Santo before being eaten. In Lunigiana *spongata* is filled with honey or fig jam and sometimes with candied peel or nuts and raisins. The once-large Jewish population of Livorno introduced several traditional cakes that even now are recognized as familiar by travelers who have tasted them in various guises all over the world. *Bucellato,* Lucca's most famous cake, is flavored with aniseed. Lucca is also known for its *torta co' becchi,* pastry filled with chocolate or sweetened Swiss chard flavored with spices. In Pisa they make *torta co' bischeri,* pastry with a rice filling. At Massa and Carrara, where the country's premier marble is quarried, the locals prepare a magnificent rice cake, rich with eggs. On the feast of St. Peter the citizens of Castelnuovo di Garfagnana honor their patron saint by serving a delicious almond cake.

Since the Middle Ages many Tuscan cakes have been seasoned with aniseed because it was thought not only to give flavor, but also to ward off evil spells. In Florence cakes are often made with *alchermes,* a sweet red liqueur that the monks of Santa Maria Novella have been producing since the Medici ruled the city.

There are also innumerable Tuscan cakes and desserts made with chestnuts or chestnut flour. These go back to the days when the people living in the mountains were so poor that their staple diet was chestnuts. *Castagnaccio* is the most traditional and originally came from Lucca, although it is now made all over Tuscany. According to the *Commentario* for 1500, a certain Pilade of Lucca was the first person to make *castagnazzi,* as it was then called. Rather dry, this flat bread is at its best served with fresh ricotta. In Lucchesia roasted chestnuts sprinkled with grappa, rum or Vin Santo often end an autumn dinner.

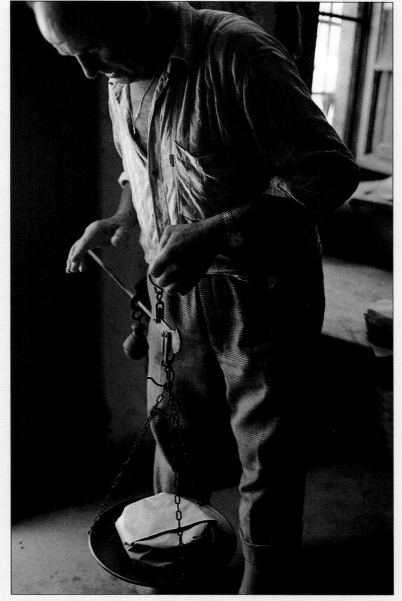

A shepherd from Pietrasanta weighs a round of pecorino *cheese. Many Tuscan meals end with a platter of cheese and fruit.*

Fresh fruit plays a starring role in local desserts. These peaches may be baked into cakes, or perhaps stuffed with meringue.

Sweet Carnival Pizza

STIACCIATA ALLA FIORENTINA

Sweet Carnival Pizza

Like most Italian cakes, this sweet Florentine pizza is linked to a religious feast: Carnival. At one time lard was used instead of butter, which added to the flavor.

¾ cup (6 fl oz/180 ml) lukewarm water (105° to 115°F/42° to 46°C)
1 oz (30 g) fresh cake yeast or 2 packages (1 scant table-spoon each) active dry yeast
2¾ cups (11 oz/330 g) all-purpose (plain) flour
pinch of salt
⅓ cup (3 oz/90 g) unsalted butter, plus extra for cake pan
⅓ cup (3 oz/90 g) granulated sugar
grated zest of 1 lemon
2 eggs
1 tablespoon confectioners' (icing) sugar

🍎 Place the lukewarm water in a small bowl. Sprinkle the yeast on top of the water and let stand until dissolved and foamy, about 10 minutes.

🍎 Heap the flour on a work surface and make a well in the center. Pour the dissolved yeast into the well and add the salt. With a fork, gradually work in the flour until all of it is absorbed. On a lightly floured surface, knead the dough until it is smooth and elastic, about 5 minutes. Shape the dough into a ball. Transfer the dough ball to a lightly floured bowl and cover with plastic wrap. Let rise at room temperature until doubled in bulk, about 2 hours.

🍎 Turn the dough out onto a floured work surface. Punch down the dough and gradually work in the ⅓ cup (3 oz/90 g) butter, granulated sugar, lemon zest and the eggs, one at a time. Lift the now-soft dough and slam it down on a hard surface several times. Using the heel of your hand, knead until the dough is no longer sticky.

🍎 Butter a 9-in (23-cm) round cake pan. Shape the dough in the

bottom of the prepared pan. Let rise at room temperature until doubled in size, about 1 hour. Meanwhile, preheat an oven to 400°F (200°C).

🍎 Bake the cake until just golden, about 30 minutes. Remove from the pan and immediately transfer to a wire rack. Sprinkle with the confectioners' sugar. Cool to room temperature before serving.

SERVES 6

CAFFÈ IN FORCHETTA

Coffee on a Fork

This pudding is called "coffee on a fork" because it is a coffee-flavored baked custard that is eaten with a fork.

1 tablespoon almond oil
4 eggs
⅓ cup (3 oz/90 g) granulated sugar
1¾ cups (14 fl oz/420 ml) milk
¼ cup (2 fl oz/60 ml) strong brewed coffee

🍎 Preheat an oven to 350°F (180°C). Brush a 9-in (23-cm) square cake pan with the almond oil.

🍎 In a bowl, whisk together the eggs and sugar until well blended and thick. Gradually whisk in the milk and coffee.

🍎 Pour the egg mixture into the prepared pan. Place the pan in a baking dish. Pour the water into the dish to a depth of 1 in (2.5 cm). Bake the pudding for 20 minutes. Cover the pan with aluminum foil and continue baking until the custard is set, about 40 minutes longer.

🍎 Remove from the oven and let cool slightly on a wire rack. Run a thin, sharp knife blade around the pan edges and invert the custard onto a platter. Serve warm.

SERVES 6

BUDINONE DI RISO

Cinnamon Rice Pudding

The Sienese have several versions of rice pudding. It is sometimes made with a little candied fruit, but the classic addition is cinnamon.

4 cups (32 fl oz/1 l) milk
1½ cups (10 oz/300 g) Arborio rice
1 tablespoon ground cinnamon
⅓ cup (3 oz/100 g) granulated sugar
6 tablespoons (3 oz/90 g) unsalted butter
3 eggs, separated

🦋 In a fairly large saucepan over moderate heat, bring the milk to a boil. Add the rice and stir well. Boil gently until all the milk is absorbed, about 30 minutes. Remove the pan from the heat and stir in the cinnamon, sugar and 5 tablespoons (2½ oz/75 g) of the butter. Let cool to room temperature. Meanwhile, preheat an oven to 350°F (180°C).

🦋 Add the egg yolks to the cold rice mixture, mixing in well. In a bowl, beat the egg whites until stiff peaks form. Fold them gently into the rice mixture.

🦋 Brush a 9-in (23-cm) round mold with the remaining 1 tablespoon butter. Press the rice mixture into the mold and smooth the top. Bake the pudding until set and lightly brown on top, about 1 hour.

🦋 Remove the pudding from the oven and let cool slightly on a wire rack. Slip a knife around the edges and invert onto a serving plate. Serve while still warm.

SERVES 6

FRITTELLE DI CREMA

Custard Fritters

At Carnival time in Siena these fritters are served hot in the cafés. They are also a popular year-round Sunday dessert.

4 eggs, separated
⅓ cup (3 oz/90 g) granulated sugar
1¼ cups (5 oz/150 g) all-purpose (plain) flour
2 cups (16 fl oz/480 ml) milk
grated zest of 1 lemon
⅔ cup (3 oz/90 g) fine dry bread crumbs
5 cups (40 fl oz/1.2 l) extra virgin olive oil for frying
1 tablespoon confectioners' (icing) sugar

🦋 Place the egg yolks in a mixing bowl. Add the granulated sugar and beat in well. Gradually add the flour, milk and lemon zest, mixing until thoroughly blended. Transfer the mixture to a shallow, heavy saucepan.

🦋 Lightly oil a large plate about 12 in (30 cm) in diameter. Place the saucepan over low heat and cook, stirring constantly, until the custard mixture begins to boil and coats a spoon. Remove the custard from the heat and pour it onto the prepared plate. It should form a layer about ⅓ in (1 cm) high. Let cool completely. When the custard is cold, slice it into 1¼-by-2-in (3-by-5-cm) rectangles. Dredge the rectangles in the bread crumbs to coat evenly on all sides.

🦋 In a deep, heavy skillet, heat the olive oil to 350°F (180°C). A few at a time, slip the rectangles into the hot oil without crowding the pan. Fry until golden, about 3 minutes. With a slotted spoon, remove to absorbent paper towels to drain briefly. Continue frying the remaining rectangles in the same manner.

🦋 Arrange the fritters on a serving dish. Sprinkle with the confectioners' sugar and serve very hot.

MAKES 20–30 FRITTERS

Custard Fritters (left) and Cinnamon Rice Pudding (right)

Sweet Bread with Fresh Grapes

PANELLO CON L'UVA

Sweet Bread with Fresh Grapes

Until very recently this recipe was made only during the grape harvest, when just-picked tiny wine grapes were available. Now, because imported grapes are in the market throughout the year, the tradition has been lost. This sweet flat bread is much tastier, however, when made with small grapes.

1 cup (8 fl oz/240 ml) lukewarm water (105° to 115°F/42° to 46°C)

1 oz (30 g) fresh cake yeast or 2 packages (1 scant tablespoon each) active dry yeast

3 cups (12 oz/360 g) all-purpose (plain) flour

¼ cup (2 oz/60 g) granulated sugar

pinch of salt

¼ cup (2 fl oz/60 ml) extra virgin olive oil

1 cup (3 oz/90 g) walnuts, chopped

10 oz (300 g) black grapes, stemmed

🍃 Place the lukewarm water in a small bowl. Sprinkle the yeast on top of the water and let stand until dissolved and foamy, about 10 minutes.

🍃 Heap the flour on a work surface and make a well in the center. Pour the dissolved yeast into the well and add the sugar and salt. With a fork, gradually work in the flour until all of it is absorbed. On a lightly floured surface, knead the dough until it is smooth and elastic, about 5 minutes. Shape the dough into a ball. Transfer the dough ball to a lightly oiled bowl, cover with plastic wrap and let rise at room temperature until doubled in bulk, about 2 hours.

🍃 Meanwhile, in a small skillet over very low heat, warm the olive oil. Add the nuts and fry gently until toasted, about 2 minutes. Remove from the heat and let the oil and nuts cool completely.

🍃 Turn the dough out onto a floured work surface. Punch down the dough and knead in the cold nuts and oil. When well mixed, shape the dough in the bottom of a round 9-in (23-cm) springform pan. Arrange the grapes on top, lightly pressing them into the dough. Let rise at room temperature until doubled in size, about 30 minutes. Meanwhile, preheat an oven to 400°F (200°C).

🍃 Bake the bread until just golden, about 30 minutes. Remove the bread from the oven and remove the pan sides. Transfer the bread to a serving plate and serve while still slightly warm.

SERVES 6

PANE TOSCANO
Tuscan White Loaf

Because Tuscan bread is saltless and keeps well, until very recently it was baked in a wood-fired oven only once a week. This is the ideal bread to use in all recipes calling for coarse country bread. It may also be seasoned with rosemary or olives and baked in a flat circle about 12 in (30 cm) in diameter. In that case, it will bake in about 20 minutes.

1 cup (8 fl oz/240 ml) lukewarm water (105° to 115°F/42° to 46°C)

1 oz (30 g) fresh cake yeast or 2 packages (1 scant table-spoon each) active dry yeast

2⅔ cups (12 oz/360 g) bread flour

❧ Place the lukewarm water in a small bowl. Sprinkle the yeast on top of the water and let stand until dissolved and foamy, about 10 minutes.

❧ Heap the flour on a work surface and make a well in the center. Pour the dissolved yeast into the well and, with a fork, gradually work in the flour until all of it is absorbed. On a lightly floured board, knead the dough until it is smooth and soft, about 5 minutes. Shape the dough into a ball. Place the dough ball in a lightly floured bowl and cover with plastic wrap. Let rise at room temperature until doubled in bulk, about 2 hours.

❧ Turn the dough out onto a floured work surface. Punch down the dough and divide it in half. Shape each half into an oval loaf about 8 in (20 cm) long.

❧ Lightly dust a baking sheet with flour and place the loaves on it. Let rise at room temperature until doubled in size, about 30 minutes. Meanwhile, preheat an oven to 400°F (200°C).

❧ Bake the bread until golden brown, about 30 minutes. Remove from the oven and let cool completely on a wire rack before slicing.

SERVES 6

BOLLI
Sweet Buns

The orange flower water and cinnamon in these buns are examples of the Middle Eastern influence present in Livorno.

1 cup (8 fl oz/240 ml) lukewarm water (105° to 115°F/42° to 46°C)

1 oz (30 g) fresh cake yeast or 2 packages (1 scant table-spoon each) active dry yeast

3 cups (12 oz/360 g) all-purpose (plain) flour

4 egg yolks

1 cup (8 oz/240 g) granulated sugar

3 tablespoons extra virgin olive oil

2 tablespoons anisette liqueur

1 tablespoon aniseed

1 teaspoon ground cinnamon

1 tablespoon orange flower water or freshly grated orange zest

1 tablespoon unsalted butter

❧ Place the lukewarm water in a medium-sized bowl. Sprinkle the yeast on top of the water and let stand until dissolved and foamy, about 10 minutes.

❧ Gradually add ⅔ cup (3 oz/90 g) of the flour to the yeast mixture, stirring constantly to prevent lumps from forming. Cover the bowl with plastic wrap and let rise at room temp-erature until doubled in bulk, about 1 hour.

❧ Heap the remaining flour on a work surface. Make a well in the center and add the yeast and flour mixture to it. With a fork, work together the yeast mixture and flour until the flour is absorbed. On a lightly floured surface, knead the dough until soft and smooth, about 5 minutes. Shape the dough into a ball. Transfer it to a lightly floured bowl. Cover with plastic wrap and let rise at room temperature until doubled in bulk, about 30 minutes.

❧ Turn the dough out onto a lightly floured work surface. Punch down the dough and add the egg yolks, one at a time. Add the sugar, the oil, anisette, aniseed, cinnamon and orange flower water (or orange zest). Knead until the dough is smooth and very soft, about 5 minutes.

❧ Grease a baking sheet with the butter and then lightly flour it. Divide the dough into pieces, each about the size of an egg, and flatten them slightly. Arrange the buns on the prepared baking sheet and let them rise at room temperature until doubled in size, about 30 minutes. Meanwhile, preheat an oven to 350°F (180°C).

❧ Bake the buns until golden, about 30 minutes. Remove to a wire rack to cool completely.

MAKES 20–30 BUNS

Tuscan White Loaf (left) and Sweet Buns (right)

DOLCE DI FARRO

Spelt Pudding

As spelt is so popular in Lucchesia, the locals prepare several different puddings with it. This particular recipe comes from the mountainous region and is especially good on cold winter evenings.

1¾ cups (10 oz/300 g) spelt
4 cups (32 fl oz/900 ml) milk
⅓ cup (3 oz/90 g) granulated sugar
4 tablespoons (2 oz/60 g) unsalted butter, plus extra for ring mold
3 eggs
¾ cup (6 oz/180 g) ricotta

🖎 In a small bowl, soak the spelt in water to cover for at least 12 hours.

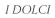

🍂 Pour the mixture into the prepared mold and smooth the top. Place the mold in a baking dish. Pour water into the dish to a depth of 1 in (2.5 cm). Bake the pudding until golden brown and firm to the touch, about 60 minutes.

🍂 Remove from the oven and let cool slightly. Serve while still warm.

SERVES 6

Arezzo

CASTAGNE UBRIACHE
Drunken Chestnuts

At one time chestnuts were widely ignored because gathering them and removing the spiky husks takes so much time. But now they are quite a luxury in the cities. They are often roasted over the fire and prepared in the following manner. This dessert is delicious served with Vin Santo or another dessert wine.

2½ lb (1.2 kg) chestnuts
1 cup (8 fl oz/240 ml) dry red wine
¼ cup (2 oz/60 g) granulated sugar

🍂 Preheat an oven to 350°F (180°C).

🍂 With a sharp knife, make a slit on the rounded side of each chestnut. Arrange the chestnuts in a single layer in a baking pan. Place in the oven and bake for 30 minutes. Remove the chestnuts from the oven.

🍂 While they are still warm, remove the hard outer shells and the furry inner skins.

🍂 In a saucepan over low heat, combine the wine and sugar. Heat, stirring to dissolve the sugar. Add the chestnuts and cook until the wine is reduced to a thick syrup, about 30 minutes.

🍂 Transfer the chestnuts to a serving dish and serve hot.

SERVES 6

Arezzo

LATTAIOLO
Baked Custard

This very simple dessert is probably the forerunner of the French crème caramel. In his book on Aretine cooking, Guido Gianni points out that originally it was made with whey rather than with milk.

few drops of almond oil
4 eggs
⅓ cup (3 oz/90 g) granulated sugar
pinch of vanilla powder or a few drops of vanilla extract
 (essence)
2 cups (16 fl oz/480 ml) milk

🍂 Preheat an oven to 350°F (180°C). Brush a 9-in (23-cm) ring mold with the almond oil.

🍂 In a mixing bowl, beat together the eggs, sugar and vanilla until well blended and thick. Gradually beat in the milk.

🍂 Pour the egg mixture into the prepared pan. Place the mold in a baking dish. Pour water into the dish to a depth of 1 in (2.5 cm). Bake the custard for 20 minutes. Cover the mold with aluminum foil and bake until the custard is set, about 40 minutes longer.

🍂 Remove from the oven and let cool slightly. Run a knife blade around the pan edges to loosen the custard, then invert onto a serving plate and let cool completely. Serve cold.

SERVES 6

Drunken Chestnuts (left), Spelt Pudding (right) and Baked Custard (rear)

🍂 Drain the spelt and place it in a heavy pot with the milk. Bring to a boil, lower the heat and simmer until all the milk has been absorbed, about 30 minutes.

🍂 Remove the pot from the heat and stir in the sugar and the 4 tablespoons (2 oz/60 g) butter. Let cool completely.

🍂 Preheat an oven to 350°F (180°C). Butter a 9-in (23-cm) ring mold.

🍂 In a bowl, whisk the eggs until well blended. Add the eggs and ricotta to the cooled spelt mixture. Blend in thoroughly.

Arezzo

Torta di Riso
Rice Cake

This cake—flatter, richer and crisper than rice pudding—may be served with a simple fruit sauce.

⅓ cup (2 oz/60 g) raisins
4 cups (32 fl oz/1 l) milk
1½ cups (10 oz/300 g) Arborio rice
pinch of salt
⅓ cup (3 oz/90 g) granulated sugar
3 oz (90 g) unsalted butter
1 tablespoon candied lemon peel, chopped
1 tablespoon candied orange peel, chopped
1 cup (3 oz/90 g) walnuts, chopped
½ cup (2 oz/60 g) fine dry bread crumbs
3 eggs, beaten

🐾 In a small bowl, soak the raisins in water to cover for 30 minutes.
🐾 Meanwhile, in a saucepan over moderate heat, bring the milk to a boil. Add the rice and simmer until the milk is absorbed and the rice is fairly dry, about 30 minutes.
🐾 Remove from the heat and add the salt, sugar and butter, saving a little to butter the cake pan. Drain the raisins and add them to the rice mixture along with the lemon and orange peels and the chopped nuts. Stir well and let cool to room temperature.
🐾 Meanwhile, preheat an oven to 350°F (180°C). Grease a 9-in (23-cm) springform pan with the remaining butter and then coat it with the bread crumbs.
🐾 When the rice mixture is completely cold, stir in the eggs. Pour the rice mixture into the prepared pan and smooth the top. Bake the cake until golden and a knife inserted in the center comes out dry, about 45 minutes.
🐾 Remove from the oven and let cool slightly. Unclip the pan sides and transfer the cake to a platter. Serve warm.
SERVES 6

Arezzo

Migliaccio al Miele
Honey Cake

In Arezzo the wheat flour in this very simple cake is sometimes replaced by cornmeal or chestnut flour.

2 tablespoons extra virgin olive oil
2½ cups (10 oz/300 g) all-purpose (plain) flour
¾ cup (6 fl oz/180 ml) milk
2 eggs, beaten
pinch of salt
½ cup (5 oz/155 g) honey, preferably chestnut

🐾 Preheat an oven to 350°F (180°C). Brush a 9-in (23-cm) square baking pan with the olive oil.
🐾 Pour the flour into a bowl. Gradually add the milk, whisking continuously to prevent lumps from forming. Stir in the eggs and salt. Pour the milk mixture into the prepared pan. Bake the cake until golden, about 40 minutes.
🐾 Remove from the oven and let cool slightly on a wire rack. Run a knife blade around the pan edges to loosen the cake, then invert onto a platter. Pour the honey on top. Serve warm.
SERVES 6 · *Photograph pages 218–219*

Rice Cake

Ring Cake

BUCCELLATO

Ring Cake

Here is Lucca's classic cake, which may be flavored with either aniseed or raisins. Traditionally, godparents would give a buccellato to their godchildren on confirmation day. This recipe is from Ristorante La Mora in Ponte a Moriano.

6 tablespoons (3 fl oz/90 ml) lukewarm water (105° to 115°F/42° to 46°C)

1 oz (30 g) fresh cake yeast or 2 packages (1 scant tablespoon each) active dry yeast

3 cups (12 oz/360 g) all-purpose (plain) flour

unsalted butter for ring mold, plus 3 tablespoons (1½ oz/ 45 g), softened

pinch of salt

⅔ cup (5 fl oz/150 ml) milk

2 whole eggs, plus 1 egg white

1 teaspoon aniseed

½ cup (4 oz/120 g) granulated sugar

🦐 Place the lukewarm water in a medium-sized bowl. Sprinkle the yeast on top of the water and let stand until dissolved and foamy, about 10 minutes.

🦐 Gradually add ½ cup (2 oz/60 g) of the flour to the yeast mixture, stirring constantly to prevent lumps from forming. Cover the bowl with plastic wrap and let rise at room temperature until doubled in bulk, about 2 hours.

🦐 Preheat an oven to 350°F (180°C). Butter a 9-in (23-cm) ring mold.

🦐 Add the salt to the remaining flour and heap it on a work surface. Make a well in the center and pour in the milk, the 2 whole eggs, aniseed, softened butter, sugar and the raised dough. With a fork, gradually work in the flour until all of it is absorbed. On a lightly floured work surface, knead the dough until it is soft and smooth, about 5 minutes.

🦐 Shape the dough in the prepared ring mold and brush the top with the egg white. Bake the cake until well risen and golden, about 45 minutes.

🦐 Remove from the oven and let cool completely on a wire rack. Remove from the pan and place on a serving plate. Serve at room temperature.

SERVES 6

CANTUCCINI
Almond Cookies of Prato

Cantuccini are a specialty of Prato, a city near Florence famous for its textiles and its cookies. Commercially produced cookies from Prato are now exported all over the world, but the homemade variety is infinitely superior. They should be dunked in a glass of sweet, amber Vin Santo before being nibbled.

unsalted butter for baking sheet
2½ cups (10 oz/300 g) all-purpose (plain) flour
¾ cup (6 oz/180 g) sugar
1½ teaspoons baking powder
2 whole eggs, plus 2 egg yolks
pinch of salt
¾ cup (4 oz/120 g) almonds, coarsely chopped
1 tablespoon milk

❧ Preheat an oven to 350°F (180°C). Butter and lightly flour a baking sheet.
❧ In a mixing bowl, combine the flour, sugar, baking powder, whole eggs, 1 of the egg yolks and the salt. Stir until a soft dough forms. Add the almonds and mix until they are evenly distributed. Divide the dough into equal portions and place them on a lightly floured work surface. Using the palms of your hands, roll each dough portion into a sausage shape about 1 in (2.5 cm) in diameter and 12 in (30 cm) long.
❧ In a small bowl, mix together the milk and the remaining egg yolk. Brush the dough rolls with the milk mixture.
❧ Arrange the dough rolls on the prepared baking sheet and bake until golden, about 20 minutes.
❧ Remove the baking sheet from the oven and, while the rolls are still soft, cut them on the diagonal into slices about ½ in (12 mm) wide. Separate the slices so they are not touching, return the baking sheet to the oven and bake until dry, 5 minutes longer.
❧ Remove to a wire rack to cool. Store in an airtight container.
MAKES 20–30 COOKIES

DOLCINI ALLE MANDORLE
Almond Biscuits

Children take these biscuits to school for the morning break. As they keep well in an airtight tin, it is worthwhile making a fairly large batch.

1 tablespoon unsalted butter
1⅞ cups (10 oz/300 g) blanched almonds, chopped
1 cup (5 oz/150 g) confectioners' (icing) sugar
5 egg whites
¼ cup (2 oz/60 g) granulated sugar

❧ Preheat an oven to 350°F (180°C). Line a baking sheet with parchment paper and grease it with the butter.
❧ In a bowl, mix together the almonds and confectioners' sugar. In a large mixing bowl, beat the egg whites until stiff, moist peaks form. Gently fold the granulated sugar and the almond mixture into the egg whites.
❧ Drop the mixture by spoonfuls onto the prepared baking sheet, spacing them about 1 in (2.5 cm) apart. Bake until golden, about 20 minutes.
❧ Lift the biscuits off the parchment and let cool completely on a wire rack. Serve at room temperature.
MAKES 20–30 BISCUITS

CAVALLUCCI
Spice Cookies

These well-known cookies, like all Sienese confectionery, are highly seasoned. They will keep well in an airtight container for several days.

⅞ cup (7 oz/210 g) granulated sugar
¾ cup (6 fl oz/180 ml) water
1¾ cups (7 oz/210 g) all-purpose (plain) flour
1 cup (4 oz/120 g) chopped walnuts
⅓ cup (2 oz/60 g) candied orange peel
pinch of ground aniseed
pinch of ground cinnamon
1 tablespoon unsalted butter

❧ Preheat an oven to 220°F (100°C).
❧ In a saucepan over low heat, combine the sugar and water. Stir until the sugar dissolves, then increase the heat to moderate and cook until mixture registers 225°F (115°C) on a candy (sugar) thermometer, or until a little of it dropped into a bowl of ice water forms long threads.
❧ Remove from the heat and gradually stir in the flour, nuts, orange peel, aniseed and cinnamon.
❧ Grease a baking sheet well with the butter, then sprinkle it lightly with flour. Drop the batter by spoonfuls onto the baking sheet, spacing the mounds about 1 in (2.5 cm) apart. Press lightly on the top of each mound to flatten it slightly.
❧ Bake the cookies until they are dry in the center but have not changed color, about 1 hour or longer. Remove to a wire rack to cool.
MAKES 20–30 COOKIES

PAN COI SANTI
Bread with Saints

This sweet bread is called "bread with saints" because it is traditionally made on the first day of November, the Feast of All Saints. Its peppery flavor is quite unusual and, when the bread becomes hard, the Sienese dunk it in red wine before taking a bite.

1 cup (8 fl oz/240 ml) lukewarm water (105° to 115°F/42° to 46°C)
1 oz (30 g) fresh cake yeast or 2 packages (1 scant tablespoon each) active dry yeast
¼ cup (2 fl oz/60 ml) extra virgin olive oil
1 cup (3 oz/90 g) walnuts, chopped
3 cups (12 oz/ 360 g) all-purpose (plain) flour
⅓ cup (3 oz/90 g) granulated sugar
1 tablespoon freshly ground black pepper
pinch of salt

❧ Place the lukewarm water in a small bowl. Sprinkle the yeast on top of the water and let stand until dissolved and foamy, about 10 minutes.
❧ Meanwhile, in a small skillet over very low heat, warm the olive oil. Add the nuts and fry gently until toasted, about 2 minutes. Remove from the heat and let the oil and nuts cool completely.
❧ Combine the flour, sugar, pepper and salt. Heap this mixture on a work surface and make a well in the center. Pour the dissolved yeast into the well along with the cooled nuts and oil. With a fork, gradually work in the flour mixture until all of it is absorbed. On a lightly floured work surface, knead the dough until it is elastic, about 10 minutes. Shape the dough into a ball. Transfer the dough ball to a lightly oiled bowl,

Almond Cookies of Prato (front), Spice Cookies (left), Almond Biscuits (right) and Bread with Saints (rear)

cover with plastic wrap and let rise at room temperature until doubled in bulk, about 2 hours.

🍂 Turn the dough out onto a floured work surface. Punch down the dough and form it into a flat oval loaf about 1 in (2.5 cm) thick at the center and ½ in (12 mm) thick at the edges. Lightly oil a baking sheet and place the loaf on it. Let rise at room temperature until doubled in size, about 30 minutes.

Meanwhile, preheat an oven to 400°F (200°C).

🍂 Bake the bread for about 30 minutes, or until a wooden toothpick inserted into the center of the loaf comes out dry. Remove the bread from the oven and let cool completely on a wire rack. Place on a serving plate and serve.

SERVES 6

Apple Cake (left) and Almond Cookies (right)

Arezzo

TORTA DI MELE

Apple Cake

Like so many Tuscan dishes, this cake is made with leftover bread. It is very simple and children love it as an afternoon snack.

6 oz (180 g) coarse country bread
2 cups (16 fl oz/480 ml) milk
1 tablespoon unsalted butter
3 eggs
⅓ cup (3 oz/90 g) granulated sugar
3 tablespoons all-purpose (plain) flour
grated zest of 1 lemon
4 Golden Delicious apples or other sweet apples

🐾 Soak the bread in 1 cup (8 fl oz/240 ml) of the milk for about 30 minutes. Drain and squeeze out any excess moisture; set aside.
🐾 Preheat an oven to 350°F (180°C). Grease a 9-in (23-cm) cake pan with the butter.
🐾 In a mixing bowl, beat together the eggs, sugar and flour. Add the remaining milk and the lemon zest and mix well.
🐾 Peel and core the apples. Cut them into fairly thick slices.
🐾 Place the soaked bread in a layer on the bottom of the prepared pan. Arrange the apples in concentric circles on top of the bread. Pour the egg mixture over the apples. Bake until the top is golden and a knife inserted in the center comes out dry, about 50 minutes.
🐾 Remove from the oven and let cool a little. Run a knife around the pan edges to loosen the cake and transfer to a platter. Serve warm.

SERVES 6

Siena

RICCIARELLI

Almond Cookies

Like most Italian almond sweetmeats, ricciarelli were probably introduced to Siena by crusaders returning from the Middle East. They are now produced commercially, but when homemade they are softer at the center, the secret of a good ricciarello. The wafers mentioned in the recipe, which are made from rice flour, look like communion hosts. If they are not available, rice paper may be used or the cookies may simply be baked on parchment paper.

2 cups (10 oz/300 g) blanched almonds
1¼ cups (10 oz/300 g) granulated sugar
1¼ cups (7 oz/210 g) confectioners' (icing) sugar
1 teaspoon vanilla powder or 1 teaspoon vanilla extract (essence)
2 egg whites
36 thin wafers (see note above), about 2 in (5 cm) in diameter

🐾 Preheat an oven to 250°F (120°C). Spread the almonds in a single layer in a shallow pan and place them in the oven to dry for 10 minutes; do not allow them to darken.
🐾 Transfer the almonds to a blender container and add the granulated sugar. Blend until evenly pulverized. Add 1 cup (5 oz/150 g) of the confectioners' sugar, the vanilla and egg whites. Blend briefly.
🐾 Sprinkle each wafer with a little of the remaining confectioners' sugar, reserving some sugar for sprinkling on later. Place a spoonful of the almond mixture on each wafer. Flatten the mounds to about ⅓ in (9 mm) and, using a sharp knife, cut each of them into diamond shapes. Arrange the diamonds on a baking sheet and let stand in a cool place for at least 12 hours.
🐾 Preheat an oven to 250°F (120°C). Place the cookies in the oven and turn off the heat immediately. Leave the cookies in the oven until dry but still soft in the center, about 3 hours. Remove from the oven and cool on a wire rack.
🐾 When completely cold, sprinkle them with the remaining confectioners' sugar and serve. Store in an airtight container.

MAKES 36 COOKIES

235

Livorno

PANNA COTTA AL CARAMELLO

Cooked Cream with Caramel

Cooked cream, an old Tuscan dish, has recently been discovered by the rest of Italy and is now very much in vogue. In Livorno it is flavored with cinnamon. The cream can be kept in the refrigerator for 24 hours, in which case the caramel will dissolve by itself and the cream will be easily inverted onto the platter.

2 tablespoons unflavored powdered gelatin
6 tablespoons (3 fl oz/90 ml) water
2 cups (16 fl oz/480 ml) heavy (double) cream
⅞ cup (7 oz/210 g) granulated sugar
1 teaspoon ground cinnamon

🌸 In a small bowl, sprinkle the gelatin over 4 tablespoons of the water and let soften for about 3 minutes without stirring.
🌸 In a heavy saucepan over low heat, warm half of the cream with half of the sugar and the cinnamon, stirring to dissolve the sugar. Heat the mixture to just below the boiling point; do not allow it to boil.
🌸 Remove from the heat and stir in the gelatin. Let cool to room temperature.
🌸 Whip the rest of the cream until stiff peaks form. When the cream-sugar mixture is at room temperature, gently fold in the whipped cream.
🌸 In a small, heavy saucepan over low heat, melt the remaining sugar in the remaining 2 tablespoons water, stirring to dissolve the sugar completely. Increase the heat and cook without stirring until the sugar caramelizes and is a rich brown, about 3 minutes.
🌸 Remove the caramelized sugar from the heat and immediately pour it into a 9-in (23-cm) ring mold. Tilt the mold so that the caramelized sugar coats the bottom and sides. When the caramel is completely cold, pour in the cream mixture. Cover and refrigerate for at least 3 hours.
🌸 Just before serving, briefly dip the bottom of the cake pan in hot water to soften the caramel. Then invert onto a plate and serve.

SERVES 6

Cooked Cream with Caramel

Bomboloni

Lucca

BOMBOLONI

Doughnuts

These particular doughnuts are one of the specialties of Forte dei Marmi, a fashionable beach resort near Lucca. Every morning and late afternoon, men dressed in white walk along the beach, carrying baskets of hot doughnuts for the hungry bathers.

1 cup (8 fl oz/240 ml) lukewarm water (105° to 115°F/42° to 46°C)

1 oz (30 g) fresh cake yeast or 2 packages (1 scant tablespoon each) active dry yeast

3 cups (12 oz/360 g) all-purpose (plain) flour

⅓ cup (3 oz/90 g) granulated sugar

¼ cup (2 oz/60 g) unsalted butter, softened

grated zest of 1 lemon

salt

5 cups (40 fl oz/1.2 l) extra virgin olive oil for frying

🐦 Place the lukewarm water in a small bowl. Sprinkle the yeast on top of the water and let stand until dissolved and foamy, about 10 minutes.

🐦 Heap the flour on a work surface and make a well in the center. Pour the dissolved yeast into the well along with ¼ cup (2 oz/60 g) of the sugar, the softened butter, lemon zest and salt. With a fork, gradually work in the flour until all of it is absorbed. On a lightly floured work surface, knead the dough with energy until it is very elastic and smooth, about 10 minutes. Shape the dough into a ball.

🐦 Transfer the dough to a lightly floured bowl, cover with plastic wrap and let rise at room temperature until doubled in bulk, about 2 hours.

🐦 Lightly flour a baking sheet. On a lightly floured work surface, punch down the dough and divide it into about 18 ovals about the size of an egg. Flatten them until they are ½ in (12 mm) thick. Arrange the doughnuts on the baking sheet and let rise at room temperature until doubled in size, about 30 minutes.

🐦 In a deep, heavy skillet, heat the olive oil to 350°F (180°C). A few at a time, slip the doughnuts into the hot oil and fry until golden on both sides, about 3 minutes. With a slotted spoon, remove to absorbent paper towels to drain. Continue frying the remaining doughnuts in the same manner.

🐦 Arrange on a serving plate and sprinkle with the remaining 2 tablespoons sugar. Serve hot.

MAKES 20–30 DOUGHNUTS

Apple and Rice Pudding

PASTICCIO DI RISO E MELE
Apple and Rice Pudding

All the fine restaurants on the island of Elba serve this delicious pudding at Christmastime.

⅓ cup (2 oz/60 g) raisins
1 cup (8 fl oz/240 ml) Vin Santo or other white dessert
  wine
4 cups (32 fl oz/900 ml) milk
pinch of salt
1½ cups (10 oz/300 g) Arborio rice
pinch of freshly grated nutmeg
1 teaspoon ground cinnamon
6 tablespoons (3 oz/90 g) granulated sugar
1 tablespoon unsalted butter
3 eggs, beaten
2 Golden Delicious apples or other sweet apples

🦋 In a small bowl, soak the raisins in the Vin Santo for 6 hours.
🦋 In a heavy saucepan over moderate heat, bring the milk to a boil with the salt. Add the rice, lower the heat and simmer until all the milk has been absorbed and the rice is fairly dry, about 30 minutes. Remove the pan from the heat and stir in the nutmeg, cinnamon and 4 tablespoons (2 oz/60 g) of the sugar. Drain the raisins and mix them in as well. Let cool completely.
🦋 Meanwhile, preheat an oven to 350°F (180°C). Butter a 9-in (23-cm) springform pan.
🦋 When the rice mixture is cold, stir in the eggs, then pour the batter into the prepared pan. Peel and core the apples, then thinly slice them. Arrange the apple slices in concentric circles on top of the batter and sprinkle them with the remaining 2 tablespoons sugar. Bake the pudding until set, about 1 hour.
🦋 Remove from the oven and let cool slightly on a wire rack. Remove the pan sides and transfer the pudding to a plate. Serve warm.

SERVES 6

CASTAGNACCIO

Chestnut Flour Cake

This is one of the most traditional Florentine cakes and it should be made with very fresh chestnut flour. If the flour is stale, it gives the cake a slightly bitter flavor. Seasoned with rosemary and pine nuts, castagnaccio *is sold in Florence during the autumn.*

2½ cups (10 oz/300 g) chestnut flour
6 tablespoons (3 fl oz/90 ml) extra virgin olive oil
1½ cups (12 fl oz/350 ml) water
pinch of salt
½ cup (2 oz/60 g) pine nuts
2 tablespoons fresh rosemary leaves

❧ Preheat an oven to 350°F (180°C).

❧ Pour the flour into a mixing bowl. Stir in 2 tablespoons of the olive oil. Gradually add the water, whisking constantly to prevent lumps from forming. Season with the salt.

❧ Pour the remaining 4 tablespoons (2 fl oz/60 ml) olive oil into an 11-in (28-cm) square cake pan, tipping the pan to coat the bottom and sides evenly. Pour the batter into the pan and sprinkle the surface with the pine nuts and rosemary. Do not be concerned if there seems to be too much oil; it is required for the cake to cook properly.

❧ Bake the cake until the surface starts to crack, about 20 minutes. Remove from the oven and pour off any excess oil.

❧ Loosen the cake with a knife, and with the help of a large spatula, transfer the cake to a serving dish. Serve while still warm.

SERVES 6

Chestnut Flour Cake

Livorno

CROCCANTINI DI FRUTTA CANDITA

Candied Fruit Macaroons

When the Medici family made Livorno a free port at the end of the sixteenth century, many immigrants were attracted to it. Among them were Spanish and Portuguese Jews who greatly influenced Livornese cooking, as this Jewish recipe illustrates.

2 egg whites
¾ cup (3 oz/90 g) slivered blanched almonds
1 tablespoon all-purpose (plain) flour
¼ cup (2 oz/60 g) granulated sugar
1 tablespoon honey
1 tablespoon candied (glacé) cherries, chopped
1 tablespoon candied (glacé) orange peel, chopped
1 tablespoon candied (glacé) lemon peel, chopped
unsalted butter for baking sheet
3 oz (90 g) bittersweet (dark) chocolate

🍂 Preheat an oven to 350°F (180°C).
🍂 In a mixing bowl, whisk the egg whites with a fork until only just frothy. Add the almonds, flour, sugar, honey, cherries and orange and lemon peels.
🍂 Brush a baking sheet with the butter. Drop the batter by spoonfuls onto the baking sheet, spacing them about 1 in (2.5 cm) apart. Flatten the tops with a wet teaspoon.
🍂 Bake the cookies until golden and set, about 10 minutes. Remove from the oven and transfer to a flat surface. Let cool completely.
🍂 Place the chocolate in a small saucepan or dish. Set the vessel inside a large pan of barely simmering water atop the stove. The

Candied Fruit Macaroons

water should reach about halfway up the sides of the vessel holding the chocolate. As soon as the chocolate melts, brush some onto the surface of each cookie. Let the chocolate cool and set, then arrange the cookies on a plate and serve.

MAKES ABOUT 18 MACAROONS

Livorno

OSSA DI MORTO

Munchy Bones

These cookies originated on the island of Elba, where they are served with Aleatico, a dessert wine produced on the island. They will keep well in an airtight tin for several days.

2⅛ cups (12 oz/360 g) blanched almonds
4 egg whites
⅞ cup (7 oz/210 g) granulated sugar
1⅝ cups (7 oz/210 g) all-purpose (plain) flour
grated zest of 1 lemon
grated zest of 1 orange
1 tablespoon unsalted butter

🍂 Preheat an oven to 350°F (180°C).
🍂 Place the almonds in a blender container and blend just until evenly pulverized.
🍂 In a mixing bowl, whisk the egg whites with a fork until only just frothy. Add the almonds, sugar, flour and lemon and orange zests. Stir until the mixture is smooth but not too stiff. Divide the mixture into sticks about 2 in (5 cm) long and ¼ in (6 mm) wide.
🍂 Grease a baking sheet with the butter and dust lightly with flour. Arrange the sticks on the baking sheet and press each slightly in the middle to form a bone shape.
🍂 Bake the cookies until golden, about 20 minutes. Remove to a wire rack to cool completely.

MAKES 20–30 COOKIES

Lucca

BRIGIDINI

Aniseed Wafers

Although these thin wafers originated in Lucchesia, they are now sold in markets throughout Tuscany. They are cooked between two hot, round flatirons called stiacce *that are about 4 in (10 cm) in diameter. They may also be baked in an oven.*

1½ cups (6 oz/180 g) all-purpose (plain) flour
½ cup (4 oz/120 g) granulated sugar
2 eggs
1 tablespoon aniseed

🍂 In a food processor, combine the flour, sugar, eggs and aniseed. Process the ingredients until you have a soft, elastic dough similar to pasta dough. Alternatively, combine all the ingredients in a bowl and beat with a wooden spoon.
🍂 Preheat the two flatirons on top of the stove over high heat. Divide the dough into balls the size of walnuts. Flatten them slightly, then, one at a time, press them between the hot irons. Hold the irons together until the wafer is crisp, about 2 minutes. Reheat the irons before cooking the next wafer.
🍂 Alternatively, preheat an oven to 350°F (180°C). On a lightly floured surface, roll out each dough ball into a very thin round about 4 in (10 cm) in diameter. Arrange the dough rounds on a baking sheet. Bake the cookies until crisp, about 3 minutes. Remove to a wire rack and let cool completely.
🍂 Arrange on a platter to serve. These wafers keep well in an airtight container.

MAKES 20–30 WAFERS

Left to right: Selection of Nut Brittles, Munchy Bones and Aniseed Wafers

Lucca

CROCCANTE

Walnut Brittle

This brittle is sold on the beaches in Versilia, as well as at village festivals.

1 tablespoon almond oil
1⅓ cups (10 oz/300 g) granulated sugar
½ cup (4 fl oz/120 ml) water
juice of 1 lemon
2¼ cups (7 oz/210 g) walnuts

🐾 Brush a board with the almond oil.
🐾 In a deep, heavy saucepan over low heat, melt the sugar in the water, stirring to dissolve the sugar. Increase the heat and cook the sugar without stirring until it caramelizes and turns a deep, rich brown, about 10 minutes.
🐾 Remove from the heat and gradually add the lemon juice and nuts, taking care not to burn yourself as the hot sugar syrup may splatter when the cold lemon juice is added.
🐾 Pour the syrup mixture onto the oiled board, forming a layer about ¼ in (6 mm) thick. Let the brittle cool completely.
🐾 Lift the brittle with a spatula and break it into pieces. Arrange on a platter to serve. Store any leftovers in an airtight container.

SERVES 6

Lucca

MANDORLATA

Almond Brittle

In the Garfagnana the bees produce particularly delicious honey. In the past, this honey-rich brittle was always made there for the feast of Santa Lucia on December 13. Nowadays it is available year-round.

1⅔ cups (1¼ lb/600 g) honey
1 tablespoon almond oil
1¾ cups (10 oz/300 g) blanched almonds, chopped

🐾 In a heavy saucepan over low heat, warm the honey until a drop poured into a cup of cold water forms a firm ball when rolled between your fingers, about 5 minutes.
🐾 Lightly brush a board with the almond oil and pour the honey on it. Let the honey stand until it is cool enough to knead by hand, then knead until it is pale yellow, about 3 minutes. Add the nuts and knead them in well to mix evenly. If the mixture becomes too hard to work with, return it to a saucepan and reheat it until it softens and is just pliable enough to spread into a thin sheet.
🐾 Smooth the mixture into an even sheet about ¼ in (6 mm) thick. Cut into 1¼-in (3-cm) squares and transfer to parchment paper. Cool to room temperature before serving.

SERVES 6

Arezzo

RICOTTA ALL'UVETTA

Ricotta with Raisins

The Aretines are very fussy about ricotta and only eat it raw on the day it is made. The next day it is used in tortelli *or* gnocchi.

⅓ cup (2 oz/60 g) raisins
1 cup (8 fl oz/250 ml) Vin Santo or other white dessert wine
2½ cups (1¼ lb/600 g) fresh ricotta
3 tablespoons granulated sugar
1 teaspoon ground cinnamon

❧ In a small bowl, soak the raisins in the Vin Santo for about 6 hours. Drain them.
❧ Position a sieve over a mixing bowl. Press the ricotta through the sieve to remove any lumps. Add the sugar and raisins and stir gently.
❧ Shape the ricotta mixture into a mound on a serving plate. Put the cinnamon in a fine sieve and sprinkle it over the ricotta. Serve at room temperature.

SERVES 6

Grosseto

TORTA AL FINOCCHIO

Fennel Cake

Rosemary, thyme and fennel are used to season cakes and breads in Tuscany. The fennel accent makes this simple cake particularly interesting.

1 tablespoon unsalted butter
1 cup (4 oz/120 g) all-purpose (plain) flour
1 cup (4 oz/120 g) ground almonds
1 cup (8 oz/240 g) granulated sugar
1 teaspoon baking powder
1 cup (8 fl oz/240 ml) milk
1 tablespoon fennel seed

❧ Preheat an oven to 350°F (180°C). Grease a 9-in (23-cm) springform pan with the butter.
❧ In a mixing bowl, combine the flour, almonds, sugar and baking powder. Mix well. Gradually stir in the milk and then mix in the fennel seed.
❧ Pour the batter into the prepared pan. Bake the cake until golden and a wooden toothpick inserted in the center comes out dry, about 1 hour.
❧ Remove from the oven and let cool completely on a wire rack. Unclip the pan sides and transfer the cake to a serving platter. Serve at room temperature.

SERVES 6

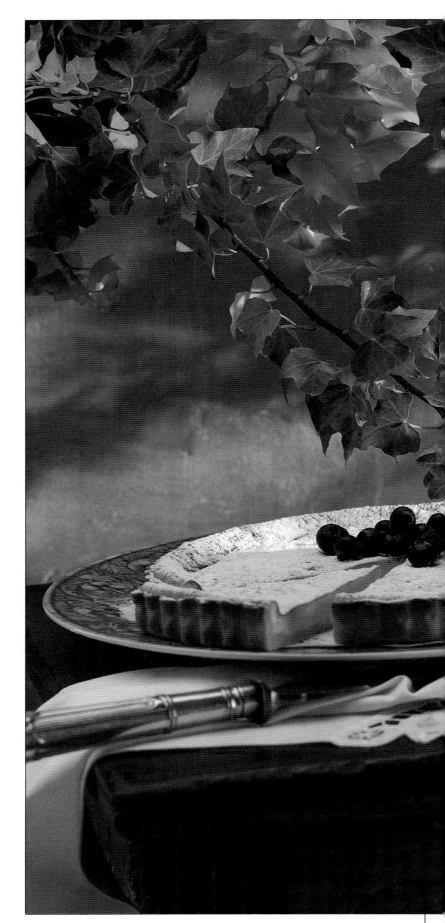

Grosseto

CROSTATA DI RICOTTA

Ricotta Tart

The Grosseto area produces a great deal of pecorino, *sheep's milk cheese. As the sheep graze close to the sea, the* pecorino *is saltier than most. Ricotta made from the whey is a local specialty.*

PASTRY
1¾ cups (7 oz/210 g) all-purpose (plain) flour
⅓ cup (3 oz/90 g) granulated sugar
grated zest of ½ lemon
⅓ cup (3 oz/90 g) butter, softened
1 egg

FILLING
1¼ cups (10 oz/300 g) ricotta
3 eggs, separated
¼ cup (2 oz/60 g) granulated sugar

½ tablespoon unsalted butter

❧ To prepare the pastry: combine the flour, sugar, lemon zest, butter and egg in the bowl of a food processor. Process with brief pulses until the dough begins to come together in a ball.

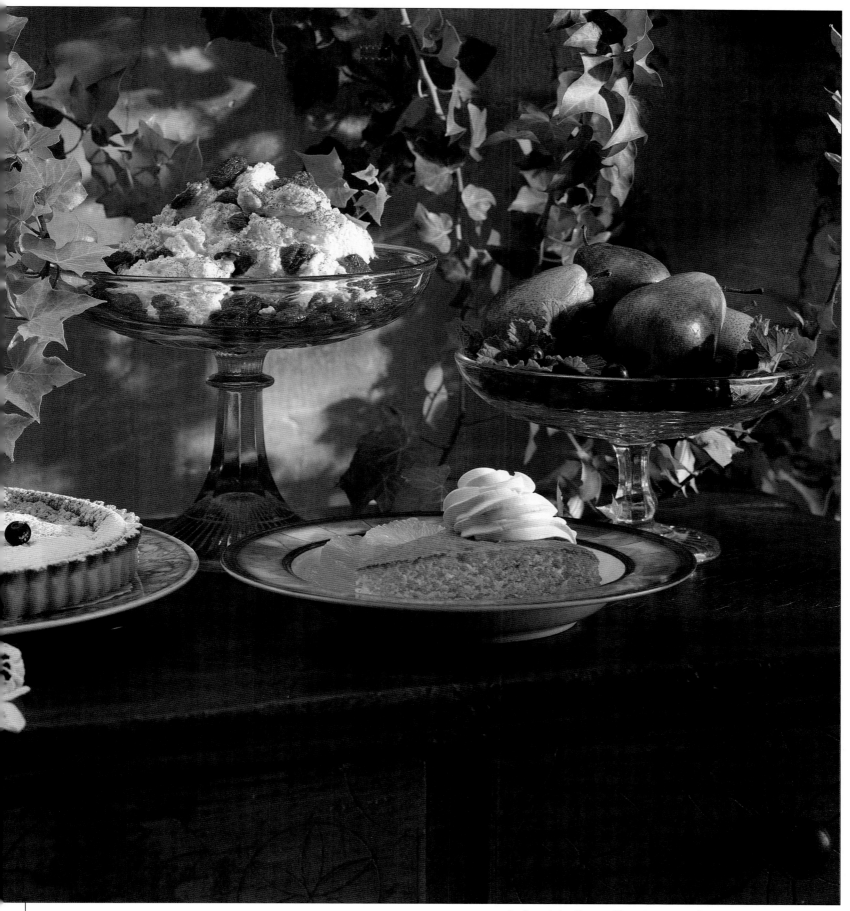

Left to right: Ricotta Tart, Ricotta with Raisins, and Fennel Cake

Alternatively, combine the ingredients in a mixing bowl and beat together with a wooden spoon until the dough begins to come together in a ball. Gather the dough into a ball, wrap in aluminum foil and refrigerate for about 1 hour.

🍃 Meanwhile, to prepare the filling: combine the ricotta, egg yolks and sugar in a large mixing bowl and blend well. In a separate bowl, beat the egg whites until stiff, moist peaks form. Gently fold the egg whites into the ricotta mixture.

🍃 Preheat an oven to 350°F (180°C). Select a 9-in (23-cm) tart pan (flan tin) with a removable bottom and grease the bottom with the butter. On a lightly floured work surface,

roll out the dough into a round about 10½ in (26.5 cm) in diameter. Carefully transfer it to the prepared pan and press gently against the bottom and sides. Trim the dough even with the rim of the tart pan. Spoon the filling into the pastry shell and smooth the surface. Bake the tart until just golden, about 45 minutes.

🍃 Remove from the oven and let cool completely on a wire rack. Transfer the tart to a platter and serve at room temperature.

SERVES 6

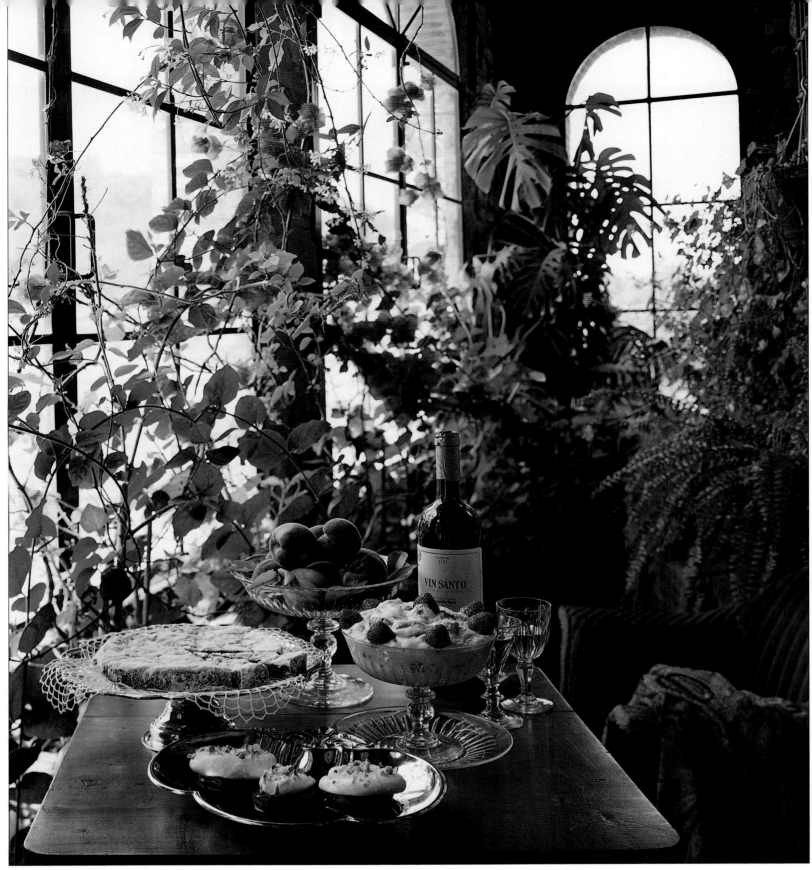

Stuffed Peaches (front), Flat Fruit Cake (left) and Strawberries and Ricotta (right)

PANFORTE

Flat Fruit Cake

Panforte, *literally "strong bread," is the most famous Sienese cake and is now exported all over the world. Originally it was a Christmas treat. Historian Giovanni Righi Parenti tells us that it was first written about in 1205. To make true* panforte *at home is not easy, because the dough is very sticky and you would need dozens of different spices. This version is much simpler but quite good.*

1¼ cups (6 oz/180 g) toasted almonds, chopped
1¼ cups (6 oz/180 g) mixed candied peel, cubed
1½ cups (6 oz/180 g) all-purpose (plain) flour
1 teaspoon ground cinnamon
1 tablespoon mixed ground spices (coriander, nutmeg, cloves, aniseed)
unsalted butter for cake pan

⅔ cup (9 oz/270 g) honey
½ teaspoon ground cinnamon mixed with 1 tablespoon all-purpose (plain) flour

🐾 In a large bowl, combine the almonds, candied peel, flour, cinnamon and mixed spices. Mix well.
🐾 Preheat an oven to 350°F (180°C). Line an 11-in (28-cm) cake pan with parchment paper and butter the paper well.
🐾 In a saucepan over low heat, heat the honey and cook, stirring continuously, for about 2 minutes. Stir the hot honey into the flour mixture, blending well. Taking care not to burn your fingers, shape the mixture into a ball.
🐾 Flatten the ball of dough evenly in the prepared pan. Pour the cinnamon-flour mixture into a sieve and shake it over the top of the cake. Bake the cake until golden brown, about 40 minutes.
🐾 Remove the cake from the pan and let cool on a wire rack. When cool, peel off the parchment and place the cake on a platter. Any leftover cake can be stored in an airtight container.

SERVES 6

RICOTTA CON LE FRAGOLE
Strawberries and Ricotta

Small, strongly flavored wild strawberries are commonly used to prepare this dessert. Larger strawberries should be sliced.

10 oz (300 g) wild strawberries, hulled
1 cup (8 fl oz/240 ml) Vin Santo or other sweet white wine
⅓ cup (3 oz/90 g) granulated sugar
2 cups (1 lb/480 g) ricotta
2 egg whites

🌢 Combine the strawberries, wine and half of the sugar in a bowl. Toss to mix and let stand for 2 hours. Drain the strawberries and set aside a few for decorating the dessert.
🌢 Position a sieve over a medium-sized bowl. Press the ricotta through the sieve to remove any lumps. Gradually stir in the strawberries and the remaining sugar.
🌢 In a separate bowl, beat the egg whites until stiff, moist peaks form. Fold the egg whites into the ricotta-strawberry mixture.
🌢 Arrange the mixture in a dome shape in the middle of a serving plate. Decorate with the reserved strawberries and serve immediately.

SERVES 6

PESCHE RIPIENE
Stuffed Peaches

Make sure that the peaches are not too ripe or they will disintegrate while cooking. When a more substantial dessert is required, the peaches are served on a slice of sponge cake sprinkled with alchermes, a sweet red liqueur.

3 underripe peaches
1 cup (8 fl oz/240 ml) dry red wine
⅓ cup (3 oz/90 g) granulated sugar
2 tablespoons blanched almonds, chopped
2 egg whites
⅓ cup (2 oz/60 g) confectioners' (icing) sugar
2 cups (16 fl oz/480 ml) milk

🌢 Cut the peaches in half and carefully remove and discard the pits. Place the peaches in a shallow saucepan with the wine and granulated sugar. Cook over low heat until the peaches are soft, about 10 minutes.
🌢 Meanwhile, preheat an oven to 350°F (180°C). Place the almonds in a small pan and toast them until golden brown, about 10 minutes. Remove from the oven and set aside.
🌢 With a slotted spoon, remove the peaches to a plate. Cook the wine over moderate heat until the sauce reduces and coats a spoon, about 5 minutes. Remove from the heat and let cool completely.
🌢 In a bowl, beat the egg whites until soft peaks form. Add the confectioners' sugar, a spoonful at a time, and continue beating until stiff, moist peaks form.
🌢 In a shallow saucepan, bring the milk to a simmer. Using 2 large spoons, shape the egg whites into oval meringues by scooping up the egg white with one spoon and gently covering it with the other. You should have 6 meringues in all. Slip the meringues into the milk without crowding the pan and poach on both sides until just firm, 1–2 minutes per side. With a slotted spoon, remove the meringues to a plate and let cool. Continue poaching the remaining egg whites in the same manner.
🌢 Arrange the peach halves flat side up on a serving dish. Place a meringue on each peach and sprinkle with the almonds. Pour the cold wine sauce over them. Serve at room temperature.

SERVES 6

PAN DI MIELE
Honey Bread

In Grosseto this bread is made with honey from hives placed near strawberry plants. Try to use a honey that has a strong flavor and is slightly bitter.

1 cup (8 fl oz/240 ml) milk, heated to lukewarm (105° to 115°F/42° to 46°C)
1 oz (30 g) fresh cake yeast or 2 packages (1 scant tablespoon each) active dry yeast
2⅔ cups (12 oz/360 g) all-purpose (plain) flour
1 tablespoon granulated sugar
2 tablespoons honey (not too sweet)
salt

🌢 Place the lukewarm milk in a small bowl. Sprinkle the yeast on top of the milk and let stand until dissolved and foamy, about 10 minutes.
🌢 Heap the flour on a work surface and make a well in the center. Pour the dissolved yeast into the well along with the sugar, honey and salt. With a fork, gradually work in the flour until all of it is absorbed. On a lightly floured surface, knead the dough until it is smooth and soft, about 5 minutes. Shape the dough into a ball.
🌢 Transfer the dough ball to a lightly floured bowl and cover with plastic wrap. Let rise at room temperature until doubled in bulk, about 2 hours.
🌢 Turn the dough out onto a floured surface. Punch down the dough and shape it into an oval loaf about 12 in (30 cm) long. Lightly dust a baking sheet and place the loaf on it. Let rise at room temperature until doubled in size, about 30 minutes.
🌢 Meanwhile, preheat an oven to 400°F (200°C). Bake the bread until golden, about 30 minutes. Remove from the oven and let cool completely on a wire rack before slicing.

SERVES 6

Honey Bread

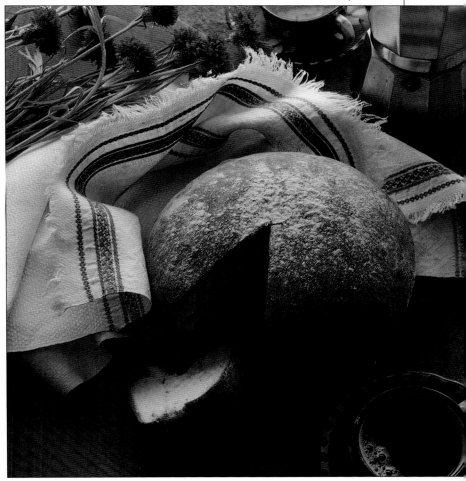

Firenze

TORTA SOFFICE DI MELE
Light Apple Cake

This family cake is particularly tasty in autumn, when the apples have just been picked and are still strongly scented and hard. Granny Smith and Golden Delicious apples are suitable for this recipe.

2½ cups (10 oz/300 g) all-purpose (plain) flour
⅔ cup (5 oz/150 g) granulated sugar
3 eggs
⅔ cup (5 oz/150 g) unsalted butter, melted, plus extra
    for pan
grated zest of 1 lemon
pinch of freshly grated nutmeg
1 teaspoon baking powder
⅓ cup (3 fl oz/90 ml) milk
3 apples

❧ Preheat an oven to 350°F (180°C).
❧ In a food processor, combine all the ingredients except the apples. Process until a smooth batter is formed. Or combine all the ingredients in a bowl and beat with an electric mixer at medium speed until a smooth batter is formed.
❧ Butter and flour a 9-in (23-cm) springform pan. Pour in the batter.
❧ Peel and core the apples, then slice them thinly. Arrange the slices in concentric circles on top of the batter; they will sink in a little.
❧ Bake the cake until a wooden toothpick inserted into the center of the cake comes out dry, about 1 hour. Remove from the oven and let cool slightly on a wire rack. Remove the pan sides and slip the cake onto a serving plate. Serve at room temperature.

SERVES 6

Grosseto

FICHI CANDITI
Candied Figs

This is another ancient recipe that Giovanni Righi Parenti mentions in his book, La grande cucina toscana, *published in 1972. Presoaked prunes may be used in place of the figs.*

⅓ cup (3 oz/90 g) granulated sugar
18 fresh figs, peeled
grated zest of 1 lemon
2 tablespoons honey
few drops of almond oil

❧ Preheat an oven to 350°F (180°C).
❧ Sprinkle half of the sugar in the bottom of a baking pan and arrange the figs in the pan side by side. Sprinkle the figs with the remaining sugar and the lemon zest. Drizzle with the honey.
❧ Bake the figs until the sugar caramelizes and is pale gold, about 30 minutes. Remove the pan from the oven.
❧ Brush a serving dish with the almond oil. With a spatula remove the figs to the dish. Serve cold.

SERVES 6   *Photograph pages 218–219*

Light Apple Cake

Africans

AFRICANI

Africans

At one time there were several Tuscan convents where the nuns prepared these cookies, but nowadays they are hard to come by. You can still find them in Greve in Chianti on Saturdays, when the weekly market is held and the local cake shop has them for sale.

6 egg yolks
¾ cup (6 oz/180 g) granulated sugar

🐑 Using a fork, combine the egg yolks and sugar in a mixing bowl. Beat together until the sugar completely dissolves and you have a white, creamy mixture, about 1 hour. (Do not use an egg beater for this step; it makes the mixture too light and dry.) Preheat an oven to 250°F (120°C).

🐑 Place small, pleated paper cups on a baking sheet and fill them with the mixture. Place the cookies in the oven and turn off the heat immediately. Leave the cookies in the oven until they have risen but are still creamy at the center, about 1 hour.

🐑 If the oven gets too cold toward the end of the cooking time, it may be reheated to 185°F (90°C). Remove the cookies to a wire rack to cool completely, then arrange on a platter and serve.

MAKES 20–30 COOKIES

crowding the pan. Fry a few at a time until just golden, about 3 minutes. With a slotted spoon, remove the fritters to absorbent paper towels to drain. Continue frying the remaining batter in the same manner.

Firenze

FRAGOLE AL VINO ROSSO

Strawberries in Red Wine

Here is the simplest and most traditional way Italians serve small wild strawberries; large cultivated ones can also be used. Florentines always use a well-aged Chianti Classico for the red wine. This makes an excellent dessert for a summer luncheon.

1¼ lb (600 g) wild strawberries, hulled
⅓ cup (3 oz/90 g) granulated sugar
1 cup (8 fl oz/240 ml) Chianti Classico Riserva
small strip of lemon peel

🦋 Place the strawberries in a large bowl. Sprinkle with the sugar and pour in the wine. Cover and refrigerate for at least 12 hours.
🦋 Drain the strawberries, reserving the marinade, and set the strawberries aside in a serving bowl. Pour the marinade into a small saucepan. Add the lemon peel and heat gently, stirring occasionally, until the wine becomes syrupy and coats a spoon.
🦋 Remove the pan from the heat. Remove and discard the lemon peel. Let the wine cool completely.
🦋 Put the strawberries in a serving bowl, pour the cold wine syrup over them and serve.

SERVES 6

Firenze

FRITTELLE DI TONDONE

Pancake Fritters

A tondone is a type of hard pancake that is crumbled, mixed with egg and made into little fritters. This recipe has been used in Florentine kitchens for centuries.

½ cup (3 oz/90 g) raisins
⅔ cup (5 fl oz/150 ml) water
2½ cups (10 oz/300 g) all-purpose (plain) flour
pinch of salt
1 tablespoon extra virgin olive oil, plus 5 cups (40 fl oz/1.2 l) for frying
6 eggs
grated zest of 1 lemon
1 tablespoon confectioners' (icing) sugar

🦋 In a small bowl, soak the raisins in warm water to cover for about 1 hour.
🦋 Pour the water into a bowl and gradually add the flour, whisking constantly to prevent lumps from forming. Stir the salt into the batter.
🦋 In a nonstick skillet, heat the 1 tablespoon olive oil. Add the batter and cook over low heat until the pancake sets, about 15 minutes or until a toothpick inserted in the center comes out dry.
🦋 Turn out onto a plate, browned side up. Slide the pancake back into the skillet and cook the other side for about 2 minutes. The pancake should be well cooked but not golden. Turn the pancake out onto a plate and let cool to room temperature.
🦋 Crumble the pancake into a blender container. Add 2 of the eggs. Separate the remaining 4 eggs and add the yolks to the blender; set the whites aside in a medium-sized bowl. Drain the raisins and add to the blender along with the lemon zest. Whirl to blend well. Pour into a large bowl.
🦋 Beat the egg whites until stiff, moist peaks form. Fold them delicately into the batter.
🦋 In a deep, heavy skillet, heat the olive oil for frying to 350°F (180°C). Drop the batter by spoonfuls into the hot oil without

🦋 Arrange the fritters on a platter, sprinkle with the confectioners' sugar and serve piping hot.

MAKES 20–30 FRITTERS

Firenze

FRITTELLE DI RISO

Rice Fritters

Florentines love sweet fritters, especially these tasty rice-studded ones. During Carnival they also prepare them with apples, semolina or just with a simple egg-and-flour batter.

4 cups (30 fl oz/900 ml) milk
6 tablespoons (3 oz/90 g) granulated sugar
2 tablespoons unsalted butter
grated zest of 1 lemon
1½ cups (10 oz/300 g) Arborio rice
2 eggs, separated
5 cups (40 fl oz/1.2 l) extra virgin olive oil for frying

🦋 In a heavy saucepan, combine the milk with half of the sugar, the butter and the lemon zest. Bring to a boil, stirring to dissolve the sugar, and add the rice. Lower the heat and simmer until the liquid is absorbed and the rice is fairly dry, about 30 minutes. Remove from the heat and let cool to room temperature.
🦋 When the rice mixture is completely cold, add the egg yolks, mixing in well. Whip the egg whites until stiff peaks form and then fold them gently into the rice mixture.
🦋 In a deep, heavy skillet, heat the olive oil to 350°F (180°C). Drop the batter by spoonfuls into the hot oil without crowding the pan. Fry a few at a time until golden, about 3 minutes. With a slotted spoon, remove the fritters to absorbent paper towels to drain. Continue frying the remaining batter in the same manner.
🦋 Arrange the fritters on a platter, sprinkle with the remaining sugar and serve very hot.

MAKES 20–30 FRITTERS

Pancake Fritters (left), Rice Fritters (right) and Strawberries in Red Wine (rear)

GLOSSARY

ACQUACOTTA is a popular Tuscan bread soup. Originally a very simple dish, it is now enriched with a variety of vegetables poured over bread.

AFFOGATO means "drowned"; in culinary terms, drowned in seasoned wine or tomato sauce.

ALLA DIAVOLA is a method of cooking chicken. The chicken is split open, flattened and grilled while being basted with olive oil. When ready it is crisp outside and soft within.

ALL'UCCELLETTO means "like a bird." Describes dishes prepared with olive oil, garlic and sage, the classic treatment for small game birds. A little tomato is added to the celebrated Tuscan beans *all'uccelletto*.

ALMOND OIL, a fragrant oil expressed from almonds, is commonly found in the kitchens of Italy, France, Spain and Portugal. Almond oil produced elsewhere is generally milder in flavor. Look for almond oil in shops specializing in southern European foods and in some health food stores. Refrigerate this oil to preserve its delicate flavor.

ANCHOVIES are preserved in oil in cans or jars, or in salt, usually in cans. Oil-packed anchovies come already filleted; if working with salt-packed anchovies, brush off all visible salt and then bone the fish before using. Anchovies in oil (preferably olive oil) can be found in supermarkets; anchovies in salt are available at well-stocked Italian shops.

ARBORIO RICE is a variety of short-grain rice grown in the Po Valley of northern Italy. Its stubby kernels absorb a remarkable amount of liquid as they cook, resulting in round, plump grains that, because of their high starch content, become quite creamy when tender. Arborio rice can be found in Italian shops and well-stocked supermarkets. If unavailable, short-grain rice may be substituted.

ARROSTO MORTO is a pot roast, cooked fairly slowly in a little wine flavored with vegetables.

ARTICHOKE, native to the Mediterranean, is grown for its flower, which is picked before it blooms. The flower, or head, is globelike, with thick, firm, thorn-topped leaves surrounding a tender heart and a prickly, inedible choke. The more mature the artichoke, the more developed the choke. Artichokes range in size from tiny buds of no more than 2 oz (60 g), which can be eaten whole after light trimming, to large globes up to 5 in (13 cm) in diameter. In this book, the larger artichokes are called globe artichokes, after the most common variety, Green Globe, to distinguish them from the tiny buds, which are referred to as small artichokes.

BACCALÀ see *salted cod*.

BATTUTO is the Tuscan term for *soffritto* (q.v.), but in Tuscany *pancetta* (q.v.) or lard is sometimes added to the chopped vegetables.

BEANS form the basis of many of Tuscany's best-known dishes. *Cannellini* are the classic Tuscan white beans. These relatively long, thin-skinned, kidney-shaped beans are at their best at the end of summer, when they are eaten fresh. *Cannellini* beans can be found in Italian shops dried or in cans. White kidney beans, Great Northern beans (which are slightly smaller and rounder) or white haricot beans (which are slightly larger and rounder) may be substituted. *Borlotti*

beans, also known as cranberry beans, are pale beige, oval beans with reddish mottling. They, too, are eaten fresh at summer's end, as well as dried. Dried *borlotti* are easily found in many supermarkets. Fava beans, also known as broad beans, are encased in flat green pods that range from about 4 in (10 cm) up to 1 foot (30 cm) or so in length. Only the very youngest fava beans may be eaten pod and all; larger pods must be discarded. Each moist, flat green bean is covered with a sturdy skin that should be removed by splitting the skin and slipping it off. Fresh fava beans can be found in the markets from spring to early summer. Fava beans are also available dried.

BIANCHETTI are tiny anchovies and sardines less than an inch (2.5 cm) long and as narrow as toothpicks. Their flavor is more delicate and they are less oily than baby eels.

BIROLDO see *sanguinaccio*.

BLACK CABBAGE, or *cavolo nero,* has long, narrow, very deep green leaves with a bumpy surface. Although in Italy cultivated only in Tuscany, black cabbage is now in demand all over the country. Its strong, slightly bitter flavor, which is most fully developed after the first frosts, is excellent in hearty Tuscan soups. Savoy cabbage may be substituted.

BLACK TRUFFLE is a roundish, highly aromatic, extremely costly fungus, usually about the size of a small mandarin orange, that grows underground and must be hunted with a dog or pig whose job it is to sniff it out. It has a rough surface, dense interior and earthy flavor. Southwest France and Umbria, which abuts Tuscany, are the sources of Europe's finest black truffles, which are exported fresh in the autumn to specialty food stores. They can also be purchased in jars or cans. If unavailable (or too expensive), omit truffles from the recipes.

BORAGE is a flowering plant native to the Mediterranean basin. When young, its bristly leaves, which taste faintly of cucumber, are used whole or chopped in salads or as a seasoning in beverages and other preparations; more mature leaves are cooked (which causes the bristles to disappear) and served in the same manner as other greens. Borage is not widely cultivated and is therefore found only in specialty vegetable markets (from late spring to early autumn) and in home gardens. Other greens such as spinach may be substituted. The lovely blue flowers, which are slightly sweet, are also edible.

BORLOTTI see *beans*.

BORRAGGINE, the wild varieties of borage (q.v.) and comfrey, grow well in Lucchesia, where they are used to flavor meats, frittatas and ravioli stuffings.

BRACIOLE are large, fairly thin slices of boneless beef, veal or pork. They may be grilled, fried or braised with tomatoes.

BROCCOLI RAAB, also known in Italian as *rapini, rape* and *cima di rape,* is a variety of foliage turnip that does not produce an enlarged base, hence its other common English name, turnip tops. It has dark green leaves on sturdy stalks topped with small flower clusters. This cool-weather vegetable is sautéed in oil with garlic or boiled and dressed with olive oil and lemon. It may also be served in tomato sauce.

BRODO means "broth" or "stock." In Italy it is made by simply putting a large piece of boneless beef or a chicken in a deep pot with a carrot, onion, celery, parsley and a pinch of salt. The meat and vegetables are abundantly covered with water and left to simmer for a couple of hours. Unlike the French method, no roasted bones or marrow bones are added. The stock is light, not fatty, and has a very fresh flavor. Herbs such as thyme and tarragon may be added.

CACCIUCCO is a famous Livornese fish soup. In Tuscany, however, the term is also used to describe a method of cooking in which fish, meat or vegetables are gently fried in chopped onion, celery, carrot and parsley before being cooked in a tomato sauce.

CALAMINT, or *nepitella,* is a perennial herb found in the Mediterranean basin and Asia. It has small grayish-green leaves and pale blue blossoms that recall those of thyme. Calamint is a member of the mint family. In Italy, where it is used to season soups and sauces, it is always tucked into the bundle when you buy fresh *porcini* (q.v.). Peppermint or a similar mint may be substituted.

CANNELLINI see *beans.*

CAPERS are the unopened flower buds of a bush native to the Mediterranean. The buds, which range in size from very tiny to about the size of a pea, are preserved in vinegar in jars or packed in salt in wooden boxes. Capers in vinegar are readily found on supermarket shelves; capers in salt are available in Italian shops. If working with the latter, rinse them briefly in cold water before using.

CARDOON, called *gobbi* in Tuscan dialect, is related to the artichoke and looks somewhat like an overgrown celery plant. The tenderest cardoons are those that have been wrapped in paper as they grow, to produce white stalks. Green cardoons are tougher and their flavor is less delicate. Cardoons can be found in better-stocked supermarkets.

CASTAGNE are chestnuts. Fortunately, chestnut woods in Tuscany survived the terrible blight that struck at the turn of the century. Chestnuts, also called *ballotte,* are used for stuffing poultry, puréed for serving with game, and are made into desserts. During the grape harvest they are at their peak. Toasted on an open fire in a special perforated pan, they are eaten hot with a glass of red wine.

CAUL FAT is the fat-ribbed transparent membrane that holds the organs of the abdominal cavity of mammals in place. It is used as a wrapping for meats to keep them moist as they cook. Caul fat can sometimes be purchased fresh, but more often frozen, in better meat markets and butcher shops.

CAVOLO NERO see *black cabbage.*

CHESTNUT FLOUR is milled from dried chestnuts and is high in both starch and sugar. The flour is used for making pasta, polenta, bread and desserts and can be purchased in shops specializing in Italian or French foods.

CHIANTI is the name of an area that lies between Siena and Florence and of the wine produced there. Chianti Classico, one of the finest wines in Italy, is a DOCG wine, meaning that it complies with strict regulations set by the government concerning grape variety, geographic origin, aging requirements and so on. It is produced in the heartland of the Chianti region and is aged not less than 18 months. In contrast, Chianti Riserva may originate anywhere in the Chianti region but must be aged for over 3 years. Chianti Classico Riserva is a higher-quality Chianti Classico and must be aged not less than 3 years. Chianti wine is principally made from the Sangiovese grape, usually with the addition of Canaiolo, Trebbiano or other grapes. The exact proportions of the grape varieties depend upon the type of Chianti being bottled. Any good-quality, full-bodied, dry red wine may be substituted.

CHICK-PEA FLOUR (garbanzo flour) is a fine flour milled from dried chick-peas, known as *ceci* in Italy. The flour can be found in shops specializing in Italian, Middle Eastern, Pakistani or Indian foods. In the latter it will be labeled *besan.*

COARSE-GRAINED CORNMEAL is most commonly eaten in Italy in the form of polenta, a thick, hot porridge that can also be cooled, sliced and fried or grilled. (Polenta is also made from other ingredients, including barley and chestnuts.) Look for coarse-grained yellow cornmeal marketed under the name polenta in Italian food stores and well-stocked supermarkets, or use any coarsely ground yellow cornmeal.

COPATE are honey biscuits enclosed in very fine wafers that for centuries were made by nuns. Each convent had its own jealously guarded recipe. They are now hard to find, but are worth looking for.

CORNMEAL see *coarse-grained cornmeal.*

COSTATA is a large T-bone steak. Cut from young beef, it is a famous Florentine specialty. Everywhere except in Tuscany it is called *bistecca alla fiorentina.*

CROCCHETTE, unlike *polpette* (q.v.), are meatballs made with cooked meat. The finely chopped meat is combined with egg, mashed potatoes and herbs. The meatballs are rolled in flour or bread crumbs before being fried in olive oil until crisp.

CROSTINI are a popular Tuscan antipasto. They are slices of bread that have been toasted, fried or quickly dipped in broth and then spread with a topping. The two most widely used toppings are made of chicken livers and spleen.

CUTTLEFISH is a marine mollusk that looks very much like a squid but with a broader, thicker oval body. It has prominent eyes on a wide head, ten tentacles and an ink sac. Cleaned and cooked in much the same way as squid, cuttlefish are enjoyed in Italy, Spain, Greece and many Asian countries. Look for cuttlefish in fish markets that cater to Asian or southern European communities.

DOLCEFORTE is an ancient, sweet and pungent sauce still used with wild boar. A little vinegar, sugar and garlic are added to the pot at the last minute. For a richer sauce, raisins, candied lemon peel and pine nuts are used.

DRAGONCELLO see *tarragon.*

ELDER FLOWERS are harvested from the elder, a large shrub that also produces an edible purple berry. The delicate white blossoms are used to flavor preserves, wines, breads and cakes.

EXTRA VIRGIN OLIVE OIL, or *olio extravergine d'oliva,* is something no Tuscan cook could live without. Butter is very seldom used and was unknown in Tuscany until quite recently. To be called extra virgin, olive oil must contain less than 1 percent acid. True extra virgin oil is quite expensive because it is cold pressed and the olives must be picked by hand to avoid bruising them, which raises the acid content. Always purchase the best-quality olive oil that you can afford.

FARRO see *spelt.*

FEGATELLI are pieces of pork liver. They are generally wrapped in a piece of caul fat (q.v.) before being sautéed with pepper and fennel seed. They are also put on skewers with sausage and chunks of bread, which absorb the fat while they are grilling.

FENNEL, or *finocchio,* grows wild all over Tuscany. Its umbels of yellow flowers are very decorative. In autumn the seeds are collected for seasoning many well-known Tuscan dishes. Fennel bulbs come from a cultivated variety of this plant.

FIASCO is a large, round-bottomed bottle wrapped in straw. Although very picturesque, these bottles usually contain inferior wine.

FINOCCHIO see *fennel.*

FRANTOIO is a mill where olives are pressed as soon as possible after picking. To get extra virgin olive oil, the olives are pressed between two huge granite grindstones. The oil flows into a special bath and is passed through a paper filter to rid it of any impurities that might cause the oil to go rancid.

FRITTURA can be deep-fried vegetables, meat, fish or sweet things, all of which are very popular in Tuscany, where extra virgin olive oil is always used for frying. Extra virgin olive oil has no bad odor when heated and even when very hot does not release toxins. Frying oil should be used only once.

GAETA OLIVES are small, salt-cured olives with wrinkled black skins. Small, black Greek or Spanish olives may be substituted.

GALLO NERO, or "black rooster," is the symbol of Chianti Classico, the wine produced in a specific area between Florence and Siena.

GARMUGIA is a celebrated soup from Lucchesia made with very young green vegetables and wild herbs; occasionally a little meat is added as well.

GNOCCHI is a generic term for small dumplings served as a first course. They are made of potatoes, ricotta and spinach, cornmeal or semolina. Potato gnocchi are generally turned against the prongs of a fork to give them their characteristic ridges.

GOBBI see *cardoon.*

GRATELLA is the Tuscan word for a grill used to cook over an open fire. It is an essential part of every Tuscan household because it is used not only for grilling meat and vegetables, but also for toasting bread that is later rubbed with garlic and sprinkled with oil.

JUNIPER BERRIES are the fruit of the evergreen shrub of the same name. The pungent, small, hard berries, which are a deep blue black, are used to make gin and to flavor game and other meat dishes. They can be found bottled in the spice section of most supermarkets.

MARSALA WINE is a rich amber wine produced in the Sicilian provinces of Trapani, Agrigento and Palermo. It is a prized dessert wine and is used in desserts as well. Any well-stocked wine shop will carry a selection of Sicilian Marsalas.

MEZZALUNA is a large two-handled knife with a semi-circular blade. It is efficient and easy to use because it is simply rolled from side to side to chop herbs, meats and vegetables. It usually has a single blade, but double-bladed knives of this type are available.

MINESTRA is a light stock enriched with pasta, egg, diced vegetables or small pieces of meat.

MINESTRONE is a very thick soup made of coarsely chopped mixed vegetables to which a little rice or pasta is added.

MORTADELLA is among the most popular of all Italian sausages, in Italy as well as abroad. Its distinctive pattern comes from the mixing of finely ground (minced) pork with coarsely diced pork fat. The slowly cooked sausage, which usually measures about 6 in (15 cm) in diameter, is a popular sandwich meat and is sold at most delicatessens.

OLIO EXTRAVERGINE D'OLIVA see *extra virgin olive oil.*

OVOLI are the most highly prized wild mushrooms in Italy. They are now very rare and extremely expensive. They have orange caps and white stalks and are generally gathered very young when they are still egg shaped. They are excellent sliced raw and dressed with olive oil, lemon and thin shavings of Parmesan cheese. Although they are not nearly as special as *ovoli,* button (cultivated) mushrooms can be used in their place.

PANCETTA is Italian bacon, usually a tightly rolled slab that is sliced crosswise to form spirals of meat and fat. In its most common form, *pancetta* is salt-cured pork belly, although a *pancetta affumicata* (smoked *pancetta*) is also made. *Pancetta* can be purchased in Italian shops and in most markets specializing in European foods. The recipes in this book call for unsmoked *pancetta;* if unavailable, unsmoked bacon may be substituted.

PANPEPATO is a Sienese fruit cake flavored with pepper. It is much like *pan coi santi,* for which the recipe is included in the Dolci chapter.

PANS travel under different names in the international kitchen. In this book, a "heavy pot" is any thick-walled, fairly deep, heavy pan equipped with a lid. It should be made of a material that retains heat well, such as enameled cast iron. The British call this type of pot a flameproof casserole; American cooks may use their Dutch ovens. A heavy sauce-pan would also work well. What is termed a skillet in these pages is the same utensil as a frying pan, while cake pans, which are round unless otherwise indicated, are the same as cake tins.

PANZANELLA is a salad originally invented to use up stale bread. In the classic version, the dampened bread is mixed with tomatoes and onion and dressed with olive oil and a little vinegar. Occasionally tuna fish, capers and cucumbers are added. In some places it is called *panmolle,* or "wet bread."

PAPPARDELLE is a homemade Tuscan pasta (q.v.). The egg-and-flour dough is rolled very thinly and cut into broad ribbons about 1¼ in (3 cm) wide and 4 in (10 cm) long. It is usually served with a hare or game sauce.

PARMESAN CHEESE, which is made from cow's milk, is a hard cheese with a granular texture and a pleasantly sharp flavor. It is used in cooking and as a condiment, especially on pastas. True Italian Parmesan is produced between April 1 and November 11 in a region that stretches from Parma Province to Mantua Province on one side and Bologna on the other. The best is *parmigiano reggiano,* marked clearly on the crust. A great deal of Parmesan is also made in the United States, Argentina, Australia and other countries with large populations of Italian descent. Italian Parmesan is quite expensive and other good-quality, aged Parmesan cheese can be substituted. Never purchase pre-grated Parmesan cheese and do not grate the cheese until you are ready to use it, as the flavor of the cheese is at its peak immediately upon grating.

PARSLEY is available in two basic varieties, curly leaf and flat leaf. Although the former is more easily found in markets outside of Italy, the latter, which has a more pungent flavor, is preferred for the recipes in this book.

PASTA. Fresh pasta is most easily made with a hand-cranked pasta machine that rolls out the dough into very thin sheets for cutting into noodles of any width or for forming stuffed pastas. (Electric machines work well, too, but are expensive; manual ones, in contrast, are quite reasonably priced.) You will need to feed the dough, a small piece at a time, through the machine's rollers, beginning with the rollers set at their widest opening and gradually adjusting the rollers to narrower settings until the desired thickness is achieved. At each degree of thickness, the dough should be put through the rollers until it is smooth and elastic, dusting it lightly with flour whenever it becomes sticky. Once you have a thin sheet of pasta, the machine blades may be adjusted to the noodle width desired. *Taglierini,* for example, would probably require the narrowest setting, while *tagliatelle* would call for a setting of slightly less than ¼ in (6 mm) wide. Rolling out pasta dough by hand is difficult for all but the most experienced cooks, as it is a challenge to produce a very thin, very even sheet of dough. If, however, no pasta machine is available, the dough can be rolled out on a lightly floured work surface. Divide the dough into 3 or 4 portions to make the rolling more manageable. Flatten the dough into a disc and roll from the center outward, using no more strokes than are necessary. To cut the dough into noodles, let it rest for a few minutes, then roll it up into a cylinder, flatten the top slightly and cut crosswise into the width desired.

PECORINO is sheep's milk cheese made in several parts of Italy, but the Tuscan variety is considered the best. Fresh *pecorino* is called *marzolino* because it is made in the spring when the ewes have just lambed and have abundant milk. The cheese is put into oval terra-cotta molds. Mature *pecorino,* which is sometimes aged under ashes, has a much stronger flavor but is never very sharp.

PEPOLINO is a small-leaved wild thyme used to flavor many soups, including the famed *ribollita,* a hearty soup of vegetables and bread. It has a much stronger aroma than cultivated thyme.

PLUM TOMATOES, also known as egg, Roma and pear tomatoes, are oval in shape and particularly suitable for making sauces because of their meaty flesh. If fresh, flavorful plum tomatoes are unavailable, canned ones may be substituted; drain before using. Look for cans that contain whole, peeled plum tomatoes imported from Italy, as the Italian tomatoes have the finest, fullest flavor.

POLENTA see *coarse-grained cornmeal.*

POLPETTE are meatballs made of raw ground (minced) meat seasoned with herbs and cooked in tomato sauce. *Polpettone* is a meat loaf, and in Italy the center is generally filled with hard-cooked eggs, slices of ham or thin omelet strips.

PORCINI is the common name of *boletus edulis,* the most sought-after wild mushrooms. Called *cèpes* by the French, they come up in early autumn after the first rain, when, as the local farmers say, "the earth boils." The stalks are broad and pale and the cap thick and dark. The darker the cap, the better the mushroom, and when buying them you should make sure the stalks are firm. In autumn they are thinly sliced and dried for use when out of season. Good-quality dried slices usually measure about 2 in (5 cm) long.

PROSCIUTTO is raw, salt-cured ham that has been aged to produce moist, lightly veined, intense pink meat with an edge of fat. Imported Italian *prosciutto* is quite costly (the best is from Parma), but many domestic products are of good

quality and can be used. Avoid *prosciutti* that taste too salty, and buy only what is needed, as cut *prosciutto* dries out rapidly. *Prosciutto* can be found in Italian shops, delicatessens and many supermarkets. If unavailable, substitute another raw, salt-cured ham, such as French Bayonne or German Westphalian; do not use a smoked ham.

RAPINI see *broccoli raab.*

RICOTTA in Tuscany is made from sheep's milk whey left after making *pecorino* cheese. The whey is reboiled, hence its name, and strained. Once it has thickened, ricotta is eaten fresh. There is also a blander cow's milk ricotta on the Italian market. Elsewhere cow's milk ricotta is often the only type available.

RISOTTO is made with Arborio (q.v.) or Vialone Nano rice. The plump grains contain a large amount of starch that is released during cooking and gives the risotto a creamy quality. Liquid is gradually added to the rice so that the kernels are always just covered but never floating in it.

ROSEMARY, a hearty shrub that belongs to the mint family, has needlelike leaves, blue flowers and a strong, woodsy scent. Italian cooks regularly use it with roasted meats such as pork, lamb and chicken. It can be found dried in bottles on supermarket spice shelves or fresh in many vegetable sections. It is also easily grown in the home garden.

SAGE, called *salvia* in Italian, has gray-green leaves and a potent flavor. Tuscans like to add the coarse-textured, oval leaves to bean dishes and meats. Better supermarkets stock fresh sage year-round; dried sage in various forms is carried on the spice shelves.

SALTED COD is cod that has been preserved by first salting and then drying. It is available both boneless and with bones and is most commonly found in Portuguese, Italian, French, Spanish, Greek and Caribbean markets. Sometimes salted cod is sold packed in small wooden boxes that hold about 1 lb (500 g); other times large pieces are stacked in a heap and you select the one you want. Before cooking salted cod, it should be soaked in cold water to cover in the refrigerator for 24 hours, changing the water 3 or 4 times, to soften it and rid it of excess salt. (In Italy it is often sold presoaked.)

SALVIA see *sage.*

SANGUINACCIO, a highly spiced sausage made with pig's blood, is sometimes called *biroldo.* There is a sweet version, flavored with raisins and pine nuts. Traditionally the sausage is made in autumn when local farmers kill pigs to make ham, salamis and sausages.

SCHIACCIATA is a flat bread, about half an inch (12 mm) thick, sprinkled with olive oil and salt. It is sometimes flavored with sage or rosemary. An even flatter variety is called *ciaccino.*

SCOTTIGLIA is a mixture of meats cooked in a tomato sauce; the greater the variety the tastier the dish. In some parts of Tuscany, however, this dish is made with only chicken, rabbit and lamb.

SOFFRITTO is chopped onion, celery, carrot and parsley gently fried in a little olive oil over low heat before the main ingredient is added to the pan. This method is used all over Italy.

SOPPRESSATA is a headcheese (brawn) made from rendered meat from a pig's head, forehock and skin, as well as the aspic from the reduced cooking liquid. It is seasoned with herbs and spices and left to set in a special mold.

SPELT, called *farro* in Italian, is an ancient variety of wheat with small, reddish brown grains. The early Romans made a dish called *puls,* which was something like a polenta, made of ground spelt. Spelt is still popular in Lazio and Umbria but above all in the Garfagnana, an area of Lucchesia. Spelt is sold in well-stocked Italian shops and some health food stores.

SPIEDINI, which are similar to kabobs, are made from pieces of meat, sausage, bread, tomatoes or peppers (capsicums) and sometimes onion. They are nearly always cooked over the embers of a wood fire. Butchers in Italy sell them ready prepared—especially in autumn and winter when fires are lit in the open hearths.

STOCCAFISSO is cod dried in the sun without salting.

STRASCICATO literally means "dragged." You will hear this word mentioned with pasta in Tuscan trattorias, where cooked pasta is often tossed into the skillet with the sauce and dragged around the pan.

SUGO DI CARNE is meat sauce, of which there are several varieties in Tuscany. Pieces of pork and beef are gently braised with a chicken liver, a little bacon, tomato and herbs. The meat is not chopped until after it is cooked.

SUGO FINTO is tomato sauce, called "fake sauce" because to Tuscans the only real sauce is made of meat.

SWEET ITALIAN SAUSAGE in northern Italy is a fresh link sausage made from pork seasoned with black pepper. In the south of Italy, they are seasoned with fennel and garlic, and a hot version includes red chili pepper in the mixture. Italian sausage is available in Italian shops and some supermarkets.

TARRAGON, called *dragoncello* in Italian, is the most popular herb in Siena, although it is used nowhere else in Tuscany or Italy. It appears in soups and sauces, and from spring to autumn every Sienese trattoria has at least one tarragon-flavored dish.

TEGAME is a wide, shallow pan that until recently was always earthenware. It is generally used for gentle cooking in wine or tomato sauce.

TOPINI, or "little mice," are oval gnocchi (q.v.) in Tuscany.

TORTELLI, TORDELLI and TORTELLONI are various names for fresh pasta (q.v.) generally stuffed with spinach and ricotta in Tuscany. The name varies according to the size; Tuscan *tortelli* are, for example, smaller than *tortelloni.*

TORTINO is another name for frittata, but with the difference that *tortini* are sometimes cooked in the oven or, if over direct heat, on one side only until the eggs are almost set but still very moist on top.

TRIPPATA means "cooked like tripe," i.e., first sautéed in a *soffritto* (q.v.), then cooked in tomato sauce.

TUSCAN COUNTRY BREAD is a coarse-textured, dense, chewy, unsalted loaf with a pleasantly tough crust (see recipe on page 227). Any bread of the same type, including a lightly salted one, may be substituted.

UMIDO is the Tuscan way of describing meat or vegetables cooked and served in a small amount of liquid that could be wine, water, stock or tomato sauce.

VIN SANTO is a Tuscan dessert wine produced from Trebbiano and Malvasia grapes. Pleasantly sweet and smooth, this brilliant amber wine is traditionally served with *cantucci* (almond cookies) for dipping. It can be found in better wine shops.

WHITEBAIT are small fish, at their best when no more than 2 to 3 in (5 to 7.5 cm) in length. They are most often fried crisp and eaten whole, bones and all. The name is given to both very young herring and smelt. Look for whitebait in better fish markets.

WHITE CELERY owes its pale color to the fact that it is blanched, or covered, as it grows. This treatment produces particularly tender stalks and a delicate heart. Young, very fresh green celery may be substituted.

WILD BOAR have long been pursued by hunters in Italy, France and Germany. These fierce, menacingly tusked descendants of domestic pigs are best when eaten fairly young; as they age their meat toughens. A number of different species can be found in Europe, Asia and the Americas. Laws restrict the sale of wild animals in many countries, but farm-raised boar is available at some supermarkets, butcher shops and game specialty suppliers. If unavailable, similar cuts of pork may be substituted.

WOODCOCK is a small game bird with a long, slender, pointed beak and dark meat. Native to Europe and North America, woodcocks are considered particularly fine eating birds and farm-raised ones can be purchased from game specialty suppliers.

ZUPPA is a soup that is poured over slices of bread. The bread is first either browned in the oven or fried in olive oil.

ACKNOWLEDGMENTS

Weldon Owen would like to thank the following people and organizations for their assistance in the preparation of this book:
Jacki Passmore, Norma MacMillan, Helen Cooney, Amy Morton, Stephanie Baartz, Ruth Jacobson, Ken DellaPenta, Italian Government Travel Office of San Francisco, Richard VanOosterhout, Fee-Ling Tan, Lesley Schwartz, Pete Friedrich, Rapid Lasergraphics (San Francisco).

Peter Johnson and Janice Baker wish to thank the following: Jennifer Grillo, for her generous hospitality and invaluable assistance on location in Tuscany; Elizabeth McLeod and Cara Hobday for assisting with food preparation and styling; Robert White for helping with the photography.

Michael Freeman thanks Romano Cagnoni, Patricia Franceschetti and Pasquale Brogini for their assistance.

Props used in this book are from the following sources in Sydney, Australia: Appley Hoare Antiques, Woollahra; The Bay Tree, Woollahra; Country Floors, Woollahra; Country Road Australia Ltd; Accoutrement, Mosman; Parterre Garden, Woollahra; Corso di Fiori, Chatswood; Ventura for Alessi; The Art of Food and Wine, Woollahra; Jacobus, Woollahra; Sentimental Journey at Mosman Antiques, Mosman; Hale Imports for Pillivuyt; Villeroy and Boch, Brookvale; The Country Trader, Woollahra; Porters Original Limewash, Sydney; The Fragrant Garden, Erina; The Lacquer Chest, London. In addition, Susan Whitter, Karen Byak, Inger Marchant, Elizabeth McLeod, Janice Baker and Peter Johnson kindly lent privately owned items for propping.